# The
# Cell Phone
# Handbook

### Everything You Wanted to Know About
### Wireless Telephony
### (But Didn't Know Who or What to Ask)

## Penelope Stetz

Aegis Publishing Group, Ltd.
796 Aquidneck Avenue
Newport, Rhode Island 02842
401-849-4200
www.aegisbooks.com

Library of Congress Catalog Card Number: 99-22666

Aegis Publishing Group, Ltd.
796 Aquidneck Avenue
Newport, Rhode Island  02842

International Standard Book Number: 1-890154-12-1
Printed in the United States of America.

10 9 8 7 6 5 4 3 2 1

**Library of Congress Cataloging-In-Publication Data**

Stetz, Penelope J., 1949-

The cell phone handbook: everything you wanted to know
about wireless telephony (but didn't know who or what to ask)/
by Penelope Stetz
        p.        cm.
Includes index.
ISBN 1-890154-12-1 (pbk.)
1. Cellular telephones.  2. Cellular telephone systems.
I. Title: The cell phone handbook: everything you wanted to know
about wireless telephony (but didn't know who or what to ask)

TK6570.M6S74    1999
384.5'3--dc21                                    99-22666
                                                      CIP

# Other Telecom Titles from Aegis Publishing Group:

**Telecom Business Opportunities**
*The Entrepreneur's Guide to Making Money in the Telecommunications Revolution*, by Steve Rosenbush
$24.95   1-890154-04-0

**Winning Communications Strategies**
*How Small Businesses Master Cutting-Edge Technology to Stay Competitive, Provide Better Service and Make More Money*, by Jeffrey Kagan
$14.95   0-9632790-8-4

**Telecom & Networking Glossary**
*Understanding Communications Technology*
$9.95   1-890154-09-4

**Telecom Made Easy**
*Money-Saving, Profit-Building Solutions for Home Businesses, Telecommuters and Small Organizations*, by June Langhoff
$19.95   0-9632790-7-6

**The Telecommuter's Advisor**
*Real World Solutions for Remote Workers*, by June Langhoff
$14.95   0-9632790-5-X

**900 Know-How**
*How to Succeed With Your Own 900 Number Business*, by Robert Mastin
$19.95   0-9632790-3-3

**The Business Traveler's Survival Guide**
*How to Get Work Done While on the Road*, by June Langhoff
$9.95   1-890154-03-2

**Getting the Most From Your Yellow Pages Advertising**
*Maximum Profits at Minimum Cost*, by Barry Maher
$19.95   1-890154-05-9

**Money-Making 900 Numbers**
*How Entrepreneurs Use the Telephone to Sell Information*
by Carol Morse Ginsburg and Robert Mastin
$19.95   0-9632790-1-7

**How to Buy the Best Phone System**
*Getting Maximum Value Without Spending a Fortune*, by Sondra Liburd Jordan
$9.95   1-890154-06-7

**1-800-Courtesy**
*Connecting With a Winning Telephone Image*, by Terry Wildemann
$9.95   1-890154-07-5

**The Telecommunication Relay Service (TRS) Handbook**
*Empowering the Hearing and Speech Impaired*, by Franklin H. Silverman, Ph.D.
$9.95   1-890154-08-3

**The Best Jobs in Telecommunications**
*Commanding Top Salaries in an Explosive $750 Billion Industry*
by Sondra Liburd Jordan
$14.95   1-890154-11-3

**The Cell Phone Handbook**
*Everything You Wanted to Know About Wireless Telephony (But Didn't Know Who or What to Ask)*, by Penelope Stetz
$14.95   1-890154-12-1

**Phone Company Services**
*Working Smarter with the Right Telecom Tools*, by June Langhoff
$9.95   1-890154-01-6

# Acknowledgements

My dream for writing this book received enthusiastic support from friends and family. Thanks to all of you for cheering me on with this endeavor. I would like to especially thank the following:

My husband, Jon Stetz, for his unending support and for designing some of the illustrations for this book.

My friends, Gisela Carrillo, Trudi Fensel, Deb Gibbons, and my father, John S. Wright, for helping me make sense of all this information.

My friend, Paul Silla, who took my portrait for the cover.

My publisher, Robert Mastin, for his enthusiasm, support, and all the other little things.

My cats, Chipmonk and Que Será Será, for forcing me to take breaks when I was working too intensely.

Nearly everyone I contacted was cooperative, and I thank each of you for your help. A few companies went out of their way to provide me with information, and I would like to specifically thank them for their support: Belkin Components, GTE Telecommunications Services, Inc., Motorola, Inc., and Nextel Communications, Inc.

The following companies also provided me with information:

21st Century Telesis
3Com Corporation
Cellular Telephone Industry Association (CTIA)
CenturyTel
CNP—Cellular Networking Perspectives
Diamond Multimedia Systems, Inc.
Everything Wireless
Federal Communications Commission (FCC)
GoAmerica Communications Corp.
Hello Direct
Novatel Wireless, Inc.
North American Numbering Plan Administrator
    (NANPA)
Personal Communication Industry Association
    (PCIA)
RCR Global Wireless
Siemens Security & Chip Card ICs
Sony PMC America
Spread Spectrum Scene Online
SRS Technologies
Technocel
Telular Corporation
Wireless Now
The World of Wireless Communications

# Table of Contents

## Introduction

Introduction . . . . . . . . . . . . . . . . . . . . . . . . . 1
Three Types of Wireless Phones . . . . . . . . . . . . 2
Getting the Most Out of This Book . . . . . . . . . . 4
   What this book will do for you . . . . . . . . . . . 4
   What this book won't do for you . . . . . . . . . . 4
How To Use This Book . . . . . . . . . . . . . . . . . 5
   If you are a first-time buyer . . . . . . . . . . . . . 5
   If you are an existing user . . . . . . . . . . . . . . 5
   As a general reference . . . . . . . . . . . . . . . . 6
   Icons . . . . . . . . . . . . . . . . . . . . . . . . . . . 6

## Chapter 1               History

From Car Phones . . . . . . . . . . . . . . . . . . . . . 7
...To Cellular Phones . . . . . . . . . . . . . . . . . . 9
   AMPS . . . . . . . . . . . . . . . . . . . . . . . . . . 11
   NAMPS . . . . . . . . . . . . . . . . . . . . . . . . . 13
   TDMA . . . . . . . . . . . . . . . . . . . . . . . . . . 13
   CDMA . . . . . . . . . . . . . . . . . . . . . . . . . . 14
   GSM-NA . . . . . . . . . . . . . . . . . . . . . . . . 15
   PACS . . . . . . . . . . . . . . . . . . . . . . . . . . . 16
   PCS . . . . . . . . . . . . . . . . . . . . . . . . . . . 17
   Nextel . . . . . . . . . . . . . . . . . . . . . . . . . . 19
Looking Ahead . . . . . . . . . . . . . . . . . . . . . . 21
   Terrestrial wireless systems . . . . . . . . . . . . 21
   Wireless local loop . . . . . . . . . . . . . . . . . . 22
   Satellite wireless telephony . . . . . . . . . . . . 22
   Atmospheric alternatives . . . . . . . . . . . . . . 24

# Chapter 2

## How Wireless Telephony Works

Background . . . . . . . . . . . . . . . . . . . . . . 27
Basic Concepts of Wireless Telephony . . . . . . 28
The System. . . . . . . . . . . . . . . . . . . . . . 29
  Registration and autonomous registration . . . 32
  Power levels . . . . . . . . . . . . . . . . . . . . . 33
  Handoffs. . . . . . . . . . . . . . . . . . . . . . . 34
  Dropped calls and system holes. . . . . . . . . . 35
  Dealing with capacity overload—how 800 MHz
  ended up with two digital technologies . . . . . 36
The Phone . . . . . . . . . . . . . . . . . . . . . . 38
  What happens when I turn my phone on? . . . 38
  What happens when I place a call? . . . . . . . . 39
  What happens when I receive a call? . . . . . . 41
  What happens when I hang up? . . . . . . . . . 41
  Phone features . . . . . . . . . . . . . . . . . . . 42
Subscribing To a Carrier . . . . . . . . . . . . . . 43
Coverage Areas and How They Are Assigned. . . 44
What Is My "Home" Market? . . . . . . . . . . . . 46
Understanding the Carrier/Agent,
  Dealer/Customer Relationship. . . . . . . . . . . 46
Resellers. . . . . . . . . . . . . . . . . . . . . . . . 48
How Do I Interface With the Carriers? . . . . . . 49
Over-the-Air Activation . . . . . . . . . . . . . . . 50

# Chapter 3

## Acquiring Wireless Equipment and Service

Where Do I Buy It? . . . . . . . . . . . . . . . . . 51
  Cellular . . . . . . . . . . . . . . . . . . . . . . . . 51
  PCS . . . . . . . . . . . . . . . . . . . . . . . . . . 52
  Nextel. . . . . . . . . . . . . . . . . . . . . . . . . 52
Choosing a Phone . . . . . . . . . . . . . . . . . . 53
  Should I buy a new phone, and why? . . . . . . 55
  What kind of phone should I get? . . . . . . . . 56
  Decide on a phone format . . . . . . . . . . . . . 58

## Table of Contents

Where do I start? . . . . . . . . . . . . . . . . . . . . . 61
First-time buyer . . . . . . . . . . . . . . . . . . . . . 61
Feature details . . . . . . . . . . . . . . . . . . . . . . 64
Choosing a Carrier . . . . . . . . . . . . . . . . . . . . 74
Cost of airtime . . . . . . . . . . . . . . . . . . . . . 76
Security user . . . . . . . . . . . . . . . . . . . . . . 76
Light user . . . . . . . . . . . . . . . . . . . . . . . . 77
Medium user . . . . . . . . . . . . . . . . . . . . . . 77
Heavy user . . . . . . . . . . . . . . . . . . . . . . . 77
Power user . . . . . . . . . . . . . . . . . . . . . . . 78
Least-cost-per-month access fees . . . . . . . . . 79
Least-cost-per-minute usage . . . . . . . . . . . . 79
Carrier considerations . . . . . . . . . . . . . . . . . 79
The Final Score . . . . . . . . . . . . . . . . . . . . . . 85
Rate Plan Analysis . . . . . . . . . . . . . . . . . . . . 86
Do the math! Calculate your savings . . . . . . . 86
Replacing Your Equipment . . . . . . . . . . . . . . . 88

## Chapter 4                                    Roaming

What Is Roaming? . . . . . . . . . . . . . . . . . . . . . 91
Making and Receiving Calls While Roaming . . . 95
Outbound roaming calls . . . . . . . . . . . . . . . 95
Inbound roaming calls . . . . . . . . . . . . . . . . 97
800 MHz analog cellular . . . . . . . . . . . . . 97
The traditional roaming way . . . . . . . . . . 97
Automatic call delivery—the new and
improved method . . . . . . . . . . . . . . . . . 100
Nonlocal automatic call delivery . . . . . . . 101
Nonlocal traditional roaming call . . . . . . 102
Digital Roaming . . . . . . . . . . . . . . . . . . . . . 102
Cellular—800 MHz digital roaming . . . . . . . 102
800 MHz CDMA roaming . . . . . . . . . . . . 104
800 MHz TDMA roaming . . . . . . . . . . . . 106
PCS—1900 MHz roaming . . . . . . . . . . . . . 108
1900 MHz CDMA roaming . . . . . . . . . . . 109
1900 MHz TDMA roaming . . . . . . . . . . . 111
1900 MHz GSM-NA roaming . . . . . . . . . . 113

1900 MHz PACS roaming . . . . . . . . . . . . . 113
Nextel roaming. . . . . . . . . . . . . . . . . . . . . 114
Enhanced Roaming Features . . . . . . . . . . . . 114
Call delivery . . . . . . . . . . . . . . . . . . . . . . . 114
International roaming . . . . . . . . . . . . . . . . 117
North American Cellular Network (NACN) . . . 117
Enhanced home network. . . . . . . . . . . . . . 118

## Chapter 5    Fraud

Cloning. . . . . . . . . . . . . . . . . . . . . . . . . . . 119
What is it? How do the thieves do it? . . . . . . 119
Fraud Prevention Measures . . . . . . . . . . . . . 120
Profiling . . . . . . . . . . . . . . . . . . . . . . . . . . 120
Radio frequency (RF) fingerprinting . . . . . . . 121
Authentication . . . . . . . . . . . . . . . . . . . . . 121
PIN codes . . . . . . . . . . . . . . . . . . . . . . . . . 122
Subscriber Fraud . . . . . . . . . . . . . . . . . . . . 122
What Can I Do to Prevent or Reduce My
Chances of Being Cloned? . . . . . . . . . . . . . 123

## Chapter 6    Using Wireless Phones For Data

Circuit-Switched Data . . . . . . . . . . . . . . . . . 125
Performance expectations . . . . . . . . . . . . . 128
Cellular Digital Packet Data (CDPD) . . . . . . . 129
General Packet Radio Services . . . . . . . . . . . 132

## Chapter 7    Accessories

Batteries. . . . . . . . . . . . . . . . . . . . . . . . . . . 133
Battery details. . . . . . . . . . . . . . . . . . . . . . 133
Nickel cadmium batteries . . . . . . . . . . . . 133
Nickel metal hydride batteries . . . . . . . . . 134
Lithium ion batteries. . . . . . . . . . . . . . . . 135
Sealed lead-acid batteries . . . . . . . . . . . . 135
Battery summary . . . . . . . . . . . . . . . . . . . . 135
The most frequently asked battery question . 136
The future of batteries. . . . . . . . . . . . . . . . 138

Antennas . . . . . . . . . . . . . . . . . . . . . . . 139

Chargers. . . . . . . . . . . . . . . . . . . . . . . . 141

Cigarette Lighter Adapters . . . . . . . . . . . . . 142

Hands-Free Adapters. . . . . . . . . . . . . . . . . 142

## Chapter 8                 Extras

Wireless Phone Etiquette. . . . . . . . . . . . . . . 145

One Phone, One Number, Anywhere! . . . . . . . 146

Enhanced 9-1-1 . . . . . . . . . . . . . . . . . . . . 148

CALEA . . . . . . . . . . . . . . . . . . . . . . . . . 150

Equal Access For Long Distance . . . . . . . . . . 151

North American Numbering Plan . . . . . . . . . . 152

Local Number Portability . . . . . . . . . . . . . . 152

## Chapter 9           Frequently Asked Questions—FAQs

Are cellular phones safe to use
(for my health)?. . . . . . . . . . . . . . . . . . . . 155

How can I prevent my wireless phone number
from being read on caller ID devices? . . . . . . 157

What is a NAM (number assignment
module)?. . . . . . . . . . . . . . . . . . . . . . . . 157

What information should I know about
my wireless phone, and why? . . . . . . . . . . . 158

What should I do if I lose my phone? . . . . . . . 159

What is a SID? . . . . . . . . . . . . . . . . . . . . . 159

How does my phone know that I am in
my home market?. . . . . . . . . . . . . . . . . . . 159

Why does my phone say NO SERVICE
when I first turn it on? . . . . . . . . . . . . . . . 160

Why do my calls drop? . . . . . . . . . . . . . . . . 160

Why doesn't my phone retain the feature
changes I made?. . . . . . . . . . . . . . . . . . . . 160

Why do I lose my signal when I go into a
building or drive into a garage or valley? . . . 161

Why do I get a system-busy indication
when I should have service (or have
had service in the same area before)?...... 161

Sometimes my call gets very staticky, and
then it clears up. What happened here?.... 162

How can I have a digital phone on an
analog system?...................... 162

How does cellular compare to the new
PCS services available?............... 163

Why can't I use my phone out of town?..... 164

What is dual NAM?.................... 167

Subscribing to more than one system—
why would I want to?................ 167

Which carrier is offering dual NAM in
my market?........................ 169

Can I have one number on two phones?..... 169

How do I erase a stored number?.......... 169

My car kit drains my car's battery. Why?
What can I do about it?............... 170

What about cellular in other countries?..... 170

Can I use a wireless phone on an airplane?.. 171

Where can I rent a wireless phone?........ 173

# Appendices

Appendix A—Equipment Manufacturers..... 175

Appendix B—Resources.................. 179
  Satellite Companies.................... 179
  Phone Rental Companies............... 181
  Miscellaneous Companies ............. 181
  Wireless Organizations ................ 183
  Wireless Publications................. 184
  Mail Order Companies................. 185
  National Resellers .................... 186

Appendix C—Cellular Market Areas
  MSA Numerical Market Listing ......... 187
  MSA/RSA Map ....................... 188
  RSA Numerical Market Listing.......... 196

Appendix D—PCS Market Areas
  MTA Numerical Market Listing.......... 207
  MTA Map ............................ 208
  BTA Numerical Market Listing.......... 211
  BTA Map ............................ 212

Appendix E—Nextel Coverage Areas
  Nextel Market Listing ................. 225
  Nextel Map .......................... 226

Appendix F—Carrier Information
  Carriers ............................. 235
  Carriers by Market, Channel Block, and
    Technology......................... 242
  Carrier Name Abbreviations............ 267

Appendix G—Frequency Charts
  Frequencies of Wireless Phone Systems .... 269
  Cellular—Transmit and Receive ......... 270
  PCS—Transmit and Receive............. 271
  Nextel—Transmit and Receive ......... 272

Glossary ............................... 273

Index .................................. 325

## Figures

Figure 2-1. . . . . . . . . . . . . . . . . . . . . . . . . . . . . 29

Figure 2-2. . . . . . . . . . . . . . . . . . . . . . . . . . . . . 30

Figure 2-3. . . . . . . . . . . . . . . . . . . . . . . . . . . . . 31

Figure 2-4. . . . . . . . . . . . . . . . . . . . . . . . . . . . . 31

Figure 4-1. . . . . . . . . . . . . . . . . . . . . . . . . . . . . 91

Figure 4-2. . . . . . . . . . . . . . . . . . . . . . . . . . . . . 94

Figure 4-3. . . . . . . . . . . . . . . . . . . . . . . . . . . . . 98

Figure 4-4. . . . . . . . . . . . . . . . . . . . . . . . . . . . . 99

Figure 4-5. . . . . . . . . . . . . . . . . . . . . . . . . . . . 100

Figure 4-6. . . . . . . . . . . . . . . . . . . . . . . . . . . . 101

Figure 4-7. . . . . . . . . . . . . . . . . . . . . . . . . . . . 104

Figure 4-8. . . . . . . . . . . . . . . . . . . . . . . . . . . . 105

Figure 4-9. . . . . . . . . . . . . . . . . . . . . . . . . . . . 107

Figure 4-10. . . . . . . . . . . . . . . . . . . . . . . . . . . . 107

Figure 4-11. . . . . . . . . . . . . . . . . . . . . . . . . . . . 109

Figure 4-12. . . . . . . . . . . . . . . . . . . . . . . . . . . . 110

Figure 4-13. . . . . . . . . . . . . . . . . . . . . . . . . . . . 111

Figure 4-14. . . . . . . . . . . . . . . . . . . . . . . . . . . . 112

Figure 4-15. . . . . . . . . . . . . . . . . . . . . . . . . . . . 116

## Introduction

Few industries have seen the explosive growth of the wireless telephone industry. Subscribers in the United States topped 70 million in just 16 years, with a growth rate of 25 percent in 1998. Analysts predict the number of domestic wireless subscribers will exceed 100 million by the year 2000. Making the right choice is a challenge. There are as many as nine wireless carriers in each market, not to mention resellers, four incompatible digital technologies plus analog, and three different frequency spectrums.

*The Cell Phone Handbook* is for you if you own or are planning to purchase a cellular/wireless phone. It is also useful if you want to gain a broader understanding of these communication devices and the various services offered. Where the user's manual explains only what or how, this book explores the why behind certain features of wireless phones. Nuances of the wireless telephone industry are edified as well.

When buying a wireless phone for the first time, you are bombarded by advertising for free phones, prepaid wireless service, and special introductory deals on digital services from both 800 MHz cellular and 1900 MHz Personal Communications Services (PCS) carriers. It is both dizzying and intimidating. If you are an experienced cellular user, you generally have a better idea of what you want from your next wireless phone, but it is still confusing trying to untangle the information available on the various technologies. Determining a sound basis for choosing the equipment and service that best suits your specific needs is a daunting task.

## Three Types of Wireless Phones

Wireless telephony encompasses three general types of technology: cordless phones, terrestrial cellular-type phones, and satellite phones. A cordless phone, which offers a 1,000-foot range from its base and interfaces directly with the local phone company, is not difficult for most people to figure out because it emulates a wall or desk phone.

Terrestrial cellular-type technologies can be further broken down into three groups: 1) 800 MHz cellular systems, 2) 1900 MHz PCS (a.k.a 1.9 GHz PCS), and 3) Nextel Communications, Inc. These technologies all process calls in a similar fashion. An outbound call from the wireless handset is transmitted via radio waves to a cell site, which is an antenna with a computer at its base. From the cell site, the call continues via wired or microwave transmission to the mobile telephone switching office (MTSO), which is the brain of the network. The call continues by wires to the public switched telephone network (PSTN)— the local telephone company—and then is processed like any other phone call. The cell sites are all ground- or terrain-based They consist of overlapping circles of coverage resembling a honeycomb, or a diagram of biological cells, ergo the name cellular.

Satellite technology involves the use of a telephone handset that communicates directly to satellite systems that interface with the PSTN. These systems orbit the earth at altitudes ranging from 1,000 miles to 22,000 miles.

This book will cover cellular, PCS, and Nextel, all of which are terrain-based wireless telephone technologies. Cellular, which began analog service in November 1983 and has two carriers in every market, has begun its transition to digital service. However, because the industry was unable to agree on a digital standard, two incompatible digital technologies have been adopted: time division multiple access (TDMA) and code division multiple access (CDMA). To provide a common thread, the industry has agreed to support analog service through the year 2015. PCS, which began commercial service in January 1996 and will have up to six carriers in each market, also could not agree on a digital standard. PCS uses four different digital technologies: TDMA, CDMA, Global Systems for Mobile communications for North America (GSM-NA), and Personal Access Communications Systems (PACS). Nextel began providing its unique digital service in 1994, which combines TDMA digital wireless telephone service with two-way radio capabilities and the features of a pager, all in the same handset.

The term cellular technology has come to be linked with anything that functions on a terrestrial network in a cellular-like fashion. When PCS was conceived, the idea was that it would provide low-power, low-cost local phone service. It would serve as an intermediate wireless telephone step between the cordless phone at home that has no per-minute charges, and the cellular phone that charges by the minute. If the average charge for cellular is 35¢ per minute, PCS would have averaged about 10¢ per minute.

Instead, many of the companies bidding for licenses in the PCS auctions were existing cellular carriers. They leapt at the chance to get additional spectrum in more markets so they could build more wireless phone networks. With the technologies available today that weren't available 16 years ago, PCS carriers are building 100 percent digital networks—no analog technology allowed. Analog cellular carriers converting their networks to digital technology are marketing their "digital" service. The new kids on the block, the 1900 MHz PCS carriers, are marketing their digital service as "PCS," and they make it sound like a panacea. Therefore, in an attempt to compete on a level playing field, 800 MHz cellular carriers are marketing their digital services as PCS. Regardless of the frequency, digital technology offers the same features. Many companies use the term PCS to refer to any digital technology that offers short messaging service (SMS), caller ID, voice mail notification, etc., and not to refer to the PCS companies operating at 1900 MHz.

# Getting the Most Out of This Book

## What this book will do for you

- Make you aware of issues to consider in selecting your carrier.
- Help you decide what is important to consider in your wireless telephone purchase.
- Show you how these two are related.
- Explain the different technologies.

## What this book won't do for you

- Tell you about all the latest wireless telephones available. That information is best found at the handset manufacturers' Web sites, in magazines, and at Web sites such as that of *Consumer Reports*.

- Evaluate and compare local calling plans from the carriers in your market. Use the tools in this book to help determine what's best for you.

- Make your decision for you. You will be able to make your own decision based on your enlightenment from reading this book.

- Provide you with details on satellite telephony. There is a brief discussion, however, to give you an idea of what's coming.

# How To Use This Book

## If you are a first-time buyer

As a first-time buyer, this book will provide you with information about the different technologies that you will encounter on your quest for a wireless carrier. Armed with knowledge, you will be able to interview prospective service providers confidently, knowing what type of service and features will fulfill your needs. You will also be prepared to discuss equipment and some of the features that are essential for your specific use.

## If you are an existing user

As an existing user, this book will give you a broader grasp of wireless telephony. For instance, if you've ever had trouble roaming and experienced difficulty resolving the problem, then understanding what is happening when you roam may expedite your service call because you are better able to describe the situation. If you are ready to purchase a new phone, information on the different technologies will help you decide which one is best for you.

## As a general reference

This book does not have to be read front to back to be useful. It can be used as a reference for targeted information.

As wireless companies merge, or declare bankruptcy, information in this book will become dated. However, contact telephone numbers often remain the same, even if the name of the company is different.

## Icons

Icons are used is this book to help you quickly identify information that is pertinent to you. If you are an 800 MHz user, you can skip the information on 1900 MHz, unless you're curious. Accordingly, as a 1900 MHz user, you can focus in on the specific technology you are interested in. The pointers and tips icon is used to draw attention to especially useful information.

| | | | |
|---|---|---|---|
| $\frac{800}{\text{AMPS}}$ | 800 MHz AMPS | $\frac{1900}{\text{GSM}}$ | 1900 MHz GSM |
| $\frac{800}{\text{CDMA}}$ | 800 MHz CDMA | $\frac{1900}{\text{CDMA}}$ | 1900 MHz CDMA |
| $\frac{800}{\text{TDMA}}$ | 800 MHz TDMA | $\frac{1900}{\text{TDMA}}$ | 1900 MHz TDMA |
| $\frac{\text{NEX}}{\text{TEL}}$ | Nextel | $\frac{1900}{\text{PACS}}$ | 1900 MHz PACS |

 Pointers and Tips

## From Car Phones...

Until 1949, two-way radios were the only form of wireless communication. At that time a car phone service called Mobile Telephone Service, or MTS, was deployed. In order to use an MTS phone, you had to have a large, luggage-sized transceiver installed in the trunk of your car. The phone itself worked a lot like a two-way radio. You pushed a button when you wanted to talk and released it to listen. When you picked up the mobile phone handset, an operator working for the MTS phone company answered. The MTS operator would connect you with the local phone company operator, who would dial your call for you. You couldn't talk and listen at the same time the way you can with today's full-duplex technology. MTS operated on VHF frequencies (152-159 MHz). Two types of companies offered competitive service: wireline companies, referred to as telcos, and non-wireline companies, called radio common carriers (RCCs).

Technology moved more slowly back then, and it took 13 years before MTS was improved upon and dubbed Improved Mobile Telephone Service, or IMTS. This improvement removed a step in the connection. Instead of picking up the phone and getting a mobile operator, who transferred you to a phone company operator, your IMTS phone was able to access the phone company network directly. This meant you could dial the call yourself. In

1964, automatic channel selection was implemented. Another improvement, which took five more years, was to add channels. As lower frequencies were being used more and more for two-way radios, channels were assigned in the UHF spectrum (450-460 MHz). Between 1969 and 1983, minor improvements were made to IMTS, such as adding full-duplex capabilities.

The IMTS phones were still large, bulky transceiver boxes that weighed more than 25 pounds. Compared to the 3-watt installed cellular phones of today, their transmitting power was quite high: 20 watts for UHF and 25 watts for VHF. There was only one powerful 75-watt transmitting tower per carrier for each major city, covering roughly 50 miles in diameter. The system itself had limited capacity. VHF had a total of 18 channels, 11 telco and 7 RCC, while UHF had 26 channels, 12 telco and 14 RCC. Each channel was used exclusively by a single conversation, so there was a maximum of 44 conversations at any given moment in an entire metropolis.

Another problem with IMTS was the nature of the equipment. The phone was actually a scanner, and if you pressed a channel button, you could hear someone's wife reminding him to stop and get milk or a critical private conversation. Consequently, privacy and capacity, or user access, became driving factors to improve upon IMTS. In 1974, the FCC allocated radio spectrum for cellular use, but the first commercial cellular service wasn't available until November of 1983. It took seven years for all 306 Metropolitan Service Areas (MSAs) designated by the FCC to have at least one carrier available.

# ...To Cellular Phones

Today, there are several different types of cellular or terrestrial wireless phones. The one we are most familiar with is 800 MHz cellular service, which uses an analog technology called Advanced Mobile Phone Service (AMPS). AMPS carriers are currently implementing digital networks that overlay their existing analog systems. The new kids on the block are Nextel and PCS, both implementing digital-only networks. As much as these wireless phone services seem the same, there are some differences. See Appendix G for more information.

The first difference is the frequencies they use:

| | |
|---|---|
| Nextel | 806-821 MHz, 851-866 MHz |
| 800 MHz cellular | 824-849 MHz, 869-894 MHz |
| 1900 MHz PCS | 1850-1910 MHz, 1930-1990 MHz |

The second difference is how they are licensed to operate by the FCC. In an attempt to create competition—unlike the local phone company—the FCC wanted to have more than one carrier per market. For 800 MHz cellular service, two 25 MHz channel blocks were designated: channel block B for existing telephone companies and channel block A for alternate companies who wanted to get into cellular. With PCS, the FCC decided that because there was more spectrum, there would be more carriers. The PCS spectrum was divided into six blocks, but not evenly. Half the blocks, designated A, B, and C, were assigned 30 MHz of spectrum, and the other half, designated D, E, and F, were assigned 10 MHz of spectrum. The spectrum licensed to Nextel is not shared.

The third difference is how the FCC defined the coverage areas. With 800 MHz cellular service, coverage lines were drawn based on Metropolitan

Service Areas (MSAs) that covered cities and on Rural Service Areas (RSAs) that covered less-populated areas grouped as counties. With PCS, there are two different coverage delineations: Major Trading Areas (MTAs) that cover entire states and Basic Trading Areas (BTAs) that are cities and counties combined into commercial marketing areas. As Nextel has no competition within their spectrum, they have access to all the markets in the United States.

Digital technologies are available from all three types of wireless services. There are several reasons for implementing digital switching equipment. A major reason is to accommodate access to the system for an increased number of users at any one time. Another big reason is to provide secure, or encrypted, transmissions. Even though analog cellular is more private than IMTS because the phone itself isn't a scanner, people can still acquire equipment that allows them to eavesdrop on your phone conversation.

It's important to note that CDMA and TDMA digital technologies work the same regardless of the frequency. Some service features available from digital carriers may replace the need for a separate paging device. The digital wireless phone can store a phone number the way a pager does and can also function as a two-way messaging pager, sending and receiving alphanumeric messages, usually limited to 15 to 20 words.

Time division multiple access (TDMA) is being implemented in 800 MHz cellular, 1900 MHz PCS, and Nextel. Code division multiple access (CDMA) is being deployed by both 800 MHz and 1900 MHz carriers. Only PCS carriers are using Global Systems for Mobile communications (GSM) and Personal Access Communications Systems (PACS).

AMPS will remain the common thread among carriers implementing TDMA and CDMA for at least the next ten years, with dual-mode and tri-mode phones available to access the different technologies and frequencies.

Some additional information about the different types of wireless services and digital technologies follows.

## AMPS

Developed by Bell Laboratories, Advanced Mobile Phone Service (AMPS) is the technology used throughout North, Central, and South America, the Caribbean, parts of Southern Asia and Russia, as well as Australia and New Zealand. This technology is analog service that operates in the 800 MHz frequency range. The original 666 channels available in AMPS were increased to 832 channels in 1988. These 832 channels are divided equally between two carriers. Channel block B was initially licensed to wireline companies. They were called wirelines because they were already in the landline phone business. Channel block A was licensed to non-wireline companies. RCC-type companies composed of groups of independent investors entering into cellular telephony were called non-wirelines because they weren't in the landline phone business. Once the initial licensing was complete, the FCC stipulated that the same company in any given market could not hold licenses to both channel blocks A and B[1]. Mergers and acquisitions have seen wireline companies gobble up non-wireline companies and vice versa. So the division is now more a block A versus block B separation. Wirelines can own licenses to channel blocks A and non-wirelines can own licenses to channel blocks B, just so long as they

[1]Code of Federal Regulations 47CFR22.942, page 190, revised as of October 1, 1996

don't own both blocks A and B in the same market. For example, the merger between Southwestern Bell and Ameritech creates a conflict in the Chicago market for the 800 MHz carriers because Southwestern Bell operates channel block A, and Ameritech operates channel block B. One of these networks will have to be sold. If the mergers between Bell Atlantic Mobility, GTE, and AirTouch are approved, then Bell Atlantic Mobility will have to divest of one of the properties in Cleveland, because AirTouch operates on channel block A, and GTE operates on channel block B.

AMPS cellular provides full-duplex technology, which means that you can hear someone trying to interrupt you while you are speaking, just the way you can on your home phone. Cellular also uses two separate channels during a phone call, one to transmit and one to receive. With 416 channels per carrier and two channels used per call (less 21 control channels), in a given market there is the potential for about 200 conversations per carrier at one time. This is an improvement over the 44 available to IMTS. Combined with other benefits, such as privacy (the phone isn't a scanner any more) and direct-dial capability, AMPS cellular offers the potential for enormous growth.

Cellular technology provides carriers with the ability to expand their networks through channel reuse, which is an integral part of any cellular network. As more cell sites are added, the power level of the towers is adjusted to accommodate the size of the cell (ranging from four to twenty miles). In this way, carriers are able to reuse channels in different parts of their networks. (See Figure 2-1.) This provides tremendous benefit to both consumers (fewer busy signals) and carriers (greater revenue from more subscribers).

# NAMPS

Introduced in 1991, Narrowband Advanced Mobile Phone Service (NAMPS) is a technology developed by Motorola that operates at the same frequencies as AMPS technology. The difference is that instead of allocating 30 kHz to each voice channel, NAMPS splits it into three 10 kHz channels, thereby providing three times the capacity of the AMPS system. This technology is a form of frequency division multiple access (FDMA).

800
AMPS

Because it is a hybrid digital/analog technology, NAMPS offers some enhanced calling features, such as digital messaging service (DMS). This technology is system and phone dependent, so if the switching equipment being used by the carrier is not updated to utilize NAMPS, then a NAMPS-capable phone will default to the AMPS technology.

AirTouch, the block B cellular carrier in the greater Los Angeles area, is an example of how a carrier can use NAMPS to enhance its network. It revamped its system in 1993, and through channel reuse and NAMPS technology, created the equivalent of 6,000 channels from only the 416 channels allocated to it.

# TDMA

Time division multiple access (TDMA) is a digital technology that breaks up the transmission into smaller, digital bursts, and then reassembles the information at the receiving end so that it becomes understandable by us mere humans. This technology is being used at both cellular (800 MHz) and PCS (1.9 GHz) frequencies. It is a proven technology that has been used by cellular companies since 1992, providing a threefold increase in capacity. With AMPS technology, two people hog one transmit and one receive channel all to them-

800
TDMA

1900
TDMA

selves. With TDMA, six people—three pairs of conversationalists—time-share one transmit and one receive channel at a time. The callers don't know it, of course, as computers are working their magic behind the scenes.

The transmission is actually broken down into digital zeros and ones, so real-time eavesdropping is impossible. Digital transmission also protects you and your equipment from cloning fraud by using a built-in feature called authentication.

## CDMA

800 CDMA

1900 CDMA

Code division multiple access (CDMA) has held the most promise for providing increased capacity, asserting a tenfold increase over that of AMPS. However, implementation of CDMA has been very slow among the 800 MHz carriers who opted for this digital technology. As the name implies, CDMA uses codes to provide separation. A unique code is assigned to each conversation that separates it from others. Multiple conversations can be transmitted over the same channel at the same time. The system and the phone work together to deliver only your conversation to you. Other conversations, with different code assignments, are filtered out so you don't hear them. The industry analogy is that ten couples are using one pair of channels, but each couple is talking in a different language. The system actually has the capacity to exceed ten conversations per channel. However, call quality will usually begin to degrade over ten.

A function of CDMA that is unique to this technology is that there are actually three receivers in the phone. They are called "rake" receivers because they are constantly "raking" the airwaves for stronger signals. Because of these rake receivers, CDMA performs "soft" handoffs. AMPS cellular hands off to another channel after it loses a signal.

This is referred to as a "break before make" connection, or hard handoff. A soft handoff uses a "make before break" connection, where the phone finds a new and stronger signal and hands off the call before it lets go of the weaker signal. CDMA can also perform "softer" handoffs, which occur within the same cell, and will perform a hard handoff to change channels or to step down to AMPS service if the CDMA network becomes unavailable.

## GSM-NA

In 1987, a committee called Groupe Speciale Mobile, comprised of representatives from four European countries, conceived and agreed upon a digital wireless phone technology that would provide uniformity of service and roaming among the countries on the Continent. Global Systems for Mobile communications (GSM), as this technology has come to be known, has been available in Europe since the fall of 1992. At the time, roaming among most of the countries was impossible, as there were nine different types of systems, none compatible with the other. There were also capacity concerns and a desire for better audio quality.

1900 GSM

GSM is based on TDMA technology with integrated encryption, which provides privacy, and an incorporated "key," which virtually eliminates fraud. GSM uses a subscriber identity module (SIM) card, which is a credit-card-sized card containing information necessary to use the phone. By putting information such as the mobile phone number, the mobile electronic identity number (MEIN—the European equivalent of an electronic serial number), and other information about the subscribing system on the SIM card, a GSM subscriber is not limited to one phone. For example, if you take your SIM card with you, and your friend has a GSM phone, you can plug your

POINTER

SIM card into his phone and you'll be using your phone number. A SIM card can also store phone numbers in its own directory. GSM includes short messaging service, as well as the ability to connect your laptop computer to the phone for data and fax capabilities.

PCS carriers introduced GSM technology to the U.S. in 1995. Because this service operates at a different frequency than the non-U.S. GSM networks, it is dubbed GSM-NA for GSM-North America. The only difference between GSM in the U.S. and elsewhere is that, in North America, GSM operates at 1900 MHz, whereas elsewhere in the world, it operates at 900 MHz or 1800 MHz.

## PACS

1900
PACS

When PCS was originally conceived, the intention was to use the new spectrum to provide a wireless phone technology that would operate somewhere between a cordless phone (costing only as much as your home phone service) and a cellular phone, (costing an average of 35¢ per minute), resulting in a low-cost, low-power local wireless phone service that would cost 10¢ or less per minute. Well, Personal Access Communications Systems (PACS) achieves this. It combines cordless phone capabilities, using wireless local loop (WLL), with wireless mobile service equal to the quality of landline phones through the use of very high-quality speech encoding (32 kbps versus 8 to 13 kbps for cellular and other PCS networks). The system uses radio ports instead of base stations. The range of the radio port is between 200 feet and one mile, and uses about as much power as an analog portable, a maximum of 800 milliwatts. PACS networks don't use tall towers as do other wireless phone networks. They can put their antennas on lampposts and other similar structures, which eliminates zoning and construction problems. The base station is small and inexpensive, about the size and cost of a laptop computer. All this contributes to a very efficient and low-cost infrastructure. The PACS wireless handsets use the same power as a cordless handset, averaging 25 milliwatts with a maximum of 200 milliwatts. PACS is expected to be adopted in most PCS markets by one of the licensees. As of early 1999, 21st Century Telesis had made the biggest commitment with licenses in 27 markets.

## PCS

The companies offering PCS service couldn't agree on a standard, so you have your choice among four digital technologies: TDMA, CDMA, GSM, and PACS. There are up to six carriers in each market, so it is likely that there will be at least one carrier offering the type of system you choose and that you will experience the ubiquity of coverage available in the AMPS arena. A total of 140 MHz of spectrum has been allocated to broadband PCS, with 20 MHz of spectrum currently unassigned. The 1,200 channels used in broadband PCS are divided into blocks: frequency blocks A, B, and C were each assigned 30 MHz of spectrum, which consists of 300 channels, while frequency blocks D, E, and F were each assigned 10 MHz of spectrum, consisting of 100 channels. Frequency blocks A and B were geographically split into 51 Major Trading Areas (MTAs) and were typically licensed to large companies already in the wireless phone business. Blocks C, D, E, and F were divided into 493 geographic areas called Basic Trading Areas (BTAs). Blocks C and F were reserved for entrepreneurial-type concerns.

1900
GSM

1900
CDMA

1900
TDMA

1900
PACS

PCS blocks A, B, and C have a two-step construction requirement: licensees have five years to provide service to one-third of the population in their service area, and they need to cover two-thirds of the population within ten years. Blocks D, E, and F only need to cover 25 percent of the people within five years. If system construction requirements aren't met, the licensee forfeits and is unable to renew the license ever! PCS licensees pay megabucks for the rights to the spectrum. To give you some idea of this investment, the auction to license spectrum for blocks A and B for PCS resulted in 18 winners receiving a total of 99 licenses for the price of $7,019,403,797. My calculator can't handle that many digits! Roughly speaking, though, this means that the 18 winners forked out an average of $390 million per company, or an average of $70.9 million per license. So you see, PCS licensees are highly motivated to construct their networks as quickly as possible.

The infrastructure of a PCS network is different from that of an 800 MHz network due to the fact that it operates at a higher frequency. RF energy requires more power to travel the same distance at higher frequencies than it does at lower frequencies. Because the FCC limits the system power levels, PCS compensates by creating an infrastructure with towers that are closer together. Typically, the range is 200 feet to six miles. The tower transmits at no greater than 100 watts, and the phone operates at a maximum of 250 milliwatts. The antennas on the handsets are shorter because the range requirements are diminished. There are no installed, higher-powered mobile phones in PCS, only handheld portable units. Thankfully, though, future PCS equipment will offer adapters that emulate the installed mobile phone. They will provide hands-free speakerphone capability, use the car's battery instead of the portable's, and possibly use an external antenna.

## Nextel

Nextel Communications, Inc. offers a unique service in that it combines cellular-like telephony with two-way radio capability and message paging functions. The system uses Motorola's iDEN (integrated digital enhanced network) technology, which combines TDMA for the wireless phone functions of the service with sophisticated switch controllers to access the private, encrypted two-way radio capability. Nextel operates at frequencies previously licensed to Specialized Mobile Radio (SMR) carriers. Some of these carriers were offering a hybrid two-way radio/wireless telephony system that would cut you off if your call was too lengthy. Also, it did not offer full duplex (there was no audio feedback until you stopped talking and freed up the channel for the other person). The services offered by Nextel are an improvement over the previous SMR services, so they are called Enhanced Specialized Mobile Radio (ESMR).

In the early '90s, Nextel began purchasing the licenses for these frequencies nationwide. As a result, it has been able to create a national network in which there is technically no roaming, because you are using the Nextel system everywhere on the network. The benefit to you is that you don't pay roaming fees. Nextel includes both cellular airtime minutes and two-way radio minutes in its package rates. With the two-way radio built into the handset, you can talk to others on the network at a reduced rate compared to what cellular would cost. This is great for families and business groups who want to communicate with each other on their "cell phones" while they are away from home or office, but don't want to pay high wireless phone bills.

Here is an example of how Nextel provides a unique benefit to certain companies. A Florida company, Independence Recycling, has offices in Orlando,

Tampa, Lakeland, and Fort Myers. All their field personnel are outfitted with Nextel equipment. The sales team and superintendents are provided with equipment that accesses the Nextel network as both a two-way radio and a wireless phone, whereas the rest of Independence Recycling's Nextel units access only the two-way radio part of the system. When Independence Recycling's sales-people or superintendents make a phone call on their Nextel equipment, there is no long distance and no roaming anywhere in the state. Vic DiGeronimo, Jr., president of Independence Recycling, said one common usage is when a superintendent in Orlando talks to a superintendent in Tampa or Fort Myers on the Nextel two-way radio network. The conversation is completely private, and because Independence Recycling subscribes to unlimited two-way radio usage plans, there is no per-minute cost for the communication. Nextel equipment can perform group communications as well as private conversation. For example, a super-intendent at the Lakeland operation can activate a group alert to let everyone at his facility know that the catering truck has arrived.

# Looking Ahead

## Terrestrial wireless systems

**GSM1800** Following the initiative of the United Kingdom, spectrum is being added for access at 1800 MHz in addition to the 900 MHz currently being used in non-U.S. GSM markets. The spectrum remains incompatible with any spectrum being used in the U.S.

**W-CDMA** W-CDMA, or wideband CDMA, is being discussed worldwide. This technology would utilize 5,000 kHz channel spacing, where CDMA currently uses 1,250 kHz channel spacing. This is in contrast to AMPS channel spacing of 30 kHz (or NAMPS of 10 kHz). Channel spacing is like a pipe: the wider it is, the more you can push through it.

**LMDS** Some local multipoint distribution services (LMDS) auctions were conducted in 1998. LMDS is wireless service at 28 to 31 GHz. It is divided geographically into 493 BTAs, the same used for blocks C through F for PCS. The frequencies were divided into two blocks: block A represents 1,150 MHz of discontiguous spectrum, and block B consists of 150 MHz of spectrum. Licensees are given ten years to complete their build-out, as compared to the five-year rule in PCS.

LMDS is expected to provide voice telephony plus high-speed data and video transmissions. The two companies winning the most licenses to LMDS spectrum are WNP Communications, Inc. and Nextband Communications LLC. WNP Communications, Inc., which is owned by Spectrum Equity Investors, LP, Chase Capital Partners, AT&T Ventures, and Columbia Capital, paid $187 million for 40 licenses, including 11 of the top 12 markets, covering 105 million potential customers. Nextband Communications LLC, a company jointly owned by Nextel

Communications, Inc. and Nextlink Communications, Inc., paid $135 million for 42 licenses covering 96 million potential customers.

## Wireless local loop

The traditional method for you to obtain phone service to your home is for your local phone company to run wires to your house. With wireless local loop (WLL), the wiring inside your home stays the same, but there are no outside wires. A wireless switch box with an antenna would replace the network interface box inside your home that currently interfaces with a landline phone company. Wireless carriers implement channel and frequency reuse patterns to maximize usage of their spectrum. WLL service offers you choices of phone service for your local phone company provider. The systems are digital, and they are expected to deliver high-speed data services in addition to high-quality voice services. This propagates the "one phone, one number, anywhere" concept.

Some underdeveloped countries that don't have landline phone companies in place are implementing WLL because it costs substantially less than installing a landline network.

## Satellite wireless telephony

Satellite networks that connect to terrestrial landline telephone systems have been around for more than twenty years, addressing the needs of global travelers. Until recently, the only systems available used satellites in geosynchronous earth orbit (GEO), those in a fixed position approximately 22,000 miles above the earth. These GEO systems have between four and twenty satellites that are used for transmitting television, telephone services, and data (paging). The distance of the satellite from the earth causes a delay in the transmission, called latency, which can be annoying in a telephone call. Typically, the equipment is bulky, often the size of a briefcase or small suitcase, and costly. In addition, usage is expensive. Designing a satellite network for telephony without a latency problem means bringing the satellites closer to the earth. Low earth orbit (LEO) systems have satellites that orbit the earth at approximately 1,000 miles. The downside to LEO systems is that they require lots more satellites to achieve the same coverage as a GEO system. Developing a satellite network and having it integrate with terrain-based systems is a very challenging endeavor.

Iridium, Inc., for example, began work on its network in 1990 and didn't begin offering service until the fall of 1998. This is not an unusual timeline for developing a global satellite telecommunications system. Iridium has 66 satellites in a low earth orbit system. Subscriber equipment is similar in size to analog wireless phones and accommodates optional plug-in modules that emulate terrestrial networks. One module operates on the GSM 900 MHz networks and another operates on AMPS/NAMPS/CDMA 800 MHz networks. This allows subscribers to use one phone anywhere in the world. You have the option of subscribing to a terrestrial system directly for the terrestrial service. This usage is less expensive than using your Iridium number on the terrestrial module, because Iridium adds a surcharge for using the module to make terrestrial calls routed through its network.

Inmarsat Communication Systems, based in England, uses a GEO network. Companies such as LandSea Communications and O'Gara Satellite Networks provide satellite telephone communication services using the Inmarsat satellites. Intelsat of Washington, DC also uses a GEO network, with Comsat Corporation using the Intelsat system for satellite telephony.

Globalstar, owned by Globalstar, Loral Space, and Qualcomm, uses a LEO satellite system and is expected to begin offering service in 1999.

Teledesic is a company founded in 1990 by Craig McCaw and Bill Gates. In 1998, Motorola, Saudi Prince Alwaleed Bin Talal, Boeing, and Matra Marconi joined this venture (of which AT&T Wireless is 15 percent owner) with the goal of creating an affordable, global "Internet in the sky." It will be a network of 288 low earth orbit satellites designed to provide ubiquitous wireless telecommunications services that include Internet access and videoconferencing. Service is expected to be available in 2003.

To date, only one company is testing the middle space between GEO (high latency) and LEO (lots of satellites) by choosing the middle earth orbit (MEO), which requires 10 to 12 satellites orbiting at an altitude of about 6,000 miles. ICO Global Communications Services, Inc. is expected to begin offering this interconnected satellite service in 2000.

For more information about these satellite companies, see Appendix B.

## Atmospheric alternatives

There are several companies testing some alternatives to terrestrial and orbital satellite service. One company, Angel Technologies Corp., hopes to hook a communications pod to the underside of a plane and have the aircraft fly in circles 50,000 feet above a major metropolitan area. Each high-altitude long-operation (HALO) aircraft will be manned by two pilots working an eight-hour shift, with three shifts per day. Services are expected to include videoconferencing and high-speed Internet access. Angel Technologies is planning to build a fleet of 100 planes at a cost of $700 million and utilize two planes per market. This is actually much less expensive than the cost of launching orbital satellites at $50 million per launch.

AeroVironment, Inc. wants to create an "atmospheric satellite," a remotely controlled airplane fueled by solar panels that would fly at 80,000 feet. Research for this high-altitude, long-endurance flight project is being funded by NASA. A record-breaking test flight in August 1998 flew for 15 hours, reaching an altitude of 80,400 feet. High-altitude solar airplanes, with energy storage for nighttime flying, are being developed to provide continuous flights lasting weeks or months for this alternative to communications satellites. More information and updates can be found at AeroVironment's Web site (*www.aerovironment.com/area-aircraft/unmanned.html*).

Sky Station International is proposing a global system that would include 250 strategicly placed platforms held in place above the earth by an ion-propulsion system designed to sustain a geostasis of 100,000 feet. Geostasis means that the platforms would be traveling at the same speed as the earth rotates. The size of football fields, these platforms would be held aloft by helium blimps. More information and updates can be found at Sky Station's Web site (*funnelweb.utcc.utk.edu/~holtzman/mystuff/skystat.htm*).

# How Wireless Telephony Works

**2**
Chapter

## Background

Heinrich Hertz first measured an electromagnetic signal in the late 1800s. He determined that the variation between different frequencies could be measured in cycles per second. Because of his work, we now refer to cycles per second as Hertz (Hz). Audio frequencies, the range of hearing by human beings, are 20 Hz to 20,000 Hz (20 kHz). Electromagnetic frequencies are above 20 kHz. Very high frequency (VHF) is any frequency in the 30 MHz to 300 MHz range. Ultra high frequency (UHF) is any frequency in the 300 MHz to 3,000 MHz range. Microwave refers to frequencies 2 GHz and higher.

| | |
|---|---|
| 1 kHz (kiloHertz) | One thousand (1,000) Hz |
| 1 MHz (megaHertz) | One million (1,000,000) Hz |
| 1 GHz (gigaHertz) | One billion (1,000,000,000) Hz |
| 1 THz (teraHertz) | One trillion (1,000,000,000,000) Hz |

To avoid uncontrollable, free-for-all use of the millions of frequencies available, the Federal Communications Commission (FCC) allocates certain spectrums for certain usages in the United States. Wireless telephony frequencies were allocated as follows:

| | | |
|---|---|---|
| Nextel | 30 MHz | 806-821 MHz (15 MHz) |
| | | 851-866 MHz (15 MHz) |
| Cellular | 50 MHz | 824-849 MHz (25 MHz) |
| | | 869-894 MHz (25 MHz) |
| PCS | 120 MHz | 1850-1910 MHz (60 MHz) |
| | | 1930-1990 MHz (60 MHz) |

Wireless telephony is a system of subscriber units (mobile phones) and cell sites that transmit radio frequency signals in a specific bandwidth of spectrum, all managed by the mobile telephone switching office (MTSO). The MTSO in turn interfaces with the public switched telephone network (PSTN), which is the worldwide wired phone system, or landline phone system. Wireless phone networks are connected to the PSTN through the MTSO. This connection makes using a wireless phone as easy as using a desktop or home phone, and allows you to call anywhere in the world.

## Basic Concepts of Wireless Telephony

Wireless telephony consists of two parts: a wireless phone and a wireless infrastructure, or network. In order to use a wireless phone, you need to subscribe to a wireless carrier or service provider. When a phone number is assigned and the wireless phone is programmed, all the information needed for the phone and system to work together is entered into the wireless phone. This is called NAM (number assignment module) programming. In addition to the wireless phone number and other information, there is a number identifying the service provider, called a system ID or SID.

It is important to understand that all wireless phones inherently want to work. This means the phone is designed to look for a wireless signal and keep on looking until it finds one. When a wireless phone is turned on, it listens to information that is constantly being broadcast by the wireless carrier in what is called an overhead signal. The overhead signal includes the SID as well as instructions to the wireless phone to identify itself by transmitting its wireless phone number and electronic serial number (ESN). The phone then matches the SID that is in the overhead signal to the SID in the phone. If they match, the phone indicates that it is in its home market. If they do not match, the phone indicates ROAM. If the wireless phone can't detect any overhead signal, then the phone gives a NO SERVICE indication.

Some newer phones have a feature called enhanced home network. With this feature, the phone indicates that it is not roaming in certain nonhome markets where the carrier charges you as if you are in your home market. For example, if you are an Ameritech cellular customer in Cincinnati, Ohio, you are charged your "home per-minute rate" when you use your phone in Dayton, Columbus, Cleveland, and Detroit. Your dealer will program your phone to recognize the SIDs of Dayton, Columbus, Cleveland, and Detroit as if they are "home" markets, and your phone won't indicate ROAM while you are visiting there.

## The System
The infrastructure of the wireless system is comprised of a network of cell sites that interface with and are managed by an MTSO.

Figure 2-1 is an image of a cell with an antenna at its center, as viewed from the top.

Figure 2-1

A wireless network is composed of clusters of cells of different sizes. Each network is configured specifically to accommodate the local terrain and the specific usage patterns of the area. For example, a more densely populated area, already well-served by the landline network, may not have as much wireless phone usage as a freeway inter-change area that backs up with slow-moving commuter traffic twice a day. A cell site may have more channels assigned to it to accommodate more wireless phone traffic, or the cell site may be divided into several smaller sites.

Figure 2-2 demonstrates how cell sites are config-ured. Cell sites are represented by hexagons, but they are actually overlapping circles.

Figure 2-2

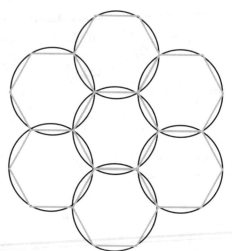

Cell site delineations can be represented even better by adjoining hexagons because a cell is divided into six sections for channel assignment. (See Figure 2-3.) Channel assignment becomes important in the design of the network because channels are reused in AMPS networks. The system engineers must be careful not to assign channels in adjacent cells in order to avoid co-channel interference, which results in cross talk—that's where you can hear another conversation and usually lose yours.

Figure 2-3

A cell site, which consists of an antenna and a base station, serves a specific geographic area called a cell. Cellular networks have larger cells than PCS because an 800 MHz signal travels farther than a 1900 MHz signal at the same power level. Cellular network cells range in size from four to twenty miles, whereas PCS network cells range from 200 feet to six miles. Channels are assigned to a cell. Cells are arranged within the network in such a fashion so that adjacent cells do not have the same channels assigned to them. Figure 2-4 is a simplistic diagram showing channel reuse with only six channels.

Figure 2-4

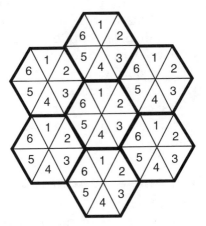

This is obviously an ideal representation. Adjacent cells aren't usually the same size. Also, an AMPS cellular system has access to 416 channels, and it uses channel pairs, one for transmitting and one for receiving. A PCS network has either 100 channels (for blocks D, E, and F) or 300 channels (for blocks A, B, and C). CDMA networks combine several channels into one larger channel. It is easy to see that the networks can be designed to reuse channels and frequencies and still allow sufficient distance separation to prevent co-channel interference.

Cell sites have base stations situated near the base of the antenna. The base station is made up of a transceiver for transmitting and receiving calls, and computer equipment that communicates with the MTSO by either wires or microwaves.

The MTSO is the brain of the wireless network. As you travel from cell to cell, the MTSO receives information from the base station of the cell you're using and analyzes your signal strength. The MTSO may ask an adjacent cell if it can receive your signal and at what strength. Then the MTSO sends instructions for your phone to increase or decrease power output and decides which cell will handle your call. Transferring the call from one cell to another is called a handoff. As you travel through your city using different cells and channels, the MTSO coordinates all the behind-the-scenes activity so that you experience continuous coverage. The base station uses control channels to "talk" to your phone, providing instructions on which channels to use.

## Registration and autonomous registration

The wireless system is constantly transmitting information about itself, as well as instructions to the phone, in what is called an overhead signal. When you first turn on your phone, it listens to the overhead signal and tunes to the strongest signal. This procedure is called registration. The MTSO makes note of where in the wireless network you are and records the information in the home location register (HLR) database. The phone continues to monitor the overhead signal, which also transmits phone numbers for inbound calls, essentially paging the phone. Your phone listens for a page that matches your mobile phone number. The system asks the phone to reidentify itself every five to fifteen minutes, a process called autonomous registration, and uses this information to update the HLR database. Then, when the MTSO receives a call for your wireless phone, it has a general idea of where in the network you are and can limit the number of cell sites it contacts, or pages, to process your call. Autonomous registration and the HLR reduce the workload of the MTSO by eliminating the need to page your phone on all the channels in the system.

## Power levels

When your phone autonomously registers, the cell site measures your phone's signal level and reports it to the MTSO. Wireless phone calls are not always processed at the maximum power output of the phone. For example, an AMPS wireless phone may process a call at .006 watts (6 milliwatts). The 3-watt phone is able to provide more power than the .6-watt (600-milliwatt) portable if the system asks for more power. In AMPS cellular networks, there are eight power steps. However, the cell site prevents portables from using the two highest power steps. This is controlled by a setting in the phone called a station class mark. The cell sites are constantly monitoring the power levels of the phone during a phone call. They send instructions to the phone to increase or decrease its power, as necessary, to maintain an adequate connection without causing interference to other phones on the network. This control minimizes potential channel interference from higher power levels as frequencies are reused within the network. With portables, control of the power level during transmission also helps maximize battery life.

CDMA technology, whether 800 MHz or 1900 MHz, controls the power of the phone somewhat differently because it creates large channels by combining several small ones. A CDMA system actually wants all the phones to be "talking" to the system at the same power level, so it checks each phone's power level up to 800 times per second and sends instructions to adjust the power level as needed.

## Handoffs

Another reason the cell sites measure signal strength levels of the phone is to determine if your call needs to be handed off to another cell site. As you travel through a wireless network, your phone moves within range of different cell sites. The MTSO is constantly monitoring the power level of your phone's signal. If your phone is transmitting at its highest power level, but the signal received by the cell site is weak, the MTSO checks other cell sites to see which one has a stronger signal from your phone. The MTSO hands off your call to the cell site that detects the strongest signal from your phone, providing there are voice channels available. If no other cell sites can detect a signal from your phone and your signal becomes too weak at the cell site you are using, your call will drop.

**Analog** As much as all the terrestrial wireless telephone systems operate in a similar fashion, there are some differences. The AMPS and NAMPS systems at 800 MHz are analog. Analog systems behave the same way FM signals do, so when they start to fade, you hear static, hissing, and dead air or silence. In other words, you get some warning that the signal is bad and that you may lose your call. In AMPS, there is actually a five-second window at the switch. If the system loses the phone's signal, the system waits five seconds before it disconnects the call. This is why you can change batteries during a call on some phones without losing the signal.

Multipath is a term used in conjunction with RF systems that describes signal reflections. This can happen in cities with tall buildings or in hilly terrain and is sometimes called signal spiraling. In AMPS, multipath is an enemy, whereas CDMA technology uses multipath to its advantage. Multipath fading in AMPS is where the reflections can seem stronger than the actual signal, which confuses the phone. It is an idiosyncrasy of FM. You might be familiar with the symptoms from experience with your car radio. As you pull up to a traffic light, your favorite song starts to fade. Then you roll forward a foot or two, and the signal comes back. Sometimes just putting your phone up to your other ear will correct the weak signal problem.

**Digital**    Digital technologies, on the other hand, function the same regardless of the frequency. When the signal gets weak, your call will be terminated without any warning noises. You might hear a slight difference in performance between 800 MHz and 1900 MHz. The main reason for this is that the 800 MHz carriers have more users on their network. A secondary reason is that the 800 MHz carriers are splitting their channels between analog and digital technologies. Digital networks will sound crisper and cleaner than analog systems, whether at 800 MHz or 1900 MHz.

## Dropped calls and system holes

No matter how carefully the system engineers design a network, there will always be weak spots. Wireless phone signals transmit along what is called "line of sight." This means that if you stand where the transmitting tower is and look out, that is where there will be coverage. If there is a "dip" you can't see into, that is where there will be weak or no coverage, or what is called a "hole" in the system.

Because wireless telephony is affected by terrain, hilly geographic areas are more prone to holes than flat areas. Cell sites are placed to optimize the coverage, of course, but when you're mobile and drive into a dip, you may lose your signal because you just entered a hole in the system. The signal is usually reestablished by just continuing to drive. If you are on foot, try walking to higher ground. This is a good reason to get a portable phone instead of an installed one. If your car breaks down while you are in the dip and you lose service, you won't be able to call for help if you can't take your phone out of the car.

POINTER | Wireless systems are also affected twice a year by the leaves on trees. When they fall off in the autumn and when they grow in the spring, carriers usually have to retune their networks to optimize the signals.

## Dealing with capacity overload— how 800 MHz ended up with two digital technologies

As more and more customers opt for wireless telephony services, the original analog cellular systems are becoming overcrowded. Carriers are always seeking ways to accommodate more users without diminishing the level of service their customers expect. To avoid busy signals and dropped calls caused by all channels being in use, the analog carriers also need to find ways to increase the capacity of their systems. One inexpensive nondigital solution is to implement

Narrowband AMPS (NAMPS) technology, which provides a threefold increase in capacity. In 1991, when NAMPS was introduced by Motorola, digital technologies were not yet available. Some larger markets that were nearing capacity limits, but had decided to adopt the forthcoming CDMA digital technology, implemented NAMPS as an interim measure to expand their capacity. This is an ongoing interim measure for carriers wanting to increase their capacity when they aren't ready yet for digital systems.

Digital technologies held the promise of capacity increases as well as enhanced service offerings. Time division multiple access (TDMA) offered a threefold increase in capacity and became available in 1992. Code division multiple access (CDMA) held the promise of at least a tenfold increase in capacity, which had greater appeal to more companies. However, despite promises to the contrary, CDMA wasn't available until 1996. This discrepancy created a split among carriers. Some of them wanted to implement digital technology as soon as possible to address capacity issues in markets such as New York, Los Angeles, and Chicago, so the A systems in those markets went with TDMA. AT&T implemented TDMA in all its markets, as did BellSouth and Southwestern Bell. Most of the rest of the carriers chose to wait for CDMA, and what a wait it turned out to be!

Both technologies are now available and being implemented by cellular and PCS carriers. As cellular carriers in your market convert to digital systems and PCS carriers get their networks up and running, you will no doubt see massive advertising campaigns. Digital sounds great, but remember, it is new technology. It may not be for everybody. Do your homework! Check out the service area footprint to make sure you are covered where you need service.

Read Chapter 3 of this book for guidance on acquiring wireless equipment and service. To see what companies are offering service in your area, check Appendix F–Carriers by Market, Channel Block, and Technology. If your town isn't listed, look for the nearest city. For wireless dealers in your area, you can check your local phone directory or yellow pages for phone numbers and locations.

## The Phone

Your wireless phone is actually a two-way radio and a miniature computer with specialized functions. Because this wireless device is able to communicate with the PSTN and behave like a wired telephone, it is called a telephone rather than a radio.

## What happens when I turn my phone on?

The wireless phone carrier is always transmitting information. When you turn your phone on, it initially shows a NO SERVICE indication while it listens to the carrier information. The phone tries to match the SID information provided by the carrier. If the SID from the carrier **matches** what is programmed into the NAM of the phone, then the phone does not indicate that it is roaming. If the SID from the carrier does **not** match what is programmed into the NAM of the phone, the ROAM indicator on the phone will be activated.

POINTER

This doesn't necessarily mean the phone will work. In fact, if the system determines that the information is not valid or is restricted, the call won't process or go through. Unfortunately, you have no way of knowing this until a call attempt is made.

When the carrier transmits its information, one of the things it does is ask the phone to identify itself by telling the carrier its phone number and ESN. The carrier matches this information with its database to verify, or validate, the information. If you are in your home market, the system makes note of where you are and which tower (cell site) is being accessed by using a home location register. This helps the carrier to manage or limit the number of cell sites it uses to page your phone on an inbound call. When the carrier knows your position, it can page the last known cell site and surrounding cell sites. The carrier asks the phone to identify itself as often as every five minutes. As mentioned previously, this is called autonomous registration. This same process occurs when you are roaming, except that the visiting location register is utilized instead of the home location register.

Automatic call delivery systems forward your inbound calls to you as you roam. When you turn on your phone in a roaming market, a message is sent from the roaming market back to your home market asking if you are a valid user. If the answer is yes, the roaming market tells your home market to send any inbound calls to your wireless phone over to the market you are visiting.

PCS carriers have taken this concept even further. Because many PCS carriers have created a national presence and may or may not have established roaming agreements with other carriers, they need a way to control which networks you roam on. Each PCS carrier has a list of authorized usable locations, which is a roaming list made up of system IDs (SIDs) and network IDs (NIDs). The NIDs identify the carrier's network and those of any "roaming part-ners." This list is programmed into the phone when the phone number is first activated. It can be updated by the carrier to include more locations as the carrier's network grows or as the list of roaming partners increases. You will need to take the phone to the dealer to have the programming updated. In the future, CDMA over-the-air activation capabilities may allow a carrier to update your list without a trip to your dealer. When the phone is looking for a network, the authorized usable location list is checked to allow or deny service.

## What happens when I place a call?

Wireless phones differ slightly from landline phones. For instance, landline phones provide you with a dial tone for auditory feedback when you lift the phone from the receiver or take the phone off-hook. Then, you get more auditory feedback in the form of dual tone multifrequency (DTMF)—the tones you hear when you press the number buttons. This process is called postorigination dialing. Wireless phones use preorigination dialing. This means you dial the number first, and then take the phone off-hook. Because we expect to hear it, wireless phones generate auditory feedback as you enter the number into the keypad. However, when you go off-hook, a dial tone is not generated and the DTMF tones are not transmitted. Wireless phone systems do not use dial tones or DTMF. Data devices such as faxes and laptop computers do generate DTMF and need dial tones, so these are generated by the data devices connected to your wireless phone. More information on using your wireless phone for data can be found in Chapter 6.

After you dial in the number you're calling and press the SEND key, it takes a few seconds before you hear ringing. In those few seconds, the cell site has verified that the phone is tuned to the strongest control channel. Then your phone transmits its own mobile number and ESN as well as the number you dialed. While the MTSO verifies the mobile number and ESN and sends the call to the PSTN, the cell site tells the phone which voice channel to use. The system and the phone exchange signaling tones, which confirm that the two-way communication channels are working properly. Fortunately for us, the system doesn't let us hear these tones. After the audio path confirmation is complete, you hear ringing sounds, which is auditory feedback that your call is being processed. When the person you called answers, you can talk to them the same way you would on any other phone.

## What happens when I receive a call?

A called placed from a landline phone is processed by the PSTN to the MTSO. The MTSO checks its home location register for your last known location and sends out a page to your mobile phone number. Your phone listens to the overhead message, hears the page, and says, "Here I am. Send the call over." The voice channel assignment and audio path confirmation tones occur as they did on the outbound call. Once verified, your phone rings to alert you that you have an incoming call.

## What happens when I hang up?

When you press the END button on your phone, it transmits a tone to the switch signaling that you request your call be terminated. The cell site forwards the request to the MTSO, alerting the PSTN to release the landline and terminate the call. If the person you were talking to hangs up first, the PSTN tells the MTSO the call is terminated. Then the MTSO tells your phone to let go of the channel you were using, which terminates your call. The latter process takes a few seconds longer and could result in a phone call being three minutes and four seconds long instead of two minutes and fifty-eight seconds long. If your carrier charges in whole-minute increments, those few extra seconds will result in your call being billed as a four-minute call instead of a three-minute call. That's why it's always best to terminate calls on your wireless phone yourself.

POINTER

## Phone features

Wireless phones have a variety of features that allow you to perform functions or take advantage of services. Some very basic necessities for operating a wireless phone are:

- a microphone and speaker so you can talk and listen during the phone call.
- a display so you can see who you are calling.
- a keypad so you can dial the number.
- a SEND or TALK key and an END key so you can make, answer, and terminate calls.
- a power button so you can turn the phone on and off.
- a power source, typically a battery, and a charger if your phone is portable.
- a subscription to a carrier.

It is most likely that the phones you come across will have more features than listed above. Features such as number storage or hands-free capability can benefit you in a variety of ways, from making the phone more user friendly to making it safer to use. All phones have some repertory memory, even if it's not a lot. Repertory memory is a storage place in the phone that retains numbers so you don't have to keep dialing them manually. This is an excellent safety feature, especially for people who use their phones while driving. Repertory memory allows you to pay more attention to your driving than to your phone!

More and more phones are coming with the option to attach a headset for hands-free capability. The headsets are usually inexpensive, running around $25 to $50. This is a very worthwhile investment for the safety it provides, allowing you to keep both hands on the wheel while driving. Compare this with the money you'd pay if you had an accident!

The list of phone options and features is quite extensive and is addressed completely in the feature details section of Chapter 3.

## Subscribing To a Carrier

To have a wireless phone ready to use whenever you want, you need to subscribe to a wireless carrier, the same way you subscribe to your local phone company in order to have phone service at your house whenever you want. In the same way that you pay a monthly fee to your local phone company to maintain active service, you will be charged a monthly access fee by the carrier you choose to subscribe to. Usage on a wireless phone is similar to long distance, where you pay a per-minute charge. Some carriers include a certain number of minutes of usage in the monthly access fee. These monthly access fees are usually a little bit higher than those with no minutes included. You are actually paying for the included minutes, but often at a lower cost per minute than if you paid for them separately. For example, a monthly access fee of $26.95 plus 27¢ per minute for 60 minutes of usage equals a total cost of $43.15. A bundled plan of $39.95, including 60 minutes, saves you $3.20 per month. You are paying for the minutes, but at the rate of 22¢ for a savings of 5¢ per minute.

| | |
|---|---|
| To calculate this, take the bundled minute rate | $39.95 |
| and subtract the unbundled monthly access. | -$26.95 |
| Then, divide the answer | $13.00 |
| by the number of minutes included. | ÷ 60 |
| The per-minute rate is : | $ .22 |

Most cellular carriers require you to sign a service contract. There is some basic language in all of them that says they are not responsible if the system goes down or if your phone breaks, etc., and that you are obligated to pay for any usage you incur. Cellular contracts usually obligate you to the carrier for a term of one, two, or three years, and if you cancel before the term is up, you are required to pay penalty fees. These penalty fees are usually a lump payment of $150 to $300, but some carriers require you to pay the balance of the monthly access fees as well. Make sure you read your contract carefully before signing it and understand what you are signing. Carriers will often give you something in return for your commitment to them, such as free airtime or a free phone, or include accessories, such as a battery or cigarette lighter adapter.

## Coverage Areas and How They Are Assigned

In the early 1980s, the FCC needed to define geographic boundaries for coverage to provide delineation for the cellular carriers. The Office of Management and Budget divided the United States into two groups: Metropolitan Service Areas (MSAs) and Rural Service Areas (RSAs). At first, 734 service areas were defined within these groups, but the FCC modified the MSAs and RSAs. It established 306 metropolitan geographic areas for cellular coverage in the U.S., each of which has two carriers: channel block A and channel block B. Once the 306 MSAs were defined, the FCC established geographic divisions for the rural areas of the United States, designating 428 RSAs, each of which has at least two carriers: channel block A and channel block B. Refer to the MSA/RSA map and accompanying list of market names in Appendix C.

The carriers in each MSA and RSA are assigned system IDs, or SIDs. Some carriers owning adjacent cellular markets received permission from the

FCC to use the same SID in multiple systems, thereby creating what is called a supersystem.

Some examples of this are in Pennsylvania, where Bell Atlantic Mobility's Philadelphia B system ID of 00008 is also used by Allentown, Trenton, New Jersey, and Wilmington, Delaware. You can travel throughout these market areas on the B system and your phone does not indicate that you are roaming. Bell Atlantic Mobility also implemented a supersystem in the western part of the state, where the Pittsburgh B system ID of 00032 is also used in the Pennsylvania markets of Altoona, Bradford, Butler, DuBois, Indiana, Johnstown, Uniontown, State College, and Somerset; in the Ohio markets of New Philadelphia and Athens; and in the West Virginia markets of Charleston, Huntington, Logan, Parkersburg, Ripley, Weston, and Wheeling. Whew! That sure is a supersystem!

AirTouch has a supersystem in Michigan and northwestern Ohio. The Detroit A system SID of 00021 is also used in the Michigan markets of Flint, Saginaw, Lansing, Grand Rapids, and Muskegon, and in the Ohio markets of Toledo and Lima. There are more supersystems around the country. Check with your carrier for details in your area.

A decade after MSAs and RSAs were established for cellular, auctions for PCS frequencies began. Once again, lines were drawn for delineating service areas. The FCC divided the spectrum into six sets of channel blocks. In the same way that block B cellular spectrum was licensed to existing Bell operating companies, most of the spectrum for blocks A and B were auctioned to large companies already in the wireless phone business. The FCC adopted Rand McNally's organization of the United States into 51 Major Trading Areas (MTAs) to define the service areas for these block A and block B carriers. See the map and accompanying list of MTA market names in Appendix D.

For the other four blocks of channels (C, D, E, and F), the FCC used Rand McNally's division of geographical service areas called Basic Trading Areas (BTAs), of which there are 493. See the map and accompanying list of BTA market names in Appendix D.

## What Is My "Home" Market?

Your home market is that market in which you subscribe. Your home market encompasses a Cellular Geographic Service Area (CGSA), or coverage area, which is usually larger than a major metropolitan area. Wireless phone calls placed to numbers within this CGSA are considered local calls and are charged for wireless usage only. Sometimes wireless calls within a CGSA are cheaper to make than using pay phones or calling long distance due to the broad area covered by the CGSA for wireless.

## Understanding the Carrier/Agent, Dealer/Customer Relationship

When a business decides to become a wireless dealer or agent, it negotiates with one of the wireless companies in the marketplace. The dealer arranges to be compensated for each new wireless phone number it activates. Dealer/carrier negotiations vary, but some dealers arrange for their compensation on a sliding scale. Here are some examples with real numbers. Remember, this information varies by dealer, by carrier, and by wireless market.

The Wireless Phone Store is compensated $100 for every line activation. With 60 lines activated in a month, the line activity revenue to the store is $6,000. However, the Wireless Phone Store has a sliding scale clause and is paid $150 for each line if it activates more than 100 lines per month. This has an impact on the behavior of the store. For example, if the store has 90 line activations by the 25th of the month and doesn't get any other sales by the end of the month, its revenues will be $9,000 for the month. If they activate another 20 phones before the end of the month, the Wireless Phone Store will be paid $16,500 (110 phones multiplied by $150). Quite obviously, the manager of the Wireless Phone Store will be very concerned with activating more than 100 lines each month. Towards the end of the month, if the store has not exceeded the 100-line goal, the manager will creatively generate the business needed to increase his store's revenues.

You can recognize these efforts as in-store sales, or "deal of the day" specials, which might include free airtime, activation fees waived, first monthly access charge free, a limited amount of free off-peak minutes, an upgraded phone, a free accessory, such as a battery or cigarette lighter adapter, etc. If these offers are advertised, they will usually have a purchase deadline of the end of the month. As much as these specials help the wireless dealer to generate more revenue, they also benefit you as a consumer.

Another means of compensating the dealer or agent is with residuals. Residual payments are a percentage of the local usage and monthly access fee. Percentages are small, usually one to two percent. However, for a dealer or agent savvy enough to negotiate a good residual contract, even one percent can generate substantial revenues for his business. The following examples show the impact residual payments can have on store revenues:

Add 100 lines per month

12 x 100 = 1,200 lines/year

After five years @ 1,200 lines/year

5 x 1,200 = 6,000 lines

6,000 lines @ $35/month usage

6,000 x $35 = $210,000

$210,000 x 1%

.01 x $210,000 = $2,100

If the average monthly usage increased to $50 and the residual was paid at one and a half percent, the $2,100 per month additional income would increase to $4,500 per month after five years.

# Resellers

The FCC mandates that a wireless carrier (whether 800 MHz cellular, 1900 MHz PCS, or 800 MHz ESMR) "must permit unrestricted resale of its service."[2] This ruling was designed to promote competition in the marketplace by giving the consumer more options for buying his or her wireless service. In January 1999, the Personal Communications Industry Association (PCIA) requested that the FCC provide relief from this mandate for carriers in markets with four or more wireless networks.

Reseller agreements are typically made at the local market level. However, some wireless companies will negotiate reseller arrangements for more than one market, depending on how they manage their businesses. A few noncarrier companies, such as Motorola Cellular Service, Inc. (MCSI) and MCI WorldCom, have developed a nationwide reseller presence. Resellers provide a benefit to large corporations that want to deal with just one company for all their users, wherever they may be. AT&T Wireless and GTE Wireless are carriers that offer national

[2]Code of Federal Regulations 47CFR20.12, page 12, revised as of October 1, 1996

account programs by combining reseller activity with their licensed market coverage to blanket the country.

So what's the difference between a dealer/agent and a reseller? A reseller buys airtime and numbers from a carrier at wholesale. It then establishes its own retail rates, solicits its own customers, maintains its own customer service, and bills its customers directly. The reseller has to pay the carrier for airtime used whether or not the costs are recouped from its customers.

An agent or dealer has no fiscal responsibility for the airtime its customers use. However, if the customer disconnects before the end of the contract period, the dealer or agent may have to repay some or all of the commission it received even though the carrier collects a cancellation penalty from the customer.

## How Do I Interface With the Carriers?

As a consumer, most likely you will deal with the carrier through one of three channels: a company-owned retail store, an independent business that is an agent of the carrier, or an independent business that is a reseller for the carrier. All the carriers have company-owned retail stores. You will recognize these stores easily as they will include the carrier's name as part of the name of the store, such as GTE Wireless, GTE Mobilnet, Ameritech Communication Center, or AirTouch Cellular, etc. Agents of the carrier can vary from a small single-shop operation to a national chain that is designated as an agent for the carrier. National chains, such as Best Buy, Circuit City, Radio Shack®, or Sears, usually arrange local affiliations with a carrier in each market where they want to distribute wireless phones. Companies such as Hello Direct, Everything Wireless, and Wireless Dimension have made these same types of affiliations and sell nationally through mail order and Internet channels. They will often align themselves with carriers that have a presence in multiple markets. For instance, Bell Atlantic Mobility covers most of New York state, Pennsylvania, Connecticut, and Baltimore in the mid-Atlantic area. AT&T Wireless has 800 MHz coverage in more than 100 markets nationally and is building new networks where it is licensed to provide 1900 MHz coverage to create a nationwide presence. Nextel and Sprint PCS are also developing their national networks.

## Over-the-Air Activation

Digital technology has brought alternatives and change to wireless telephony. One dramatic change in the way you and the carrier interface is called over-the-air activation. The process of activating a phone usually requires a technician to program your new or used phone. With over-the-air activation, you can call the carrier you choose, and, providing you have a compatible phone and the carrier doesn't need you to sign any paperwork, the carrier will activate your phone remotely. You will be given a code to dial into the phone, which sends a signal to the carrier identifying itself as the phone needing to be programmed. You may be prompted to enter some information for identification and credit check purposes, such as your social security number and birth date. The switch, in turn, broadcasts information that the phone receives and then updates its own programming.

This process will be quite helpful as PCS carriers continue to add markets to their national network and expand their roaming markets. Over-the-air activation will enable you to call your service provider to add this information to your phone remotely and thereby improve your roaming capabilities.

**3**

## Where Do I Buy It?

Phones are not usually sold without service as one is useless without the other. If you want to purchase a phone without service, dealers often charge more. The carrier pays an activation fee to the dealer when you sign up for airtime service. Many dealers choose to use some of this commission to offset the cost of the wireless handset in order to make the phone more affordable to you. This subsidy frequently results in the dealer selling the phone for less than the cost of the unit. If you aren't getting airtime service, the dealer won't get the activation fee and has to charge a price that covers the cost of the equipment as well as a bit of profit. For example, if the dealer pays $100 for a phone and receives a $150 activation commission, he might sell the phone to you for $50. If you don't want service, the dealer will sell it for no less than $100, and often $125 to $150. This practice of subsidizing wireless phone purchases is more common among cellular dealers than PCS dealers.

### Cellular

Cellular phone stores are most commonly owned by the local carriers, but there are many independent dealers or agents as well. Other major distributors of cellular phones include the more recently authorized retail outlets such as Best Buy, Circuit City, KMart, Montgomery Ward, Office Depot, Office Max, Radio Shack®, Sears, Wal-Mart, and probably your local department store and stereo store. You will even see car dealers as cellular agents.

Many of these cellular stores have Internet online ordering available, but their Web sites may not reflect the deal of the day that the retail stores offer. Some companies offer cellular phone subscriptions and purchases through an 800 number.

Resellers are another channel for acquiring cellular phones and service. Unlike agents, resellers don't represent themselves as being affiliated with the carrier they resell for, so they often appear to be an alternate carrier.

## PCS

The PCS carriers have established company-owned and company-branded phone stores in the markets where they offer service. In addition, most PCS providers have established toll-free and/or Internet online ordering setups. Some have also aligned themselves with national retail stores. An example is the affiliation Sprint PCS has with Radio Shack®, Best Buy, Circuit City, The Good Guys, Dillard's, The Sharper Image, Office Depot, Office Max, and the following May Company department stores: Hecht Company, Foley's, Robinson's May, Kaufmann's, Filene's, Famous Barr, and Meier & Frank.

## Nextel

Nextel has established a national direct sales team with offices in the top 78 markets in the United States. It also has a network of over 1200 local dealers across the country, as well as some nationwide dealers such as Hello Direct, BearCom, American Wireless, Next Wireless, DH Brothers, USOP, Home Depot, and TIC. At the time of this writing, Nextel did not have any resellers.

# Choosing a Phone

Deciding where to buy your phone can be narrowed down by defining the level of equipment you want. There are as many different varieties of phones as General Motors has models of cars. Your mission is to decide whether you need only a Chevette-type phone, the status and features that come with a Cadillac-type phone, or something in between. Manufacturers of handsets use several different channels to distribute equipment. One channel is Original Equipment Manufacturer (OEM), where handset manufacturers sell phones to automobile makers that integrate the phone into the manufacturing of the vehicle. The carrier channel is another avenue of distribution. Handset manufacturers sell phones to the carriers. The carriers, in turn, sell the phones to their dealers, who ultimately sell the phones to end users. A third sales channel is the retail channel where national retail chains buy handsets directly from the manufacturers to sell to end users.

Some of the automobile makers participating with the handset manufacturers' OEM distribution include Lexus, Infinity, Acura, Mercedes, Cadillac, Lincoln, and Rolls Royce. Wireless phones are prewired into vehicles at the factory. These phones are usually higher-tiered and installed units. Often they provide features that are tied right into the function of the car, such as lowering the volume of the radio when the phone rings or putting speaker controls on the steering wheel. If you don't have an existing wireless number that can be moved into this phone, the car dealer becomes your wireless phone dealer.

The retail channel includes national chains such as Sears, Montgomery Ward, Best Buy, Circuit City, KMart, Office Depot, Office Max, Radio Shack®, Wal-Mart, as well as your local department stores.

As mentioned earlier, these retail stores have aligned themselves with a local carrier. The handset manufacturers sometimes have specific tiers of products designated to sell through this retail channel.

The carrier channel offers the widest selection of equipment, running the gamut from entry-level phones to feature-rich business user units. Some handset manufacturers sell phones to wholesalers, so dealers can order phones that may not be available through their carrier channel connection.

A little known and exclusive (or should I say elusive—it's hard to find!) place to buy very high-tier Motorola phones is Motorola's VIP Direct sales. Contrary to common perception, VIP Direct does not provide cheaper pricing, but rather top-of-the-line equipment featuring the latest technology with premium benefits at a premium price. Motorola is the only cellular telephone manufacturer with a field sales team selling equipment directly to the public. For more information about their phones and service, contact Motorola VIP Sales on the Internet (*www.mot.com/GSS/CSG/ WhereToBuy/MotorolaDirect/vip.html*).

One of the key differences you will notice among the various places to buy wireless phones is the level of knowledge that the salespeople have. Although not always true, the more you pay for the phone, the more knowledgeable the salespeople seem to be. A friend of mine asked me to accompany her to a local wireless dealer. She already had service with this carrier, but wanted to buy a new phone. My friend had a bag phone and was fairly certain she wanted to get a handheld portable. The wireless phone store had a couple of models that I knew had internal fast chargers, which would have been helpful to my friend at her lake property where she uses her cellular phone as her only phone. When I asked the sales clerk if either of the wireless models plugged directly into the wall, she disappeared for a few minutes, and then returned with a technician carrying two boxes containing the models in question. Neither the sales clerk nor the technician could answer the question about the phones' charging capabilities, and could only show us what accessories the phones came with.

My friend, Paul Silla, told me that when he went wireless phone shopping, he asked the salesman at the wireless dealer whether the carrier the dealer represented was operating on the A system or the B system. The sales clerk didn't know and offered to ask his manager. Unfortunately, the manager was unable to answer the question either.

## Should I buy a new phone, and why?

One school of thought states, "if it isn't broken, don't fix it." In other words, if the phone you have is doing everything you want it to do, then there is no need to replace your cellular phone. If, on the other hand, your phone is not performing correctly, you should determine if the unit is under warranty. If it is, then you may want to get the phone repaired, as this is probably the least costly option. If your cellular phone is out of warranty, you still have the option of getting the unit repaired, but the cost of the repair should be weighed against the cost of buying a new phone with a new warranty. (Most companies performing repairs on units out of warranty will warrant the phone for a short time, say 30 to 90 days.)

If you've decided you are going to replace your phone, then you will want to purchase the most current technology available. Also, make sure that a new technology requiring new equipment isn't forthcoming. See Chapter 1 for an overview of the different technologies and services available.

Once the new digital technologies are introduced, some people might try to tell you that analog cellular is obsolete. This is not totally correct. In the conventional United States cellular arena, there are two different digital technologies. Because of this, the members of the Cellular Telephone Industry Association (CTIA) have committed to keeping analog systems in place until at least 2015. This will provide a common thread for users who may travel between markets offering different technologies. Equipment for both digital technologies will be dual mode: TDMA/AMPS or CDMA/AMPS. It is important for you to know that your analog-only phone will be usable for quite some time. However, as handset makers gradually phase them out of manufacturing, new analog-only phones will be in short supply.

Cellular 800 MHz markets each have two carriers. As these carriers introduce digital overlays to their analog systems, some markets will have one TDMA 800 MHz carrier and one CDMA 800 MHz carrier, as do Chicago and New York. Other markets will have two CDMA 800 MHz carriers, as do Detroit and Cincinnati. This means that a Chicago TDMA subscriber traveling to Detroit with his TDMA/AMPS 800 MHz phone will access the AMPS system, as no TDMA 800 MHz system is available.

## What kind of phone should I get?

Your choice depends on how you plan to use the wireless phone. There are three basic phone formats:

- Mobile phone
- Bag phone
- Handheld phone

Both the mobile phone and the bag phone are 3-watt units, transmitting at the maximum amount of power allowed by the FCC. The mobile unit is designed to be permanently installed into a vehicle, utilizes an external antenna, and provides hands-free capability through the use of a microphone and speaker. The key components are a transceiver (a combination transmitter and receiver) and a handset. The handset provides the user with a keypad, a display, a speaker, and a microphone with which to make and receive phone calls.

A bag phone is actually a mobile phone modified to be carried around rather than installed. Because this phone has mobile components, it usually weighs two to four pounds and may be missing hands-free components. A bag phone is powered either through the cigarette lighter of a vehicle or by using an attach-able battery, which will increase the weight of the bag phone by one to two pounds. Some manufacturers sell mobile phones with bag phone adapters. This is ideal for those people who want the stability of an installed unit, but may also want to remove their phone for other activities such as boating or camping. An installation kit for your second car allows you to move the phone between cars.

The third and most popular form of wireless phone is a handheld phone. This category is often broken down further into portable phones, which weigh about one pound, and personal phones, which weigh a half pound or less. The power level of hand-held phones is regulated by the federal government for health and safety reasons and may not exceed .6 watts because the phone's antenna is so close to your head during use. If you are a high-volume user, such as a real estate agent or customer service representative, you can minimize your health risks by using hands-free accessories in the form of either a car kit or a headset.

POINTER

## Decide on a phone format

There are three main formats of wireless phones: mobile phones, bag phones, and portable phones. Each of these formats has specific advantages. To determine which format is best for you, envision how you will use a wireless phone. To help you with this process, some of the benefits and advantages of each format are listed below. Place a check mark in the box for the phone features and benefits that are most important to you, and the format that will work best for you will become evident. How do you see yourself using a wireless phone?

### Mobile phone
❑ 3 watts
❑ Hands-free is important to you
❑ No need to take the phone out of the vehicle
❑ You live in a remote area or an area with hilly terrain
❑ You only use the phone in one vehicle
❑ Installation expense is not an issue
❑ Wide range of prices and features

### Bag phone
❑ Inexpensive
❑ 3 watts
❑ Portable: car to boat to picnic to cottage to job site
❑ Lunch box size
❑ Weighs 2 to 4 pounds
❑ Hands-free options
❑ External antenna option for enhanced reception
❑ Good for security purposes

### Handheld phone
❑ 600 milliwatts (.6 watts)
❑ Small size
❑ Lightweight
❑ Good for security purposes
❑ Carry in pocket, purse, or briefcase
❑ Optional hands-free
❑ Optional car kit
❑ Move the phone from car to car
❑ Lend the phone to a relative or business associate

Three things usually separate one phone from another, especially when they "look the same."

- Features
- Accessories included
- Warranties and protection

If you are going to use the phone for business rather than for personal use, you might want to consider a phone that will provide you with features that better accommodate business use. If you plan on updating your equipment every year or so to have the latest technology, you may not want to pay the additional price involved with longer warranties.

## Phone acquisition

Free phone. Rent or lease a phone. Purchase a phone. Which one is for you?

How long do you plan on having a wireless phone? The general consensus is that once you get one, you won't give it up, the way that you wouldn't give up your home phone. With wireless telephony, however, there is competition. You have choices. Carriers often present their offerings as fruit baskets, so sometimes it's difficult to compare apples to apples. Use the information in this section to decide what factors are important to you so that when you go shopping, you can select the fruit basket that is right for you.

Free phones sound great until you read the fine print. The hardware is free, but the usage isn't. Find out what it's going to cost you and for how long. Is the "free" phone worth it, or are you better off buying a phone and choosing a rate plan that is more suited to your needs?

Some carriers offer rental or lease programs. Paying $5 per month sounds like a bargain until you realize that you have to sign a two-year agreement. You're paying $120 for something that you don't own at the end of the contract. You can buy a respectable phone for under $100 that is yours from day one, plus choose your carrier and rate plan.

## Summary of steps

1) Decide on the format of the wireless phone.

2) Decide on features, accessories, and warranty. What level or tier of equipment do you want?

3) Shop for the right carrier and rate plan. Key issues include:

    A) Length of term required for service
       What does a longer term provide in the way of benefits?
         -Free phone?
         -Activation fee waived?
         -Free airtime?

    B) Cancellation penalties
       How much will it cost you if:
         -You decide that the wireless phone isn't working out
         -The service (carrier) isn't good in the areas you frequent, and you need to change to an alternate carrier
         -You move and want to cancel service in your old home market

    C) Monthly access fees
       Do you want the lowest monthly rate possible (emergency use only)?
       Do you want minutes included?
       (This usually reduces the cost on minutes, but make sure you'll use them all, or that you can change out of the plan at no charge if it isn't right for your usage.)

# Where do I start?

This section is broken down into two parts: considerations for the first-time buyer and considerations for those of you replacing your equipment. Rating the different elements to consider when buying a phone will only be discussed in the first-time buyer section, even though they also apply if you are replacing your phone.

## First-time buyer

As a first-time buyer, you are faced with decisions concerning equipment and airtime. Following is a list of items and issues for you to consider. The listed items are each explained at the end of this section, as well as why you want to consider them. To make this an interactive exercise, there is a line next to each item or issue for consideration. Place a number from zero to five on the line, with zero representing no interest in the issue and five showing the most interest.

Once you have completed this exercise, make a list of the features that are important to you and take it with you when you go shopping for a phone.

# Choosing a Phone

What is the price of the phone? _____

Is the phone "free"? _____

(What will this "cost" you in monthly access charges for the length of your contract? Are there penalty charges if you disconnect early?)

How long is the warranty?

• One year _____

• Three years _____

• Five years _____

Does the phone have the features you want?

• Speed dial _____

• One-touch buttons (one, two, or three) _____

• Directory number storage (repertory memory)

-Less than 10 memory locations _____

-20 to 50 memory locations _____

-100+ memory locations _____

• Alphanumeric directory _____

• Credit card dialing _____

• Password dialing storage _____

• Display

-One-line _____

-Two-line _____

-Segmented _____

-Dot matrix _____

-LED _____

-LCD with backlighting _____

• Battery meter _____

• Signal strength meter _____

• Dual mode _____

- Dual frequency                                                _____
- Ringer tone selection                                         _____
- Answering machine recording capabilities                      _____
- Long tone DTMF                                                _____
- Dual registration                                            _____
- Vibration and/or ringer notification                         _____
- Incoming call notification                                   _____
- Call timers                                                  _____
- Automatic lock/manual lock                                   _____
- Clock/alarm clock                                            _____
- Automatic answer                                             _____
- Mute (one-way hold)                                          _____
- Keypad lock
- Call restrictions                                            _____
- System registration                                         _____

Are loaner phones available if your phone
  needs servicing?                                            _____

Is insurance included or available if the phone is
  lost, stolen, or damaged?                                   _____

What accessories come with the phone?

- Battery                                                     _____
- Nickel cadmium                                              _____
- Nickel metal hydride                                        _____
- Lithium ion                                                 _____
- Charger                                                     _____
- Cigarette lighter adapter                                   _____
- Spare battery                                               _____
- Hands-free headset                                          _____
- 3-watt car kit                                              _____

# Feature details

**What is the price of the phone?** Wireless phone prices range from free to almost $2,000. The price of the hardware varies directly in proportion to the features, accessories, and benefits that come with your phone. Carriers may offset the price of the wireless phone, but not without benefit to themselves. Usually the catch is that you are locked into a service agreement of two or three years, often with hefty early cancellation penalties. In addition, you may have to sign up for a specific rate plan, especially with free phones, and often you can't change your rate plan during the term of the contract.

**Is the phone "free"?** This sounds great! But what will this "cost" you in monthly access charges for the length of your contract? If you decide after a year into your three-year contract that you don't want the phone anymore, what are the disconnect penalties? Is the free phone really worth it, or are you better off buying a phone outright and signing up for the service package of your choice?

**How long is the warranty?** The length of the warranty is going to affect the cost. Longer warranties increase the price of the phone. Do you want to gamble on whether the phone will last two or three years even though it only has a one-year warranty? Will you want to replace it when it breaks, and is out of warranty, to get newer equipment? Would you rather pay to have the phone repaired? Purchasing extended warranties can cost $75 per year. This is a personal financial decision and you will need to decide if the extra cost is worth it to you. Don't pay more than 15 percent of the price of the wireless phone for the extended warranty, and never pay for a warranty on a free phone.

**Does the phone have the features you want?**
There are lots of features available on phones. Do you really need them? If you use your phone for business, you might find a lot of them helpful. If you only want a phone for security, you may be paying for something you'll never use.

Most phones include the following standard features:

- **Volume controls**    You can regulate the transmit and receive volume levels of your wireless phone to offset the anomalies of the system.

- **Last number redial**    Phones have as many as ten last number redials, so there's no need to redial all those numbers. Just redial the way you do at home. For those times when someone says to call back in five minutes, having more than one last number redial slot can be an advantage. You can make a few more calls and then access the last number redialed list. That way you won't risk misdialing.

Optional features that have an impact on the price of the phone are:

- **Speed dial**    Preprogramming your phone with numbers you call frequently makes dialing as easy as 1-2-3. Just press a single or two-digit number followed by the SEND button. If you make lots of calls, you will extend the life of your keypad by using speed dial.

- **One-touch buttons (one, two, or three)**    Just as your home phone has buttons that you can program for emergency or special numbers, some wireless models have one-touch buttons that include the SEND command with the programmed number.

POINTER

- **Directory number storage (repertory memory)**
  Who needs this? If you have a phone for security, you may be too upset to dial 9-1-1 SEND. Storing 9-1-1 into a one-touch memory location is best. The next best thing is to store 9-1-1 into memory location 1 or 9, so you only have to press one button and the SEND key. Storing the numbers of close relatives or friends helps when you're under stress and can't remember their numbers. Business users can store their customer contact numbers in the phone. If you're on the road a lot, you may need to use two slots per person, one for local calls and one for long-distance calls. You can see how quickly the memory locations can fill up. Keep this in mind when deciding whether you need less than 10, 20 to 50, or 100+ memory locations. Like RAM on a computer, you can never have too much.

- **Alphanumeric directory** It's easy to store a slew of numbers in your phone, but where, oh, where did you put them? Alphanumeric capability allows you to put a name with the number, and the phone stores this list alphabetically, like an electronic Rolodex. Choices include all capital letters (OFFICE), upper and lower case alpha characters (Office), and enhanced alpha characters (Office 800#). The greater the character set options, the easier it is to use, but the phone will be pricier.

- **Credit card dialing** Your company's long-distance card is billed at 10¢ per minute and the carrier charges 27¢ per minute for direct-dial long distance. You call the 800 number to access the company's long-distance network (11 digits), then you dial the number you're calling (10 digits), and then you enter the authorization code (14 digits). Whew! Thirty-five numbers! While you were driving! What a road hazard! Good thing you didn't make a mistake, or you'd have to start all over. Credit card dialing can shorten those 35 numbers to about 13: one for the memory location (1), then SEND (1), ten digits for the phone number you're calling (10), then SEND (1) to transmit the authorization code. That's a lot safer than 35 digits!

- **Password dialing storage** Some markets don't have authentication or RF fingerprinting in place. Hence, if you buy an analog phone, you are required to dial a PIN code with every phone number you call. It is more convenient to let the phone do this for you with the touch of a single key .

- **Display** The display is your visual interface with the phone. The more information it gives you, the easier the phone is for you to use. Two-line dot matrix displays provide the most options for messaging, help screens, alphanumeric nametags, etc. One-line segmented displays give you feedback on the phone calls you make, but they aren't much help otherwise.

  - Segmented displays are either seven-segment or fourteen-segment. Segmented displays can best be explained using the numeral eight. A seven-segment display has two lines on the left side (one above the other) and two lines on the right side (one above the other) with three lines connecting them. One is across the top, another in the middle, and one at the bottom (**8**). Words can seem cryptic on a seven-segment display. A fourteen-segment display breaks each of these lines in two, thereby creating greater flexibility when creating alphabetical characters.

- Dot matrix displays have dots over the entire display area. Creating recognizable messages becomes easy.

- LED (light-emitting diode) displays are bright, colorful, and easy to read in sunlight or at night. Because they require more energy than LCD displays, they are less common. Handset manufacturers usually opt for LCD displays to provide longer battery life.

- LCDs (liquid crystal displays) are usually duotone gray and are more readable when they are backlit.

- **Battery meter**   You are on a call with your best customer when your battery dies. It sounds as if you hung up on him! Knowing how much charge you have left in your battery allows you to plug in, change batteries, or make some polite excuse for ending the call.

- **Signal strength meter**   You're trying to make a call and you keep getting that annoying fast-busy sound. No wonder! Weak signal! You should have checked the signal meter first. This feature is very handy if you are in hilly terrain or in a building in the city. Changing locations, even slightly, can improve your reception.

- **Dual mode**   Given the size and weight issues, it is unlikely that more than one digital tech-nology will be in a phone in the near future. It is easy, however, to combine one of the digital technologies with AMPS, and this will help you when you're traveling. Because AMPS tech-nology is so well established, you can use a dual mode phone on the digital technology where available, and the AMPS mode is there to back you up until digital coverage areas develop more fully.

- **Dual frequency**   Cellular and PCS operate on different frequencies. To access both sets of frequencies, you need a phone capable of doing so. Some existing cellular companies have PCS licenses to complement their cellular service areas. Dual frequency phones give you access to these markets as you travel.

- **Ringer tone selection**   A phone is ringing. Is it yours? Your friend's? They all sound alike! Now you can get a phone with your choice of ringer. Make yourself stand out in a crowd. Know when it's your phone that's ringing.

- **Answering machine recording capabilities** You're expecting some important details for your client, but you're in a meeting and don't want to be rude. Turn on the answering machine and put the phone in vibration mode. No more phone tag for that vital piece of information. The caller just leaves the message, and it's electronically recorded right in your phone.

- **Long tone DTMF**   Home answering machines, voice mail systems, long-distance calling card services, etc. all depend on DTMF. Sometimes the timed burst sent by the wireless phone isn't long enough for these systems to recognize it. Long tone DTMF lets you control how long the tone will be transmitted by pressing and holding each key. The tone will transmit for as long as you hold down the key.

- **Dual registration**   If you do business in more than one city, roaming charges can get hefty. Dual (or more) NAM capability allows you to have more than one "home" market. Even though you're paying monthly access fees to two companies, your per-minute rate is greatly reduced. Do the math before you jump into this option, though. New one-rate plans are making dual registration unnecessary for travelers. See the roaming analysis form in Chapter 9.

- **Vibration and/or ringer incoming call notification** As the sound of ringing phones in restaurants, supermarkets, ball games, and theaters becomes increasingly annoying, the option of having your phone vibrate to notify you of an incoming call, instead of ringing, is more appealing. If you're phone dependent, insist on this and use it. Your friends will thank you.

- **Call timers** You're on hold on a wireless phone and the meter is ticking. How long has it been? An ongoing call timer lets you know. If that last call seemed as if it lasted forever, check the call timer. When you get your bill, you won't be shocked; you'll remember. Incoming calls from a client aren't identified on your call detail. Check the call timer and write down the duration of the call so you can include the charges on your client's invoice.

- **Automatic lock/manual lock** Your PIN code is programmed into the phone. So is your long-distance calling card, and all your clients' names and numbers. This is not information you want in the wrong hands. Setting your phone to lock every time you turn it off is just plain smart. If a thief gets his hands on your phone, it is useless to him without the unlock code. It isn't inconvenient for you either, as you only have to dial three or four numbers each time you turn your phone on.

- **Clock/alarm clock** Who needs a watch? Get accurate time and even a reminder to return that phone call on time.

- **Automatic answer**  You're expecting a call-back from your office. You're driving and you have your headset on. The phone rings. Just keep driving. There's no need to fumble for the phone and the SEND key. Within two rings, the phone answers.

- **Mute (one-way hold)**  You've been driving for hours and you're starving, so you pull into your favorite fast food restaurant. As you're waiting in line, your boss calls. It's now your turn to order, so you say to your boss, "Hold, please." You mute your microphone so that he can't hear you order the hamburger and fries you're drooling for. Once you've pulled away, you unmute the phone. Meanwhile, you have heard him talking to your office nemesis about you.

- **Keypad lock**  Various objects in purses and pockets can press the buttons of exposed keypads and inadvertently make calls. This function is handy if you don't have a covered keypad.

- **Call restrictions**  You want your daughter to take your phone with her on her first date, but only for emergency. Set the call restriction so that she can only dial from memory, which you've programmed with 9-1-1 and home. Perhaps you're issuing phones to your delivery fleet, but you only want them calling local numbers. Set the call restriction to dial seven digits only.

- **System registration**  Wouldn't it be nice if you could control which system you access? Well, with this feature you can. Let's say you're an 800 MHz B system subscriber in Toledo. You take your phone out on your boat in Lake Erie. The water amplifies the cellular signal, and now your phone actually sees several other different systems (all 800 MHz) as well as your home system: Toledo A, Detroit A, Detroit B, Cleveland A, Cleveland B, Windsor, Ontario A, and Windsor, Ontario B. If your phone is set to a standard system registration selection, your phone will look for the strongest B system first (and this may not be Toledo, your home market), but it may also see an extremely strong A system. Regardless, you run the risk of roaming onto multiple systems if you can't control your phone. By changing the setting, you can lock your phone onto your HOME system so you don't incur roaming charges. Check your manual for specifics for your phone. There are usually other options as well, and if you have a dual mode/dual frequency phone, you'll want to be familiar with how you can maximize roamer programs offered by your home market carrier. PCS phones look for networks either automatically or manually. Read your equipment manual for specific details on how to control, or override, the automatic network, or system, registration.

**Are loaner phones available if your phone needs servicing?** This is a must for those of you who are phone dependent and a nice perk if you're not. Your service provider will put your phone number into a loaner phone while your phone is being repaired.

**Is insurance included or available if the phone is lost, stolen, or damaged?** Warranties are fine if the phone breaks due to a manufacturing error. What if the damage is your fault? You drop it; you run over it; you lose it at the ball game. Are you just out a phone? Do you have to pay for the repair? Can you get insurance? Is it included? What is the deductible? How long are you covered? Be sure to read the fine print.

## What accessories come with the phone?

- **Battery**   Portable wireless phones come with at least one battery. At least one spare is essential for phone-dependent people. Different types of batteries include nickel cadmium, nickel metal hydride, and lithium ion. Check the battery section in Chapter 7 for details.

- **Charger**   The one you want may not be the one you get. A slow charger that fully discharges the battery first will enhance the life of your nickel cadmium batteries. Be sure to get the special charger that lithium ion batteries need if you opted for these lightweight energy cells. A charger built into the phone (internal charger) is very handy for travelers.

- **Cigarette lighter adapter**   This is a great way to conserve your battery while in your car, and some cigarette lighter adapters also recharge your battery in the process.

- **Spare battery**   Don't buy it too far in advance. Most batteries won't perform all that well after one year, even if they're just sitting in a drawer.

- **Hands-free headset**   One thing portable phones don't have that mobile phones do is hands-free capabilities. Or do they? By adding a hands-free headset, you can have this convenience with your portable phone, too. This inexpensive option can also be a lifesaver when you're driving. See Chapter 7 for more information.

- **3-watt car kit**   The ultimate! When you're in your car, it's a mobile phone. When you're out and about, you have a portable. You enjoy both options with just one phone number. It is the best way to add a hands-free speakerphone, bypass and conserve your battery, and secure the phone in your vehicle.

## Choosing a Carrier

Deciding who is going to provide your airtime service for the next year or so is more important than deciding on your equipment. Choosing the right rate plan may save you hundreds of dollars per year. The listed items are each explained at the end of this section, as well as why you want to consider them. To make this an interactive exercise, there is a line next to each item or issue for consideration. Place a number from zero to five on the line, with zero representing no interest in the issue and five showing the most interest. Medium, heavy, and power user usage is calculated on a 25-day month. A working month consists of 21 days, and four days have been added for the workaholics.

Following are detailed explanations of all the issues to consider when evaluating your needs for an airtime carrier. The definitions for the different types of users are designed to help you determine which category you fit into. Ask yourself the question, "How do I plan to use my wireless phone?" In answering this question, you will be able to match your anticipated use of the wireless phone with one of the five types of users. This is important to determine before you go shopping for wireless service. Otherwise, you might sign up for a plan that has too few minutes for your usage (you will pay more for the extra minutes than if they were included), or too many minutes for your usage (you will be paying for minutes you don't use).

# Choosing a Carrier

Cost of airtime

- Security user
(emergency use only)                                        _____

- Light user
(around 60 minutes per month or 2 minutes per day)          _____

- Medium user
(around 250 minutes per month or 10 minutes per day)        _____

- Heavy user
(around 750 minutes per month or 30 minutes per day)        _____

- Power user
(around 1,500 minutes per month or 60 minutes per day)

- Least-cost-per-month access                               _____

- Least-cost-per-minute usage                               _____

Carrier considerations

- Cheap or free off-peak time                               _____

- Ubiquitous roaming                                        _____

- One-rate (low-cost) roaming                               _____

- Secure communications                                     _____

- Private two-way radio capability                          _____

- Rate charging policies                                    _____

Carrier features

- Call waiting                                              _____

- Three-way calling                                         _____

- Call forwarding                                           _____

- No-answer transfer                                        _____

- Busy transfer                                             _____

- Short messaging service                                   _____

- Caller ID                                                 _____

- Voice mail                                                _____

- Call detail                                               _____

- Calling party pays                                        _____

- Prepaid wireless service                                  _____

- One-rate plan                                             _____

## Cost of airtime

The real expense of a wireless phone is the airtime bill. It consists of a monthly access fee, local airtime charges, any operator-assisted calls you made (such as 4-1-1), roaming charges (both daily fees and usage minutes), long-distance charges, and taxes. Your challenge is to keep this bill as low as possible. Each market charges different rates according to what that market will bear, so you will need to apply perspective to the following examples based on your knowledge of your market.

## Security user (emergency use only)

Try to get the lowest monthly access rate you can. When you do need to use the phone, it will probably cost you 65¢ to 95¢ per minute, but you will consider it money well spent to handle your emergency! Using this approach will keep your annual expense for this security device to less than the cost of a cup of coffee each day.

If you think the wireless phone may become more than just a security device, then ask your service provider if you can change your rate plan midterm and whether you can change back, too. Sometimes the carrier lets you change to a rate plan with bundled minutes that costs more per month for the bundle, but won't let you switch to a rate plan with a monthly access that costs you less. For example, you are on a $12.95-per-month plan with all minutes charged at 65¢ per minute. You switch to a $29.95 plan that includes 60 minutes per month. After four months, you decide to change back to the $12.95-per-month plan, but the carrier won't let you.

# Light user
### (60 minutes per month or 2 minutes per day)

You are a light user if you make one or two quick calls a day, or if you only use your phone four or five days a month for 10 to 15 minutes at a time. Your best bet is to find a rate plan that includes 30 to 60 peak minutes. Make sure that you don't trade free minutes for high peak usage charges if you exceed the free time. Pay attention to the per-minute rate if you exceed the included minutes.

# Medium user
### (250 minutes per month or 10 minutes per day)

You make four to five three-minute calls a day. A bundled rate plan that includes 200 to 300 minutes per month should fare you well. Make sure you can change to a different plan if your usage habits change. If most of your conversations are local with friends, family, or coworkers, consider a Nextel digital phone. The people you talk to will need to sign up for Nextel also, but you can use the private two-way radio for about half the cost of wireless telephony rates.

# Heavy user
### (750 minutes per month or 30 minutes per day)

You're always on the go and you still carry a pager, as you're often near landline phones. Nevertheless, you use your wireless phone 30 to 45 minutes a day. Consider a carrier offering digital service if the digital footprint will cover the geography where you travel. A digital phone, whether 800 MHz, 1900 MHz, or Nextel, will eliminate the need for a sepa-rate pager and wireless phone, saving you $10 to $25 per month right away. Also, take advantage of the short messaging service (SMS) available on digital. You can communicate with someone via text messages at less than the cost of a wireless phone call. Caller ID is usually an included feature or available at a nominal charge (about $1.95), so you can screen your calls. Digital phones with SMS also act as pagers. You can actually turn the phone off while in that important meeting. Then, when you turn on your phone, the numeric pages or text messages are instantly available. You also get alerted to any voice mail messages left while you were unavailable. Look for a rate plan that includes 600 to 750 minutes a month.

## Power user
### (1,500 minutes per month or 60 minutes per day)

You know who you are: totally phone dependent and a national traveler. You spend an hour or more a day on your wireless phone. Without doubt, you want the least-cost-per-month, least-cost-per-minute plan bundled with 1,000 minutes or more peak usage and with cheap or free off-peak time. As a nationwide roamer, it is important to check with your service provider for roaming coverage areas before you sign on the dotted line. Check with several carriers to see if they offer one-rate (low-cost) roaming. You're probably discussing some delicate business matters on your wireless phone, so be sure the service you commit to is digital. Find out where in the country your dual or tri-mode phone will default to analog and curb your discussions while there. Ask your service provider for custom calling features that will enhance your business use of the phone. For instance, caller ID lets you see who's calling. Call waiting allows you to answer one call while on another, and voice mail takes the call if you don't want to interrupt your conversation. Three-way calling lets you join the two conversations. Call forwarding lets you forward your wireless calls to another phone number, and short messaging service (SMS) will give your wireless phone both digital and alphanumeric pager capabilities as well as voice mail notification.

## Least-cost-per-month access fees

A security user is most concerned with what the cost per month will be, because the phone will only be used for emergency. If you're lucky enough to find a monthly access of $10 or $15 per month that includes 10 to 20 minutes, you probably won't have to pay extra for your emergency calls.

## Least-cost-per-minute usage

Business users need to be concerned with how much they are paying per minute for use. When you sign up for a bundled package, calculate what you are actually paying for your free minutes to make sure it's a deal. For example, if a bundled package that includes 60 local minutes costs $34.95 per month, and a basic rate plan without bundled minutes costs $19.95, the difference is $15.00. Now, divide the $15.00 by 60 minutes. You'll see that you're paying 25¢ per minute for the bundled time.

## Carrier considerations

- **Cheap or free off-peak time**   More and more carriers are offering off-peak programs. Some charge a monthly fee for unlimited off-peak airtime, usually $9.95 to $12.95. Other companies offer free off-peak time for a limited period as an incentive for signing up for a specific length of term. Read the fine print. You may get unlimited off-peak calling for two years of a three-year contract. After you've gotten used to spending three hours a day each weekend making free calls to friends and family, now, in year three, you'll be paying for it.

- **Ubiquitous roaming**   The analog coverage in the United States has become quite comprehensive after 16 years of development. Traveling with a wireless phone is becoming more popular than ever, even if the phone is only for emergencies. If you travel and want to use your phone everywhere you go, don't settle for unclear answers about roaming coverage and costs. Most carriers have roaming agreements with other companies and some have special rates.

- **One-rate (low-cost) roaming** Some markets have specific roaming rate plans where you pay a little bit more per month, but don't pay daily access fees or excessive roaming rates in a specific group of markets. One example of this is in markets in North Carolina, which let you roam into South Carolina and Virginia at home per-minute rates. Another is the Indianapolis market, where you can travel to Michigan, Indiana, Illinois, and Ohio with no extra fees in the major markets once you've enrolled in the executive roamer rate plan. Check with your local carrier for a plan of this kind.

- **Secure communications (digital network)** Although it may be illegal to use any information garnered from listening in on a cellular call, people still like to eavesdrop. If you're using the right eavesdropping equipment, an analog cellular call sounds the same as a landline call. Digital technology, though, is transmitted as binary code, and the human ear is unable to decipher the communication. Sophisticated decoding equipment may be able to determine what is being said, but it could take days. If you discuss business on your wireless phone, digital is a must.

- **Private two-way radio capability (Nextel)** A group at your office is involved in customer service work, and all of you are constantly in and out of the office. You need to communicate with one another, but don't want to pay the expenses of a wireless phone call. Consider the private two-way radio capability in the Nextel equipment. Two people can talk as securely as if they're on a digital wireless phone. More people can be added to the conversation as needed, and the cost is a fraction of that of wireless telephony. This is a great idea for groups of families or friends, too. Ericsson may be adding capabilities similar to this to their equipment. Check with their Web site or your local carrier for more details.

- **Rate charging policies**  Some digital rate plans don't charge you for the first minute of use. If you make a lot of short phone calls, this is a great option. Another way to save on your airtime costs is by signing up for a rate plan that charges you for usage in tenth-of-a-minute increments instead of rounding to the whole minute.

## Carrier features

- **Call waiting**  This switch-based feature alerts you that you have a new incoming call while you are on an existing call. You can answer the new call using a switchhook function the way you do on your home phone. On your wireless phone, press the SEND or TALK key. You can alternate between the calls, but you can't create a three-way conversation. You are charged for the airtime on both connections.

- **Three-way calling**  This is a switch-based feature that allows you to create a three-way conversation between yourself and two other parties. The conference call is set up by calling one party and then calling the second party. If someone calls you, you can put him or her "on hold" while you establish the third-party connection. You then complete the conference call by bringing the first party back on line. You will pay airtime charges for both calls.

- **Call forwarding** This switch-based feature, which works the same as it does on landline phones, forwards a call inbound to the wireless phone over to another number. The inbound call will not ring on the wireless phone. Some carriers charge airtime usage fees for this feature. This means that if you forward calls from your wireless phone to your office, then when someone calls your wireless phone and you answer it in your office, you may not realize the call was routed through your wireless phone. If you talk for twenty minutes, you will be charged wireless phone airtime. Sprint PCS, for example, charges 10¢ per minute for calls forwarded from wireless phones. Accordingly, that twenty-minute call will cost you $2.

POINTER

Here's a suggestion. If you only have one phone line at home, and you want to surf the Internet but don't want to miss any voice calls, then subscribe to call forwarding on your home land-line phone. This should only cost about $2 to $4 per month. Then, before you log on to the Internet, forward your calls to your wireless phone. This way, you'll at least know someone is trying to reach you, even if you can't afford to talk to them on your wireless phone. You can then log off the Internet and call the person back. Don't forget to turn the forwarding off when you've finished surfing the Internet. If you subscribe to voice mail on your wireless phone, you can leave your wireless phone turned off, let the call go to voice mail, and then check it when you're done on the Web.

- **No-answer transfer** This call diversion feature is another switch-based function where the call first rings into the wireless unit. If it is not answered within a specific number of rings (usually four), it will transfer to a predesignated number. No-answer transfer cannot be used at the same time as the voice mail feature, as this is how the calls are transferred to the voice mail system.

- **Busy transfer** You can designate an alternate phone number to receive your calls when your wireless phone is busy. Busy transfer is also a switch-based function and can't be used at the same time as voice mail.

- **Short messaging service (digital)** Digital phones offer you enhanced services. Among them is the ability to send and receive short messages using the display and keypad of your digital wireless phone, similar to text messages on pagers. Two other benefits, offshoots of SMS, are that the system will notify you of a voice mail message, even while you're on a call, and will store alphanumeric pager-like messages when your phone is turned off. When you turn on your phone, the message appears and, if it is a numeric message, it is available for automatic callback.

- **Caller ID** This is a service enhancement that shows the number (and sometimes the name) of the person calling on the display of your phone. This feature works the same as on your home phone service. Often, there is an additional monthly charge from your wireless carrier for this feature.

- **Voice mail** You can enjoy the benefit of an electronic secretary, similar to your home answering machine, but better. Whether your phone is turned off, you are out of the service area, or you're on another call, voice mail answers your phone when you can't. Digital services offer voice mail notification. When you power up the phone, if you have a voice mail message waiting, you receive a notification. You will also receive voice mail notification while the phone is turned on if a message was left for you while you were on another call, or if you left the phone unattended.

- **Call detail** If you want to see a list of the calls you made or received, the way you do on your home long-distance phone bill, you may have to pay extra—up to $5 in some markets. This feature is very handy for business users, especially those who pass the charges on to their clients. Most carriers offer you the choice of seeing the call detail chronologically (by the date of the call) or numerically (by the phone number called).

- **Calling party pays (CPP)** As the name implies, the person calling the wireless phone pays the airtime charges of the call. Because the financial burden isn't borne wholly by the subscriber, who pays only for outgoing calls, this concept usually increases wireless usage. Inbound call charges are spread among the various callers. CPP is very popular in other parts of the world and is slowly being implemented across the U.S.

- **Prepaid wireless service** Wireless services typically send you a bill each month for the airtime you use. This is considered postpaid because you pay after you've incurred charges. An alternative is being offered that allows you to pay in advance for a specific amount of use. This prepaid service is available to all applicants and requires no credit check. If you thought you couldn't get a wireless phone because your credit was poor or nonexistent, this service is for you. It's great for college students and for those who want to budget usage.

- **One-rate plan**    At the time this book was being written, many companies were following the lead of AT&T Wireless by implementing plans similar to its Digital One-Rate$^{SM}$. These plans charge a per-minute rate that is the same for local or roaming calls and includes any long-distance charges. This is great for the high user and power user, but overkill for the security user.

## The Final Score

If you add up the score of the features you wanted in the above lists, you'll see that the lower the score, the less you should pay for a phone and service. If features don't mean anything to you, don't pay for them. If you aren't going to talk much on your wireless phone, then don't sign up for a rate plan with lots of minutes. You'll be paying for something you won't use.

If your score is 180 or above, look for a fully featured phone, a long warranty, insurance, and a rate plan with a big bundle of minutes. Also, check to see what roaming agreements are available. Sometimes carriers offer roaming rate plans, where you can roam into specific markets at special rates for a slight increase in your monthly access fee.

# Rate Plan Analysis

You've done your homework. You have four rate plans in front of you. Which one do you choose? If you already have a phone, you have an advantage because you can use your actual usage in your calculations. If not, make your best guess and plug in those numbers. When calculating your off-peak usage, remember that off-peak time doesn't start at 5:00 P.M. It often starts at 7:00 P.M., 8:00 P.M., or 9:00 P.M.

## Do the math! Calculate your savings

First, figure out what your plan is costing you now. Exclude tax, long-distance charges, roaming charges, and other miscellaneous land-based fees. So that you can use it again, use a pencil on the following worksheet, or photocopy this page (for your own personal use). Have a calculator handy. Then fill in the blanks.

### Rate plan analysis

| | Your Info | New Plan | Example |
|---|---|---|---|
| Write down what you pay for your monthly access fee. | (1) _____ | _____ | $27.95 |
| Does this include any free minutes? | Yes No | Yes No | No |
| If yes, how many? | _____ | _____ | 0 |
| Subtract this number from the total number of peak minutes or off-peak minutes you use in the following calculations. For example, if you use 100 minutes per month and have 60 minutes included, use 40 minutes in the calculation. | | | |
| How many peak minutes do you use on average each month? (use at least three months of typical usage to determine this) | _____ | _____ | 50 min. |
| What do you pay for peak usage? | _____ | _____ | 27¢ |

| | | | |
|---|---|---|---|
| Multiply the peak minutes times the peak usage: | | _____ _____ | 50 x 27¢ |
| Total peak usage | (2) | _____ _____ | = $13.50 |
| How many off-peak minutes do you use on average each month? (use at least three months of typical usage to determine this) | | _____ _____ | 20 min. |
| What do you pay for off-peak usage? | | _____ _____ | 27¢ |
| Multiply the off-peak minutes times the off-peak usage: | | _____ _____ | 20 x 27¢ |
| Total off-peak usage | (3) | _____ _____ | = $5.40 |
| Now add: | | | |
| the monthly access fee (1) | | _____ _____ | $27.95 |
| the peak usage charges (2) | | _____ _____ | $13.50 |
| the off-peak usage charges (3) | | _____ _____ | $5.40 |
| **Final Total** | | _____ _____ | $46.85 |

Next to the numbers on the rate plan analysis form, apply the competitive rates you are considering and see what you can save. If the new calculation is less than you are paying now, consider how much this will save you over the length of the contract you are required to sign.

Will a competitor offering rates of $19.95 for the monthly access fee, 35¢ per minute for peak usage, and 20¢ per minute for off-peak usage save you money based on the above example? The monthly access fee is low, as is the off-peak minute charge, but your peak charge will increase by 8¢ per minute. Let's do the math.

| | | |
|---|---|---|
| 50 minutes x 35¢ per minute | = | $17.50 |
| 20 minutes x 20¢ per minute | = | $ 4.00 |
| Monthly access fee | = | $19.95 |
| Total | = | $41.45 |

The total cost of $41.45 is lower than the rate plan in our example by $5.40 per month, or $64.80 per year. Even after paying a $25.00 activation fee, and despite the increased peak per-minute rate, you will be ahead at the end of one year by $39.80.

## Replacing Your Equipment

As an existing user, you have a definite advantage. You know what you **don't** want! You also have a much better idea of what you do want. Make a list of the features you've envied in your friends' phones. Check the list of features under the section on choosing a phone. If it helps, rate them.

- Did you buy too much phone last time?

- Do you really need a digital phone? Is it worth the extra expense? Can you wait until digital coverage is more developed?

- Which carrier offered the rate plan you wished you had subscribed to? Maybe it's even better now!

- Pull out your bills and see how much airtime you really use. Evaluate no less than three average months. How much time do you spend talking during peak time? How much during off-peak time? Take this information with you when you go phone shopping. Look for bundles that work best for your usage. Don't trust what you think is your usage. Know for sure! Digital rates are often less expensive than analog rates, but you are usually required to sign up for a rate plan that includes a specific quantity of minutes to get these reduced rates. Taking your existing usage history with you on your quest for a new wireless phone will enable you to make the right decision.

The following story illustrates my point. Jack Smith signed up for a rate plan in Columbus, Ohio, for $99 per month that included 250 minutes. He thought this was a terrific deal! The problem was that he only used 100 minutes per month in Columbus, but he talked 150 minutes per month in Cleveland, Ohio! His local bundled rate plan didn't include the roaming minutes, so he was paying for 150 minutes he didn't use in Columbus and then paying again for the 150 minutes he did use in Cleveland. Because of an unusual arrangement in Ohio, Jack roams at his home per-minute rate in the major cities, so he wasn't paying high roaming rates. However, he was paying to use airtime in Cleveland. By changing his home market to Cleveland (where he actually talks more on his wireless phone), Jack pays $49.95 for a bundled plan that includes 150 minutes and charges 27¢ per minute for each minute exceeded. Now, when he's in Columbus, he pays 27¢ per minute for the 100 minutes. His total bill ($49.95 + $27.00) is only $76.95. Jack saves $22 per month, or $264 per year, by paying for what he uses instead of what he thinks is a terrific deal.

## What Is Roaming?

With a wireless phone, you can do something you can't do with your home phone: leave town and take your phone and phone number with you. This is called roaming. Roaming with wireless telephones means you are using a system that is not the one you subscribe to. Your home system is also referred to as a service area, or market, and

Figure 4-1

Your home market

The market you
are visiting

Your phone
indicates ROAM

represents the geographic area covered by your carrier where all calls are local. As you travel beyond the boundaries of your local wireless phone service area, you enter the service area of another company's system. At this point, your phone's roaming indicator is activated to alert you to the fact that you are no longer in your home market.

Sometimes, you don't need to travel to roam. In some service areas, your phone roams right in your home market between competing service providers. Traditionally, though, because you had a choice of service provider when you signed up for wireless service, the ones you didn't choose will not let you use their system. Not that you'd want to! Roaming can be an expensive proposition.

Roaming charges can be as little as your home per-minute rate with no daily fees, or it can cost $1 per minute or more plus a daily access fee, often about $3 per day. You see, the carrier charges its regular subscribers a monthly access fee. As a roamer, you want only temporary access to the system, so some carriers charge daily access fees. The per-minute usage fees are higher than your home rates because your home carrier charges you for the usage it missed out on. The roaming carrier charges you premium usage rates as well, because you don't subscribe in that market.

**Reduced roaming rates**   Many of the carriers are moving to reduce roaming rates. One way this happens is when your home market carrier doesn't "re-rate" the charges it receives from the roaming markets. It merely "passes through" the charges. In this instance, the only charges you see on your invoice are those billed by the roaming market to your home market for your usage.

POINTER

**Network selection**   Once you leave your home market, most phones are set to look for a system that is of the same type as the one you subscribe to. For example, if you are an A system subscriber, the phone will look for an A system in the market where you are roaming. If the phone can't find an A system, it will look for a B system, etc., until it finds a system. At this point, even though the phone has found a working system, whether A or B, you still may not be able to use your phone. If there is no reciprocal agreement in place that allows the roaming company to bill your usage charges back to your home market, you cannot use your phone.

**Brownout** A reciprocal agreement may exist between two carriers, but it is sometimes temporarily suspended due to excessive fraudulent charges from the market that you are roaming in. This suspension is called a brownout. The temporary blockage can last anywhere from days to six months. If this happens to your phone number, you may need to use a major credit card to pay for your usage charges. An alternative may be to manually change your network selection to another block of channels that does not have roaming restrictions. If it is critical that you use your phone while roaming, check with your carrier before you leave on your trip.

**Roaming rules** Most cellular markets have a rule: you are not able to roam on the opposing carrier in your home market. Because you had a choice of carriers, the one(s) you didn't pick usually will not let you use their system. They block you by restricting access of your area code (NPA) and three-digit exchange (NXX). Certain markets have overlapping coverage in multiple cities by one carrier, but not the other. In these markets, it is possible to roam on the opposing carrier.

An example of this is the Detroit/Toledo area. The AMPS B system in Toledo is operated by Alltel,

POINTER

whereas the AMPS B system in Detroit is operated by Ameritech. AirTouch operates the A system in both Toledo and Detroit. The Toledo AirTouch A system can't block Toledo B system subscribers

Figure 4-2

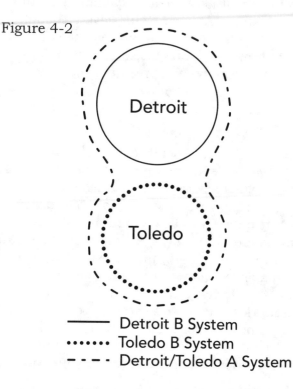

—————— Detroit B System
•••••• Toledo B System
– – – – Detroit/Toledo A System

from using their A system in Toledo without also blocking them from the A system in Detroit, so they don't block the Toledo users at all. The reverse situation works the same way. A Detroit B system user isn't restricted from using the A system in Detroit because that would block his Toledo usage. This sounds pretty good, so why should you be concerned? If you subscribe to the Detroit B system and your phone picks up the Detroit A system signal instead, then, when you make a call, you may think it's a local call in your home market. It isn't, and the call could cost considerably more than expected, perhaps three to five times more.

# Making and Receiving Calls While Roaming

Roaming involves two types of calls: outbound roaming calls and inbound roaming calls. Inbound roaming can be broken down further into four types of calls:

1) receiving a call using traditional roamer access methods from someone in:

   a) the market you are visiting

   b) another market

2) receiving a call using the automatic call delivery method from someone in:

   a) the market you are visiting

   b) another market

Let's look at what happens in each of these situations and what costs are associated with each.

## Outbound roaming calls

Placing a roaming call is usually transparent for wireless phone users. This means that you don't have to do anything differently to place a call when you roam than when you are in your home market. Call completion problems may arise if the carrier on which you are roaming uses a different dialing pattern than what you usually use. Typically, if you are making a local call in the roaming market, you dial a number consisting of the area code (three digits) and the phone number (seven digits) for a total of ten (10) digits. No "1" precedes the ten digits. You do this instead of just dialing seven digits because the roaming carrier "reads" your area code from the phone. Some places will process a seven-digit dialed number by sending it back to your home market. However, there are some markets that will process a local call in the roaming market when you merely dial seven (7) digits. If you are making a long-distance call, one that is outside the visiting market, dialing one plus the area code and phone number (1+10) will usually complete the call. Occasionally, you will be roaming with a carrier that doesn't want to deal with your long-distance charges. It won't process the call until you dial zero plus the area code and phone number (0 +10), and then provide a long-distance credit card.

If your call won't go through, you may get an inter-cept message that your call can't be completed as dialed. More likely, you will just get a fast busy signal or some other noise, which gives you no clue on how to proceed. A high-low siren is often indicative of NO SERVICE. Check to make sure your phone indica-tors are confirming the presence of a service provider. If your phone is indicating you have service, try altering your dialing pattern. Here are the four choices and the order in which to try them:

1+10 (carriers are trying to develop a universal dialing pattern for home and roaming calls)

10 (this was the original universal dialing pattern goal)

7 (this is only for roamers calling within the local roaming area)

0+10 (this will require either a long-distance or major credit card depending on the rela-tionship between your home market carrier and the visiting market carrier)

The following story illustrates how dialing patterns can affect the way your call is processed. One of my Cleveland customers traveled to Las Vegas. Once there, he dialed a seven-digit number to call someone locally in Las Vegas, but the system processed the call by sending it back to the 216 area code. My customer hadn't specified an area code, and the Las Vegas system processed seven-digit calls by reading the area code programmed into the caller's phone and routing calls to that area code.

## Inbound roaming calls

Receiving calls is more transparent than it used to be. However, when the new systems fail, it's nice to have a fallback plan. So here's an explanation of the whole process. Because the different types of technology addressed in this book present different experiences in roaming, several examples will be used.

### 800 MHz analog cellular

Let's address the analog user first. Understanding this process will give you a good basis for understanding roaming in general.

Lois and Clark are both driving from Metropolis to Smallville, but in separate cars. As they near Smallville, their cars get separated. Lois calls Clark to find out where he is. There are two ways she can accomplish this: the traditional roaming way or the new and improved method—automatic call delivery.

#### The traditional roaming way

Before leaving on her trip, Lois contacts her service provider and gets the latest roamer access numbers for the markets she plans to visit. Then Lois checks with Clark to see if he uses the A or B network in Metropolis. (When roaming, Clark's phone will look for the same type of system as that of his home carrier.) Clark is a B system subscriber in his home market, so Lois looks up Smallville in her roamer access list and finds the access number for the B system. Then Lois dials the area code and seven-digit number to access the local B system switch. This call is a "local roamer" call, which means that Lois will pay roamer charges, but not long-distance charges. After this call is completed, Lois will hear a second steady dial tone or a stuttered dial tone followed by a steady dial tone. Once Lois hears the steady tone, she dials Clark's area code and seven-digit phone number (10 digits). Lois

Figure 4-3

**Metropolis**

**Traditional Roaming Method**
- Making a local call
- Using a roamer access number to reach a roamer
- Receiving a call while roaming
- No long-distance charges to roamer

**Smallville**

**Lois's Phone**     **Clark's Phone**

**MTSO**

- Lois makes local call to local access number
- Lois pays roaming rates

- Call is local roaming to Clark
- Clark pays roaming rates

doesn't dial "1" here because she has dialed into the local switch already, and the switch only needs to know what phone number (10 digits) Lois is trying to reach. Notice that Lois doesn't need to do anything to use her phone because her home market carrier has a reciprocal, or roaming, agreement with the visiting carrier in Smallville. It also doesn't matter that Lois is an A system subscriber. Clark will pay roaming charges to talk to Lois, but not long-distance charges, as this call is being processed completely at the local switch. (See Figure 4-3.)

This two-step dialing process may seem rather involved and requires knowledge of the access

Figure 4-4

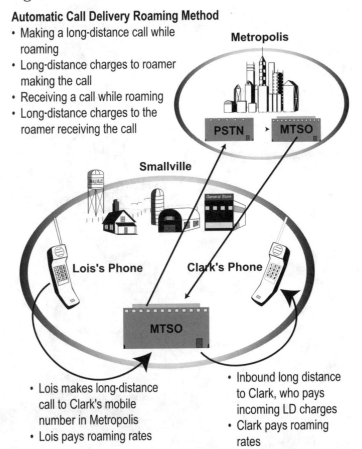

**Automatic Call Delivery Roaming Method**
- Making a long-distance call while roaming
- Long-distance charges to roamer making the call
- Receiving a call while roaming
- Long-distance charges to the roamer receiving the call

**Metropolis**

PSTN ▸ MTSO

**Smallville**

**Lois's Phone**    **Clark's Phone**

MTSO

- Lois makes long-distance call to Clark's mobile number in Metropolis
- Lois pays roaming rates

- Inbound long distance to Clark, who pays incoming LD charges
- Clark pays roaming rates

number, but it invariably works when the "new and improved" method doesn't.

### Automatic call delivery—the new and improved method

Lois dials Clark's cellular phone number as a long-distance call from Smallville to Metropolis. Lois pays roaming charges in Smallville, as well as long-distance charges from Smallville to Metropolis. The Metropolis B system switch knows Clark is in Smallville because his phone autonomously registered when he arrived in town. The Smallville B system immediately notified the Metropolis system that Clark (his phone, actually) was in Smallville, with instructions to forward all his inbound calls to

Figure 4-5

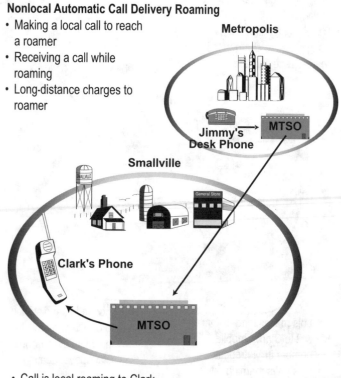

**Nonlocal Automatic Call Delivery Roaming**
- Making a local call to reach a roamer
- Receiving a call while roaming
- Long-distance charges to roamer

- Call is local roaming to Clark
- Clark pays roaming rates

Figure 4-6

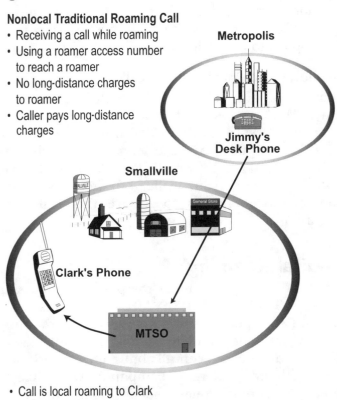

**Nonlocal Traditional Roaming Call**
- Receiving a call while roaming
- Using a roamer access number to reach a roamer
- No long-distance charges to roamer
- Caller pays long-distance charges

Metropolis

Jimmy's Desk Phone

Smallville

Clark's Phone

MTSO

- Call is local roaming to Clark
- Clark pays roaming rates

Smallville. Clark's phone rings and he answers it. He hears that it's Lois calling. Clark pays roaming fees in Smallville and also pays long-distance charges for the call to follow him from Metropolis to Smallville.

As you can see, this method requires little or no forethought or planning. However, if the system breaks down, it is almost impossible to reach your party. In addition, both callers incur long-distance charges. (See Figure 4-4.)

### Nonlocal automatic call delivery

Jimmy, from Clark's office, calls Clark using automatic call delivery. To do this, he dials Clark's cellular phone number in Metropolis. This is a local call for Jimmy, but Clark pays roaming charges in Smallville, as well as long-distance charges from Metropolis to Smallville. (See Figure 4-5.)

### Nonlocal traditional roaming call

Jimmy can also call Clark the traditional roaming way. This means that when Jimmy uses the roamer access number to dial into the Smallville MTSO, his office pays the long-distance charges from Metropolis to Smallville. Clark still pays roaming rates in Smallville, but he doesn't pay long-distance charges to receive this call. (See Figure 4-6.)

# Digital Roaming

Digital roaming introduces the possibility of using both 800 MHz and 1900 MHz spectrums. This should be good news for wireless roaming customers. The problem is that roaming agreements have never been all that easy to work out. Only a handful of large companies were able to create national wireless service footprints as a result of the PCS spectrum auctions. Some smaller companies are reluctant to make roaming agreements with these large companies. The thinking is: Why give the big guy more of an edge than he already has? Other new players are insecure about their service and don't want you roaming onto another's digital service in case you like the service you're roaming on better.

## Cellular—800 MHz digital roaming

800
CDMA

800
TDMA

Now let's talk about the 800 MHz digital roaming subscriber. It is important to understand that the 800 MHz cellular carriers that are offering digital service already have an established analog business. The coverage offered by their analog service is quite mature. This means they have a well-developed coverage area, or footprint. The digital service they are offering is less mature, which means the footprint is usually smaller. The digital coverage area overlays the analog footprint. As you travel within the carrier's coverage area, if you are outside the digital footprint, the phone will not be in digital mode. In this case, you will access the analog service within the analog footprint.

Another thing to remember is that if you start a call in the digital mode on an 800 MHz carrier, and move outside the digital footprint, the phone will hand off to analog service. However, if you start a call in the analog area of coverage and move into 800 MHz digital coverage, the phone will not hand off to digital service. If you subscribe to a package with *digital* minutes included, you'll want to pay close attention to the digital indicator on your phone to minimize the analog charges you accrue.

POINTER

The digital footprint will continue to grow as the number of subscribers supporting the digital network increases. Digital networks are expensive to build, and it is unrealistic to expect them to be as large and developed in their first few years as the 16-year-old analog networks. However, the growth will probably be faster than AMPS cellular's growth because an established and rapidly growing customer base already exists.

The 800 MHz AMPS carriers implementing digital technology offer dual mode or tri-mode equipment. The following charts demonstrate the way that the phone will seek out systems for roaming.

At this point, we need to break this discussion down into separate sections to look more closely at the different technologies. Remember that CDMA and TDMA are competing, incompatible technologies. CDMA will be addressed first, as it is being adopted by more carriers than TDMA.

## 800 MHz CDMA roaming

It is likely that the 800 MHz CDMA digital phone you purchased is also capable of operating in analog, or AMPS, mode. As you roam into another market, the 800 MHz CDMA digital phone will seek out other 800 MHz CDMA digital networks, first trying the same block of channels as the one you subscribe to, and then trying the opposing block of channels. If the phone can't find a CDMA provider, it will look for an analog system on the same block of channels as your home market. This ability to revert to the analog mode ensures you will have no less coverage when roaming with your digital phone than you did with your analog phone. Because the digital technologies are not compatible, carriers have committed to maintaining analog AMPS networks for at least the next ten years in order to provide a common thread.

**Your phone's roaming selection process** The following tables allow you to see at a glance how

Figure 4-7

Dual Mode Phone on 800 MHz Carrier

### 800 MHz CDMA/AMPS Phone

|  | Frequency | |
|---|---|---|
| Technology | 800 MHz | 1900 MHz |
| AMPS | **2nd** | |
| TDMA | Incompatible | Incompatible |
| CDMA | **1st** | Not Available |
| GSM-NA | | Incompatible |
| PACS | | Incompatible |

this works. The premise is that you subscribe to a CDMA 800 MHz service provider. These tables show you your options, depending on the equipment you use: a single mode digital 800 MHz phone is virtually impossible to find; the dual mode phone is the most common phone used; and the dual mode/dual frequency (tri-mode) phone will cost the most, but provide greater roaming access.

The best way to explain the order in which the phone will seek and find a system is to use a specific market example. You have a dual mode/dual frequency CDMA/AMPS phone as in Figure 4-8. You subscribe to Ameritech in Cincinnati, which is offering 800 MHz CDMA (block B) service (they are also the block B analog service provider in Cincinnati). You decide to head north to Cleveland. As you drive through Columbus, you access the 800 MHz CDMA (block B) network licensed to Ameritech. When you get to Cleveland, however, the 800 MHz CDMA networks are GTE Wireless (B) and AirTouch (A). Roaming agreements with both of these carriers are in place, but Ameritech operates the 1900 MHz CDMA (block

Figure 4-8

Tri-Mode Phone on 800 MHz Carrier

**800/1900 MHz CDMA/AMPS Phone**

|  |  | Frequency | |
|---|---|---|---|
|  |  | 800 MHz | 1900 MHz |
| **T**<br>**e**<br>**c**<br>**h**<br>**n**<br>**o**<br>**l**<br>**o**<br>**g**<br>**y** | AMPS | **3rd** |  |
|  | TDMA | Incompatible | Incompatible |
|  | CDMA | **1st** | **2nd** |
|  | GSM-NA |  | Incompatible |
|  | PACS |  | Incompatible |

A) network in Cleveland. Because the phone is programmed to scan for the company you subscribe to first, regardless of the channel block or frequency, you won't need to change any settings. Your phone will access the 1900 MHz CDMA Ameritech system instead of the competitors' 800 MHz CDMA systems, and you are charged the special rates you already have from Ameritech. As you travel southeast to Pittsburgh, the systems you will find are Aerial (1900 MHz GSM block B), Sprint PCS (1900 MHz CDMA block A), AT&T (1900 MHz CDMA block D), AT&T (800 MHz TDMA and AMPS block A), and Bell Atlantic Mobility (800 MHz CDMA and AMPS block B). Your phone will access a roaming partner system as Ameritech doesn't offer service in Pittsburgh. This happens to be Bell Atlantic Mobility, using the digital CDMA network.

### 800 MHz TDMA roaming

800
TDMA

This is similar to 800 MHz CDMA roaming. The difference is that TDMA technology has been available for several years. The companies that offer 800 MHz TDMA service obtained licenses for PCS spectrum and are operating 1900 MHz TDMA networks as well.

The roaming options available to you are defined by the wireless phone you have. Figures 4-9 and 4-10 demonstrate your roaming potential, assuming you subscribe to an 800 MHz TDMA carrier. The different options are based on your equipment.

A single mode 800 MHz TDMA phone is rare, and, if you get one, you can only roam on other 800 MHz TDMA networks. The companies who adopted TDMA digital technology are existing analog AMPS providers. These carriers offer a dual mode or dual mode/dual frequency (tri-mode) phone.

You can see that if you plan on traveling and want to use your phone, getting a dual mode/dual frequency (tri-mode) phone will be important to you and probably worth the additional expense. If you don't travel outside your home market, then a single mode or dual mode (TDMA/AMPS) phone will serve you well.

Figure 4-9

Dual Mode Phone on 800 MHz Carrier

**800 MHz TDMA/AMPS Phone**

| Technology | Frequency | |
| --- | --- | --- |
| | 800 MHz | 1900 MHz |
| AMPS | **2nd** | |
| TDMA | **1st** | Not Available |
| CDMA | Incompatible | Incompatible |
| GSM-NA | | Incompatible |
| PACS | | Incompatible |

Figure 4-10

Tri-Mode Phone on 800 MHz Carrier

**800/1900 MHz TDMA/AMPS Phone**

| Technology | Frequency | |
| --- | --- | --- |
| | 800 MHz | 1900 MHz |
| AMPS | **3rd** | |
| TDMA | **1st** | **2nd** |
| CDMA | Incompatible | Incompatible |
| GSM-NA | | Incompatible |
| PACS | | Incompatible |

## PCS—1900 MHz roaming

<table>
<tr><td>1900<br>CDMA</td></tr>
<tr><td>1900<br>GSM</td></tr>
<tr><td>1900<br>PACS</td></tr>
<tr><td>1900<br>TDMA</td></tr>
</table>

When roaming among the PCS carriers and other wireless telephony providers, you enter new levels of challenge. First, PCS has four different technologies: CDMA, TDMA, GSM, and PACS. Second, because the digital footprints are not fully developed, carriers offer equipment choices: phones that will roam only in their markets, or dual or tri-mode phones that will work almost anywhere wireless service is available.

In an attempt to demonstrate the options available, a combination of charts and explanations will be used. The charts are based on two elements: 1) the type of carrier you subscribe to and 2) the type of equipment you purchased. Applying this information to the matrix will give you an overview of where your phone will work. Use these matrices in conjunction with Appendix F when you travel.

You will want to remember that there are potentially six PCS carriers in each market. Now it's likely that each of the four technologies will be represented in every market. For some markets, though, the question will be when. Blocks A and B were all licensed first and to large companies, which means they have the financial resources to build their networks faster than the block C, D, E, and F licensees. Blocks A and B are geographically divided into 51 MTAs and are technologically divided as follows: 50 licensees chose CDMA, 24 licensees chose TDMA, 22 licensees chose GSM, one chose PACS, and five were uncommitted at the time of this writing.

Some PCS carriers offer single mode equipment. Even though the phone may be compatible with service offered by other carriers, these PCS carriers may configure settings in the phone so that it is usable only in their markets. Check their coverage area before buying this type of unit to make sure it matches your needs.

## 1900 MHz CDMA roaming

A dual mode/dual frequency phone costs a bit more than a single mode phone. However, if you travel outside your home market, this phone will ensure that you have virtually ubiquitous coverage, even if it's not all digital. Figure 4-12 illustrates this point.

1900
CDMA

Let's say you're a Sprint PCS (CDMA) subscriber in Miami. Your service is PCS block A, and your home Figure 4-11

Dual Mode Phone on 1900 MHz Carrier

### 1900 MHz CDMA/AMPS Phone

Frequency

| Technology | | 800 MHz | 1900 MHz |
|---|---|---|---|
| | AMPS | 2nd | |
| | TDMA | Incompatible | Incompatible |
| | CDMA | Not Available | 1st |
| | GSM-NA | | Incompatible |
| | PACS | | Incompatible |

market covers from the Florida Keys up the east coast to Vero Beach, and up the west coast to Fort Myers. When you want to go up to Walt Disney World® in Orlando, your phone will pick up the PCS block D, which is licensed by Sprint PCS. The same holds true for your visit to Busch Gardens in Tampa or a trip to Jacksonville.

Your dual mode/dual frequency (tri-mode) phone remains on the Sprint PCS digital service even

Figure 4-12

Tri-Mode Phone on 1900 MHz Carrier

## 1900/800 MHz CDMA/AMPS Phone

|  |  | Frequency | |
|---|---|---|---|
| | | 800 MHz | 1900 MHz |
| T e c h n o l o g y | AMPS | **3rd** | |
| | TDMA | Incompatible | Incompatible |
| | CDMA | **2nd** | **1st** |
| | GSM-NA | | Incompatible |
| | PACS | | Incompatible |

though the channel blocks are different. This example assumes that Sprint PCS has full market coverage in all the markets mentioned. However, building out a wireless network is expensive and is driven by subscribers. As you drive from Miami to Orlando, it is possible that the Sprint PCS networks are not yet complete in less-urban areas. Your dual mode/ dual frequency phone will seek out 800 MHz CDMA networks first. Because both AMPS carriers in the Miami and Orlando markets implemented TDMA digital technology on their 800 MHz networks, no CDMA networks are available, so your phone will seek out the 800 MHz AMPS network. Assuming that roaming agreements are in place, you will have access to a wireless phone for your entire trip, even if it isn't all digital.

## 1900 MHz TDMA roaming

A single mode 1900 MHz TDMA phone is rare. The companies implementing TDMA technology on PCS have licenses in 800 MHz AMPS/TDMA markets and are usually offering dual mode/dual frequency (tri-mode) phones. Therefore, you can access all their markets, regardless of the frequency. If you find a single mode phone, you will be able to roam only on other 1900 MHz TDMA carriers.

<u>1900</u>
TDMA

What you will commonly find is either a dual mode 1900 MHz TDMA/800 MHz AMPS phone or a tri-mode 800 MHz TDMA/1900 MHz TDMA/800 MHz AMPS phone. The way these phones select which system to use to roam onto is shown in Figures 4-13 and 4-14.

Figure 4-13

Dual Mode Phone on 1900 MHz Carrier

### 1900 MHz TDMA/800 MHz AMPS Phone

|  |  | Frequency | |
|  |  | 800 MHz | 1900 MHz |
|---|---|---|---|
| T e c h n o l o g y | AMPS | **2nd** |  |
|  | TDMA | Not Available | **1st** |
|  | CDMA | Incompatible | Incompatible |
|  | GSM-NA |  | Incompatible |
|  | PACS |  | Incompatible |

When you subscribe to a PCS 1900 MHz TDMA carrier, using a dual mode/dual frequency phone provides you with ubiquitous roaming coverage.

Figure 4-14

Tri-Mode Phone on 1900 MHz Carrier

**1900/800 MHz TDMA/AMPS Phone**

|  | | Frequency | |
|---|---|---|---|
|  | | 800 MHz | 1900 MHz |
| T e c h n o l o g y | AMPS | **3rd** | |
| | TDMA | **2nd** | **1st** |
| | CDMA | Incompatible | Incompatible |
| | GSM-NA | | Incompatible |
| | PACS | | Incompatible |

When you're roaming, the phone will seek out 1900 MHz TDMA carriers first. The phone has a special built-in function that causes it to look for the brand name of the carrier you subscribe to, regardless of the channel block licensed to your carrier in the market you are visiting.

For example, if you subscribe to AT&T Wireless 1900 MHz in Cleveland (the PCS block B licensee) and you travel to Chicago, where AT&T is the 1900 MHz block A licensee, the phone will figure this out. It will then access channel block A so you can make your phone call. The PCS block B in Chicago is operated by PrimeCo, which uses CDMA technology, so if the phone tried to access the PCS block B in Chicago, you wouldn't be able to use your phone. Continuing your trip up to Milwaukee, your phone seeks out the 1900 MHz block D as that is licensed by AT&T.

However, while vacationing in Tampa, Florida, your phone will end up on the 800 MHz block A because AT&T operates the 800 MHz TDMA network there.

If perchance you travel into a market where AT&T doesn't have a license on either the 800 MHz or 1900 MHz spectrum, or if their system isn't active yet, your phone will access a TDMA digital roaming partner or default to the 800 MHz analog system.

## 1900 MHz GSM-NA roaming

The most common GSM-NA equipment is a single mode phone capable of roaming only on other GSM-NA networks. GSM phones are designed to take full advantage of the robust feature set that GSM technology provides. In the future, it is likely that handset manufacturers will introduce GSM equipment that includes AMPS technology. Multimode phones are also probable, and they will work on 1900 MHz GSM and AMPS networks as well as on international GSM networks at either 900 MHz or 1800 MHz. 1900 GSM

Global travelers may want to inquire about the Bosch WorldPhone introduced in the spring of 1998, which is a GSM phone that operates at 1900 MHz in the U.S. and at 900 MHz throughout the rest of the planet. U.S.-based GSM companies that offer this equipment often have international roaming agreements in place. If not, just get a SIM card in the country you visit most often overseas. These SIM cards have built-in international roaming agreements.

## 1900 MHz PACS roaming

The uniqueness of PACS technology makes it less suitable for roaming as it is designed to be a low-powered local system. However, as PACS networks are constructed in markets across the country, it is likely that roaming agreements will be implemented, and those subscribing to PACS who wish to take and use their phones out of town will find they can. Because the carriers have been slow to adopt this technology, it is too early to tell if multimode phones will be available.

## Nextel roaming

NEX
TEL

The 800 MHz cellular and 1900 MHz PCS networks are made up of lots of different companies. You are required to subscribe to one of them and roam on the rest.

In contrast, Nextel owns all its markets and its phones only work on Nextel frequencies. Therefore, as a Nextel subscriber, you are always using the phone on your subscriber company's service. Even though you're not always in the market where you subscribe, there is still only one company to pay for your airtime charges when you use the phone outside your home market. In addition, Nextel offers you home per-minute roaming. You pay the home per-minute rate for all your airtime regardless of where you use the phone. Nextel also offers bundled minute rate plans that include roaming minutes, as it's all one big company network.

# Enhanced Roaming Features

## Call delivery

**Follow-Me-Roaming**    Follow-Me-Roaming was the first program that allowed someone to call you when you were roaming by just dialing your cellular number. Initially devised to allow Houston GTE subscribers to receive calls while traveling to Dallas, Follow-Me-Roaming was a manual program that required that you dial *18 SEND to activate the feature. Dialing *18 SEND sent a message from the Dallas GTE network to a clearing house facility in Houston, which in turn sent a message to the Houston GTE system that you were in Dallas. The Follow-Me-Roaming feature expired at midnight each night. You needed to dial *18 SEND each day you were in the roaming market to reactivate Follow-Me-Roaming. It often took an hour or more to activate. In order for this to work in more than one market in a given day, Follow-Me-Roaming had to be cancelled first, usually by dialing *19 SEND before you left the market.

**Follow-Me-Roaming+**  Follow-Me-Roaming+ was an interim evolutionary step that expanded the program to a national level. As you traveled to more than one market in a given day, dialing *18 SEND in each new market overrode, or deactivated, the previous market's information.

**Automatic call delivery**  Automatic call delivery is a part of Interim Standard 41 Revision A (IS-41 RevA). IS-41 is the roaming protocol standard for AMPS, NAMPS, TDMA, and CDMA, whether 800 MHz or 1900 MHz carriers. Now, automatic call delivery is an automated system. However, even though it is automated, automatic call delivery still requires the wireless carriers in both your home market and your visiting market to subscribe to a call delivery service provider. This service provider establishes a subscriber service profile when your phone autonomously registers in the roaming market. The subscriber service profile tells the roaming carrier what services and features your home market carrier will allow the roaming market to support, as well as how many times the roaming carrier has to check with the home carrier to continue your roaming privileges.

Assuming that your home market carrier and the roaming market carrier both subscribe to call delivery service providers, here's how it works. When you turn on your phone while you are roaming, your phone autonomously registers. A message is sent from the roaming market to your home market that tells your home market where you are and gives instructions to send your calls to the roaming market. Any calls to your wireless phone will automatically be forwarded to you while you are roaming. This verification and authorization process takes a

Figure 4-15

## Automatic Call Delivery

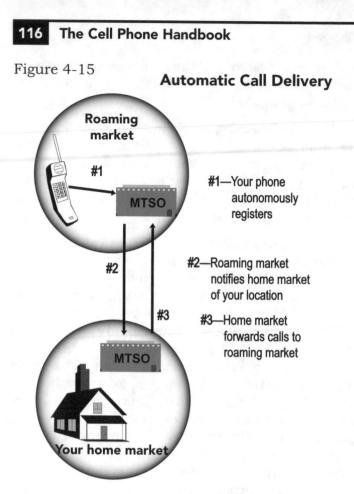

#1—Your phone autonomously registers

#2—Roaming market notifies home market of your location

#3—Home market forwards calls to roaming market

mere six seconds for the switches to complete! (See Figure 4-15.)

This process repeats itself as you travel from market to market, allowing people who need to reach you to stay in touch.

There are still some markets, however, that aren't using IS-41 RevA yet. If it's important for you to get calls when you're roaming, test the automatic call delivery system when you arrive in the roaming market. If the call doesn't process automatically, then dial *18 SEND to activate the Follow-Me-Roaming+ feature. If you don't want to receive calls while roaming, either turn off your phone or dial *19 SEND

POINTER

to deactivate Follow-Me-Roaming+ (in participating markets).

With my sales job, I traveled to Toledo from Cleveland once or twice a month. My husband would usually call me about 4:00 P.M. to see what time I would be home. He had no idea where I was, whether I was in Cleveland, still in Toledo, or somewhere in between. Automatic call delivery made it possible for his call to find me regardless of the market I was in, and without me having to do anything to make this happen.

## International roaming

GlobalRoam is an international roaming program offered to wireless carriers by GTE Telecommunications Services, Inc. If you travel internationally and are phone dependent, this is for you! Now, you can use a phone abroad, and your usage appears on your domestic wireless phone bill in U.S. currency. Even better, anyone calling your domestic wireless phone number will automatically be forwarded to your international wireless number wherever you are in more than 50 countries on four continents. For details on this program, contact your local wireless service provider.

## North American Cellular Network (NACN)

NACN, or North American Cellular Network, is a competitor of GTE TSI. Initially, GTE contracted with B system cellular carriers for Follow-Me-Roaming. NACN contracted with A system cellular carriers to offer similar call delivery services. With IS-41 RevA, the channel block and frequency constraints are no longer in place.

If the market isn't IS-41 compliant, the code to activate this feature among participating NACN carriers is *31 SEND. Deactivate by dialing *30 SEND.

A third player contributing to all the behind-the-scenes magic is a company called ILLUMINET.

## Enhanced home network

Your phone knows whether or not it is in its home market because it matches the system ID programmed into the phone with what it hears in the overhead signal that is broadcast by the carrier. When the system ID in the phone and the system ID that is broadcast in the overhead signal don't match, the phone indicates it is roaming.

Some newer phones have a feature called enhanced home network. The dealer programs the phone with multiple SIDs so the phone indicates it is not roaming in certain nonhome markets. These markets are designated by your carrier, and you are charged home per-minute rates. In effect, your carrier has extended, or enhanced, the area considered your home market.

# Fraud

**Chapter 5**

## Cloning

### What is it? How do the thieves do it?

Although there are different types of wireless telephony fraud, the most prevalent is cloning of an analog cellular phone. Here's how it works. A thief uses special scanning equipment to listen for your mobile phone number and ESN to be transmitted to the carrier (which occurs when you turn on your phone, when you make a call, or any time your phone autonomously registers). Then he reprograms the information into an older analog phone. Only phones manufactured prior to 1995 have ESNs that can be reprogrammed. The thief then sells the "cloned" phone, and the buyer uses the phone until it stops working. Cloned phones are typically used outside your home market because the local carrier can easily detect when two phones with the same information are being used on its switch at the same time.

You know you've been cloned when you see an outrageous phone bill, where your mastery of space/time travel is evidenced by the fact that you placed roaming calls from two different markets at the same time! It is also obvious to the carrier that your phone was cloned; it can recognize the patterns. The carrier credits you for the fraudulent charges, which then become a fraud write-off to the carrier. You are issued a new phone number, and your phone is reprogrammed with this new number. This breaks the mobile number/ESN combination by matching a new mobile number to your ESN and renders the old mobile number/ESN combination useless. If keeping your mobile number is important to you, see if you can arrange to have your ESN changed.

POINTER

The FCC made cloning illegal, and, in 1995, it also made altering the ESN by anyone other than the manufacturer illegal. Now, the government has taken another step to crack down on cloning. In the spring of 1998, the Wireless Telephone Protection Act (H.R. 2460) passed, making it illegal to "knowingly use, produce, traffic in, have control or custody of, or possess hardware or software, knowing it has been configured for altering or modifying a telecommunications instrument so that such instrument may be used to obtain unauthorized access to telecommunications services." This means that both the customers who are buying illegally altered equipment, as well as the people who actually do the cloning, are subject to prosecution. First-time convictions are punishable by fine and/or imprisonment up to 15 years. Second convictions are punishable by fine and/or imprisonment up to 20 years.

# Fraud Prevention Measures

## Profiling

The magnitude of fraud charges written off by carriers in the United States exceeds $1 million a day! Carriers have taken proactive approaches to reduce fraud write-offs, such as implementing usage profiles. This is a measure that raises a flag if your usage deviates from your established profile. Say, for example, you usually don't roam, or very little, and your normal usage averages 10 minutes a day. If your phone is used 60 minutes a day in a roaming market, you will probably get a call from the carrier asking if the usage is legitimate. If the carrier can't reach you, your phone number may be suspended, requiring you to call your service provider to get your phone working again. Profiling isn't limited to roaming activity. It applies to usage in your home market, as well.

## Radio frequency (RF) fingerprinting

In addition to profiling, the carriers are implementing RF fingerprinting (which is switch dependent) and authentication (which is phone and switch dependent). With RF fingerprinting, each wireless phone has a unique and distinguishable RF signature. Cell site RF fingerprinting units build a wireless phone RF fingerprint of your phone by collecting data from several transmissions. This RF fingerprint is stored at the MTSO. Then, all subsequent calls you place are validated with the stored RF fingerprint information to determine if you are a legitimate subscriber. This validation process takes place before the call is actually processed so that a thief using your mobile number/ESN combination in another phone will not be able to place a call.

## Authentication

Authentication is being implemented on analog equipment, but it is built into digital systems. Authentication uses an A-key, which is 26 characters in length. Only the phone and the switch know the A-key. Think of it as a numeric version of your mother's maiden name. If only you and I know your mother's maiden name, and I ask you what the fifth letter is, you can tell me. A thief may have your mobile number/ESN combination, but as the A-key is never transmitted, he is unable to obtain this vital element to respond to the challenge and, therefore, is unable to place a call. Because the A-key is 26 characters long and contains numbers, the switch has an endless variety of challenges for the phone. The challenge occurs when you initiate a call and takes only seconds to complete.

## PIN codes

A fraud deterrent that has been around for a few years is the use of a PIN code. PIN codes can be used several ways. Some carriers require you to dial the PIN code immediately following your outbound number each time you place a call, so your dialing sequence will be: 1-800-555-1212 SEND (stuttered dial tone) 1234 (PIN code) SEND.

Other carriers require you to "open" your phone use by dialing *560-XXXX (the Xs are your four-digit PIN) SEND. Then you "close" your usage when you are finished making calls by dialing *56 SEND. Sometimes carriers require you to establish a PIN code that will be used only when you roam. Usually, you are prompted for the PIN code the first time you try to place a call in the roaming market. Depending on the market and the relationship between the carriers, this may be the only time you are prompted to enter your PIN code for the dura-tion of your visit. On the other hand, you may need to reenter it with the first call you make each day you are roaming.

## Subscriber Fraud

As fraud-deterrent measures are implemented in analog cellular and as digital service becomes more available, cloning is less accessible to the thief. A growing kind of fraud being perpetrated on wireless carriers is subscriber fraud. In this case, someone subscribes to a carrier for wireless service with no intention of paying for his or her airtime charges. This is accomplished through the deliberate use of invalid or false credentials such as name, address, social security number, tax ID, etc.

## What Can I Do to Prevent or Reduce My Chances of Being Cloned?

There are several steps you can take to reduce or prevent your chances of being cloned. First, pay attention to your phone bill. Sometimes cloning fraud goes on for months, gradually building up. Noticing fraudulent activity on your phone bill and report it promptly should reduce the amount of fraud charges, but won't necessarily eliminate the need to change your phone number. Second, if you are replacing your old phone and buying an analog phone, ask if it is capable of authentication and whether or not the carrier supports authentication. If it fits into your budget, consider buying a digital phone, which all but eliminates your risk of being cloned.

More information about carrier solutions to fraud can be found at CTIA's Web site (*www.wow-com.com /professional/fraud*).

# Using Wireless Phones For Data

We all know that we can talk on a wireless phone. This is often referred to as "voice" in the telephone industry. What you may not realize is that these phones are also capable of transmitting data—electronic information such as faxes, e-mail, electronic file transfers, and mainframe log-ins, for example. There are two different types of wireless data currently available: circuit-switched data (CSD) and cellular digital packet data (CDPD).

## Circuit-Switched Data

AMPS telephones have the capability to transmit data using the same process as your home phone. Some of the digital technologies, such as TDMA, have limited data capabilities, and the ability to connect to your laptop computer in TDMA mode is still forthcoming. Meanwhile, your dual mode TDMA phone can be forced into the AMPS mode so that you can connect to your laptop computer.

You will need certain equipment to make a data call on AMPS (analog) cellular (circuit-switched data). The first thing you need is a data-ready cellular phone. If your manual doesn't tell you that your phone is data capable, then ask the dealer where you purchased your phone. If the dealer doesn't know, then you will need to contact the manufacturer of the cellular phone.

Once you have established that you have a data-capable phone, you'll need to look at the data device you'll be using. If, for instance, you'll be using a laptop computer, you will need to evaluate your modem. Some modem manufacturers have made cellular-ready modems. This capability is usually prominently marked on the modem or in the manual. Cellular-ready modems are often slightly more expensive than non-cellular-ready modems. Contact the modem manufacturer to obtain the cable you need to connect your PC card cellular-ready modem to your cellular phone. The cables are not sold in retail stores.

POINTER

If you don't have a cellular-ready modem or you are using a fax machine or other device, you will need a cellular data interface, which will provide the following:

- dial tone (cellular doesn't use dial tone)

- interpretation and/or conversion of DTMF (cellular doesn't use this either)

- RJ-11 interface (standard phone plug connection)

Several companies manufacture devices that perform these functions, such as Motorola's The Cellular Connection™ interface.

Now that you have everything you need, what's next? You need to connect your cellular phone to your data device. If you have a PC card modem, use the proprietary cable you purchased from the modem manufacturer. Otherwise, you will use your cellular interface device to connect your cellular phone to the RJ-11 in your data device. Now, all you have to do is proceed as if you were plugged in to a landline.

Here are two examples of how I have used my wireless phone to transmit data while away from my desk. In both cases, I routinely performed the same functions from my desk using my laptop computer and internal modem with a landline.

One day, I had been in meetings from 8:30 A.M. until 4:30 P.M. I was thirty minutes from home. I hadn't called my voice mail for messages all day, so I used my wireless phone to call and retrieve them. One message was from a Cleveland customer asking me to get him a new phone number in Houston. The customer was flying to Houston on a 7:00 A.M. flight the next morning and wanted to take a phone with him that had a local Houston number in it. In order to get the phone number for my customer, I had to generate a fax to my company to order it. I pulled off the freeway into a parking lot and typed up the order request in my word processing program. Then I hooked up the internal fax/modem installed in my laptop computer to a Motorola Cellular Connection™ interface that was connected to my cell phone. At this point, I transmitted the document using the faxing software in my computer. After the fax completed, I used the wireless phone to follow up and ensure that the Houston phone number I needed was assigned immediately. I got back on the freeway to continue my drive home. As I finished my commute, I called the customer, whose office closed at 5:00 P.M., and walked him through reprogramming the phone with the new Houston number. Without data on wireless capabilities, I would have been unable to fulfill this customer's needs.

The second example concerns connecting to a mainframe. My company provided me with access to a mainframe to check on the status of my orders. During a visit with a national account customer, the buyer asked me the status of several orders he had placed with me days before our meeting. I had my computer with me, as well as my wireless phone. All the phone jacks in my customer's office were digital, so I was unable to plug into his phone system. I connected my wireless phone to my computer's modem using the Cellular Connection™ interface, and then used communications software to access my company's mainframe. Because I used this software at my office to check on orders, I kept most of the settings the same, except for the connection speed. I reduced it from the 14,400 bps that I used for landline connections to 4800 bps for the wireless connection. My goal was to stay connected, not achieve high-speed transfers.

## Performance expectations

Keep in mind that cellular is a noisy environment. The human ear is very forgiving of pops, crackles, and static that can occur on a cellular phone call. Even the "click" noise made during a handoff can sound like an information bit on a data call. This can cause an error in the data transmission, often resulting in the device(s) terminating the call.

To optimize data transmission performance, the following is recommended:

- Try to obtain the strongest signal by optimizing your location. Drive to the top of a hill, or locate yourself near a window.

- Don't expect high speeds. Under ideal conditions, most cellular-enhanced modems have a default connection speed of 7200 bps (providing the host modem supports this speed). If the modem detects a noisy environment, it will default to slower speeds.

- Being stationary is not required, but it is preferred for circuit-switched data.

- Connecting at a slower speed once may be less time-consuming than trying to connect at a higher speed and failing numerous times.

- For file transfers, try to use Z-modem file transfer protocol, which is a software-based standard providing error correction. If transmission is interrupted, you don't have to start again from the beginning.

This last suggestion comes from personal experience. About eight years ago, I was downloading a file from Compuserve on my 2400-baud modem. After about an hour, with 90 percent of the file downloaded to my hard drive, I was disconnected! Because I wasn't using Z-modem file transfer protocol, I had to start over from the beginning! Today, many online companies incorporate Z-modem file transfer protocol into their download functions (America Online is one). AOL's download manager remembers how much of a file has downloaded if your connection terminates.

# Cellular Digital Packet Data (CDPD)

As you can see, using wireless to transmit data isn't difficult, and even more opportunities are available with digital technologies. Cellular digital packet data (CDPD) provides wireless digital connectivity through devices that are actually cellular phones devoid of any human interface capability. This means that there is no microphone or speaker for voice transmission, no keypad for dialing, and no display for visual feedback. These devices talk exclusively with and are connected directly to laptop computers and personal digital assistants (PDAs). CDPD units communicate only in bits and bytes (data) and rely on the connecting device to provide the interface for you to use them.

For example, GoAmerica offers a CDPD unit called the Minstrel Wireless IP Modem, which was custom designed by Novatel Wireless for the PalmPilot by 3Com. This allows someone using the Pilot PDA to have wireless Internet capabilities by using Go.Mail and Go.Web software from GoAmerica. Imagine, two-way text messaging via Internet

3Com's PalmPilot with Minstrel Wireless IP Modem

e-mail, all with something small enough to fit in your shirt pocket or purse! If you're so inclined, Minstrel also allows you to surf the Web while you're on the go, using a text-based Web browser.

GoAmerica's service is an additional charge to your wireless voice service. The cost is $49.95 per month for unlimited nationwide access. There are no extra charges for roaming. An entry-level package is also available for $14.95. You might want to check with GoAmerica for its coverage areas. The coverage for CDPD is smaller than the analog footprints we have come to know, but it is quite extensive, covering more than 3,000 cities.

Minstrel is one example of wireless data using a CDPD device. There are also CDPD PCMCIA (PC card) devices that plug into your laptop PC card port. Some of these PC card CDPD units can receive a message even if they are not inserted in your PC card port. There is an indicator that alerts

CDPD PC Card Modem by AirCard available from GoAmerica

you when you have a message waiting. You can then plug in your CDPD unit to receive the message at your convenience.

CDPD service, sometimes called wireless IP service, is also offered by companies such as GTE Wireless Data Services, AT&T Wireless Services, Ameritech Cellular Services, SNET Wireless Data Services, and Bell Atlantic Mobile. AT&T Wireless Services' Web site (*wddsales.entp.airdata.com/wireless/coverage/zip_coverate.html*) has the best CDPD national coverage map. This Web site also allows you to enter your state or zip code to determine coverage in a specific market.

The best list of CDPD-covered markets, with links to local coverage maps, can be found at GTE Wireless Data Services' Web page (*www.gte.com/wds/wdsmaps.html*).

Limited data capability is built into the phones and networks of digital service at both 800 MHz and 1900 MHz. One example is called short messaging service (SMS). SMS allows you to send and receive a short text message (about 100 to 160 characters—letters or numbers) to or from someone who has a phone, a pager, or an e-mail account. This is a nice benefit often included with your wireless voice phone service, or you may be charged a nominal fee. It is awkward trying to "type" when you have only 10 keys (the 0 to 9 keys), so there are connection cables available that plug into some of the digital phones and couple to the PalmPilot PDA. These cables enable you to use the Pilot to enter your text message response and then send it via the SMS capability of the phone.

With TDMA/AMPS equipment, circuit-switched data capability is only available when in AMPS mode. You will need to refer to your manual to learn how to force the phone to stay in AMPS mode so you can complete your data call.

Mitsubishi has a phone called Mobile Access that has built-in data capabilities. It includes a modem to use for circuit-switched data as well as a CDPD modem. There is a direct connection from the phone to your laptop computer's serial port (DB-9). No PC card is necessary. One nice bonus is that software comes with the phone, called Phonebook Manager, which allows you to enter names and phone numbers into your computer that you want to store in your phone's directory (repertory memory). Then, when you connect the phone to your laptop computer, the information is transferred into the phone. Phonebook Manager software can also import .csv data files from your personal information manager (PIM) software.

## General Packet Radio Services

In February of 1999, Ericsson began U.S. field trials with Omnipoint to test general packet radio services (GPRS), which offer wireless data access to the internet and other IP-based services on GSM networks. GSM currently supports data in the form of circuit-switched transmissions at speeds of 9600 bps, whereas the GPRS will reach speeds of up to 115 kbps using packet data. Using packets of data will increase the efficiency of the network and reduce costs to users. Charges are based on the actual data sent or received, not for how long you are connected. Look for commercial availability sometime in 2000.

# Accessories

**Chapter 7**

## Batteries

An integral element of electronic devices is a power supply. Batteries are essential for all types of portable phones: bag or carry phones, handheld phones, and personal or pocket phones.

## Battery details

### Nickel cadmium batteries

Nickel cadmium (NiCd) batteries, the most prevalent type, have been used by the wireless phone industry since its inception. This type of battery will experience its longest life if fully drained and then fully recharged, preferably on a slow or trickle charger. This is important for NiCd batteries because they are subject to "memory effect." Memory effect results when a battery is about 80 percent used, but not fully drained. The battery recharges, thinking that 80 percent is 100 percent. The next time it is 80 percent used and recharged, it charges 80 percent of 80 percent, which is really only 64 percent. This decline in recharge due to the battery not being fully drained and fully recharged is termed memory effect. The result is that the usable amount of charge in the battery becomes less and less. Fully draining and fully recharging a battery two or three times can reverse memory effect. This is also referred to as cycling your battery. Another way of preventing memory effect is to purchase a charger that has the ability to fully

POINTER

drain the NiCd battery before recharging it. NiCd batteries should not be stored on a charger. This could result in overcharging and considerably shorten the life of the battery.

If you keep your phone turned on all day, which will probably drain the battery, and then put the battery on an overnight or trickle charger, you should see maximum usage from a nickel cadmium battery. It is a good idea to cycle your battery once a week by fully draining and fully recharging the battery.

If you have a phone for emergency use only, you probably have a NiCd battery. There should be identification of the battery type on its label. As you probably keep the phone turned off, it is important for you to cycle your battery occasionally so it will work when you need it. NiCd batteries will lose about five to eight percent of their charge per week if they are not used. At a five percent loss, the battery will have only a 50 percent charge after three months. Sitting idle without a recharge, it will take a year for a nickel cadmium battery to lose all its charge, but it may be impossible to revive the battery at this point.

POINTER

### Nickel metal hydride batteries

A nickel metal hydride (NiMH) battery will typically weigh the same as a nickel cadmium battery when rated for the same milliamps. Unlike a NiCd, a NiMH battery won't develop memory effect. It prefers to be topped off and likes a fast charger. NiMH batteries should not be stored on their chargers.

This type of battery is for you if you are a medium- to high-volume user who doesn't want to be without your phone and you have a fast charger both at home and at the office. You will be able to recharge your NiMH battery after using it for short periods of time.

## Lithium ion batteries

The biggest advantage of lithium ion (Li Ion) batteries is that they are lightweight—almost half that of their NiCd and NiMH counterparts when rated for the same milliamps. Lithium ion batteries are also more environmentally friendly than nickel-based batteries. Because you need a special charger, Li Ion batteries can be stored on a charger. A lithium ion battery actually has electronic circuitry built into it that "talks" to the charger, preventing this type of battery from being over-charged. Li Ion batteries are not subject to memory effect the way NiCd batteries are. The Li Ion battery needs to be charged at a higher voltage than NiCd or NiMH batteries. Hence, you can use a Li Ion battery charger to charge NiCd or NiMH batteries, but you won't successfully charge a Li Ion battery on a charger designed for NiCd or NiMH batteries.

As a high-volume user, you can appreciate the benefits of a Li Ion battery. You enjoy either the same talk time as a NiCd but with less weight or the same weight as a NiCd but with more talk time. Chances are, the full-featured phone you require came with one. Keeping the phone turned on and in the charger at the office ensures you won't miss a call.

## Sealed lead-acid batteries

A sealed lead-acid battery is the same as your car's battery. It prefers to be topped off, meaning that you can drain it a little bit and then charge it up. This type of battery is immune to memory effect. It is used for carry or bag phones, but is less common than the VCR-sized nickel cadmium battery usd with bag phones.

## Battery summary

So why don't all phones come with Li Ion batteries? Li Ion batteries are more expensive than NiCd or NiMH batteries. The NiCd, being the least expensive, is usually the type of battery included with phones that are given away or sold at the lower price points. You can shave weight off your phone by buying a Li Ion battery. Remember, though, that there's more than the price of the battery to consider. You will need to invest in a Li Ion-compliant charger in order for the Li Ion battery to work properly.

When you first get your wireless phone batteries, it is best to charge them for 14 to 24 hours. Batteries will typically be sold "DOA" (dead on arrival), and they need to be "woken up" by giving them a good solid charge. For maximum battery life, follow the directions that come with the battery.

### The most frequently asked battery question

Why doesn't my battery last as long as the manufacturer said it would?

Batteries usually have two types of usage ratings: talk time and standby time. If the battery doesn't seem to be lasting as long as the ratings indicate it should, there may be several reasons why:

- If the battery is made of nickel cadmium, it could have memory effect.

- The battery could just be old. Check with the manufacturer for the expected life of the battery. This is more typically expressed in time rather than in charging cycles. For example, if a battery has a one-year warranty, any usage after that is a bonus. Although you may have hardly used the battery and didn't charge it much, a two-year-old battery probably needs to be replaced.

- If the battery is new, it could be that the manufacturer complied with industry standards instead of exceeding them. The battery industry only requires manufacturers to meet its specifications within 80 percent. That means if a battery is rated for up to 100 minutes of talk time, the battery is within industry parameters if it only gives you 80 minutes of talk time!

- If the battery is new, the reason it could be underperforming is that you overcharged the battery by leaving it on a charger for more than 24 hours.

- If your phone is a CDMA digital unit, the carrier may be draining your battery more than you realize. CDMA phones have a sleep mode in addition to a standby mode, which can greatly increase the battery's standby times. The carrier has a setting at the switch level that determines how often the phone is awakened from its sleep mode. The carrier does this so the phone can check the network for messages and pending calls. There are eight settings. The lower the setting, the more frequently the phone is polled. This reduces the standby time of the battery. The higher the setting, the less frequently the phone is polled. This causes less drain on the battery, thereby giving you more standby time. However, you won't be alerted to messages and phones calls on as timely a basis as the lower setting. This is not something you can control in the phone, and it can vary from market to market. Most CDMA carriers use settings of 0 to 2.

After evaluating the above, if you feel that the battery is not functioning properly and it is under warranty, contact the manufacturer for a replacement.

## Batteries at a glance

| Battery Type | Features | Used By |
|---|---|---|
| **Nickel Cadmium**<br>Abbreviated: NiCd<br>Pronounced: ni-cad | Cheapest<br>Heaviest<br>Fully Drain & Fully Recharge<br>Slow/Trickle Charge<br>Subject to Memory Effect | Handheld Phones<br>Pocket or Personal Phones<br>Bag or Carry Phones |
| **Nickel Metal Hydride**<br>Abbreviated: NiMH<br>Pronounced: nim | Top Off<br>Fast Charge | Handheld Phones<br>Pocket or Personal Phones |
| **Lithium Ion**<br>Abbreviated: Li Ion<br>Pronounced: li-on | Lightest Weight<br>Environmentally Friendly<br>Expensive<br>Store on Charger<br>Top Off<br>Needs Special Fast Charger | Handheld Phones<br>Pocket or Personal Phones |
| **Sealed Lead-Acid** | Top Off<br>Fast Charge | Bag or Carry Phones |

## The future of batteries

Lithium batteries are going to be developed to new levels. Here's why:

- Lithium is the lightest metal on earth
- Lithium is plentiful
- Lithium is electrochemically active
- Lithium readily gives up one of its three electrons

Lithium polymer, which uses lithium in a thin film to create thinner, flatter batteries, will be available not only for wireless phones, but also for laptop computers, video cameras, and even automobiles.

# Antennas

The antenna of your wireless phone is as critical for reception as are the antennas for your TV or radio. Wireless phones are designed to be optimally effective when the antenna is used correctly. Never use your wireless phone without an antenna, even if it works without one. The system will ask the phone to keep increasing its signal, which can damage the phone. It is also a potential health hazard, especially with handheld portables and bag phones. Health and safety parameters are established based on using a phone with its antenna.

- For portables, the antenna should be fully extended.

- For installed mobile phones, antennas should be perpendicular to the ground, pointing straight up to the sky (not angled backward or forward to look good on your car).

- For bag or carry phones, the antennas should be at least at window height inside your vehicle. Putting your 3-watt bag phone on the floor of your car, without an external antenna, will make it perform worse than a .6-watt handheld portable.

The best type of antenna for a mobile phone is a roof-mount antenna installed in the center of the roof of the car. The metal roof surrounding the antenna creates a ground plane that amplifies and enhances the signal, and literally becomes part of the antenna system. Most people don't want to drill a hole in the roof of their car, though, so the most common type of antenna is glass mounted. No holes are required for glass-mount antennas. Two small parts are silicon-glued to both sides of the glass, and the glass conducts the signal. Ideally, install the glass-mount antenna in the center of the rear window, which allows it to take advantage of 50 percent of the ground plane effect. Soft tops and convertibles often have their antennas mounted on the trunk lip. The top of the antenna needs to be above the roofline of the car in order to be effective, so an elevated-feed trunk-lip-mount antenna works best for these types of cars.

The ultimate antenna system is one that takes advantage of diversity reception, which employs two antennas. The transceiver needs to have the intelligence and antenna ports to accommodate this technology. This two-antenna system is used by installed mobile phones. One antenna is designated as the primary antenna, the other is secondary. When the phone detects the signal weakening from the first antenna, it determines whether the second antenna has a stronger signal. If the second antenna's signal is stronger, then the phone switches to the second antenna. The phone continues to monitor which antenna is providing the stronger signal and continually transfers to the best one. High-end vehicles often have diversity reception antenna systems for their FM radios.

Portable phones sometimes include the ability to remove the short antenna by unscrewing it and attaching an external antenna, such as a magnetic-mount or window-clip antenna. The connection is often called a mini-UHF connection, similar to your television cable connection. Sometimes, the connection is a bayonet N connector (BNC), which requires only one-quarter of a turn instead of unscrewing the connector. An external antenna for a portable greatly enhances reception. Usually, these antennas provide a signal boost by changing the way the signal radiates from the antenna. A 5 dB gain antenna attached to a .6-watt analog phone will improved its performance to 2 watts effective radiated power (e.r.p.).

# Chargers

Most portable wireless phones come with a charger. The type of charger and its features are usually commensurate with the price of the phone. In other words, if the phone was free, the charger will probably be the cheapest available. However, if you paid $500 or more for your equipment, you may end up with a Li Ion battery and charger.

Overnight or trickle chargers are the least expensive. They are best used with nickel cadmium (NiCd) batteries. If you have a choice or are purchasing a charger outright, get one that will completely discharge the NiCd battery before recharging it. This activity extends the useful life of the battery. Do not store a battery on this charger.

Rapid or fast chargers can be used for either NiCd or NiMH batteries. Usually, these types of chargers will fast charge a battery to 80 to 90 percent of its capacity and trickle charge the remaining 10 to 20 percent. If your NiCd battery begins to demonstrate substandard performance, improper charging may have induced memory effect. NiMH batteries prefer to be topped off, and they like a fast charger. They typically do not need to be fully drained and fully recharged the way the NiCd battery does. Do not store a battery on this charger either.

A lithium ion (Li Ion) battery charger can be used for NiCd and NiMH batteries also. When used with Li Ion batteries, this charger is able to regulate the amount of charge the battery receives so that the battery doesn't get overcharged. You can store Li Ion batteries on a Li Ion charger.

Internal chargers (chargers built right into the phone) are usually fast chargers. The plug that connects to the charger base plugs into the phone as well. You can literally have one end of the cord plugged into the phone with the other end plugged into a 120-volt wall outlet. This is great if you don't want to take your charger base with you on a trip. Just take the power cord. Also, if you have a vacation retreat where you don't subscribe to regular phone service, but there is wireless phone coverage, you can take your wireless phone and not worry about keeping your battery charged for when you need to use the phone. Just plug the cord into the wall, and use the phone while you're recharging. Plugging the phone into a cigarette lighter adapter in your vehicle also activates the internal fast charger built into your wireless phones.

## Cigarette Lighter Adapters

Cigarette lighter adapters (CLAs) plug into the cigarette lighter receptacle in your car, van, or boat and allow you to bypass the battery, thereby conserving whatever charge remains. Most CLAs today will also provide some level of charge to the battery so that you can replace any power you used up. This is a must if you are a medium to power user and you spend a lot of time in your car talking on the phone. If you don't have any hands-free capabilities with your phone, check out a CLA that incorporates hands-free capabilities. Belkin Components, Everything Wireless, Hello Direct, and Technocel are among the companies offering hands-free CLA accessories for a variety of handset manufacturers.

## Hands-Free Adapters

There are two components to hands-free capability: a microphone for speaking and a speaker for listening. Hands-free capability is available in a variety of formats. The most costly, in terms of both hardware and installation, is an installed car kit.

An installed hands-free kit may also offer additional boost to the power of your phone while connected to the car kit. These kits provide the best application of hands-free, but usually the cost of labor to install hands-free car kits is a deterrent. It is not necessarily the initial installation, but the cost of subsequent removals and reinstalls when moving the unit into a new or different car. Alternatives include headsets and cigarette lighter adapters that feature an integrated hands-free speaker and microphone. Headsets are included with many portables today. They usually consist of an earpiece speaker that rests in your ear and a microphone located about three inches down the cable from the earpiece. The microphone dangles between your chin and your shoulder, and functions adequately. Some headsets are available with boom microphones similar to those on home phone headsets.

# Wireless Phone Etiquette

It can be very exciting to get your first wireless phone, and sure, you want to show it off. Taking your phone with you wherever you go is a new experience for most people. It may be fitting in business environments, but not always so in social settings.

In certain parts of the world, wireless phone jamming devices are being installed in public places so that your phone just plain won't work. These areas include concert halls, theaters, restaurants, and other places where people may be disturbed by the ringing of a phone and a noisy conversation. Many judges in the U.S. confiscate equipment that sounds off while court is in session, such as phones and pagers.

You can be a part of the problem or a part of the solution. By demonstrating consideration for others, you help reduce the need for jamming devices in the U.S. If you have a vibration alert feature on your phone, use it. This cuts down on the auditory intrusion from phones ringing. If you have an answering machine on your phone, let it take the call while you attend a concert. If you're phone dependent or "on call," get a digital phone that can be used as a pager. Let the phone ring in vibration alert mode, but don't answer it. Then, excuse yourself and return the call when you're beyond earshot of the other theater or restaurant patrons.

POINTER

Even business users need to demonstrate consideration for others. For example, pagers and wireless phones have no place in a business meeting. Set them on vibration alert, turn them off, or leave them at your desk.

Don't forget to use your wireless phone to report accidents, driving hazards, and crimes. Calling 9-1-1 from your wireless phone is a free call and should go through even if you don't have service.

## One Phone, One Number, Anywhere!

In the spring of 1995, Motorola introduced a technology that combines two wireless telephony functions. The concept is that your cellular phone serves as a cordless phone while you are at home or at the office. The one-phone, one-number, anywhere system consists of two parts: TeleReach™, which is part of the infrastructure, and the Personal Phone Series™ of products, which is what the subscriber uses.

Operating on the 800 MHz network, Motorola's Personal Phone Series™ is called PPS™ 800. It gives you the benefits of a cordless phone on your cellular phone. Instead of giving people your home number and your cellular number, you just give them your cellular number. If you're at home and your cellular phone rings, you don't pay cellular airtime charges, because your cellular phone has transformed into a cordless phone! The PPS™ 800 system takes advantage of unused cellular spectrum near your house, with as many as 125 channels available for cordless use. The quality and range are what you're familiar with on 900 MHz cordless phones. If your office has in-building wireless private branch exchange (PBX) service adapted to work with the PPS™ 800 system, then your PPS™ 800 phone works in cordless mode there, also.

In order to make this service enhancement available to you, your carrier has to add a spectrum- and call-management device to its switch, called authorization and call routing equipment (ACRE). The cordless base station plugs into your home phone wall jack and contains an identification number that is programmed into the ACRE. When the wireless handset comes within range of the cordless base station, the base station calls the ACRE to alert it to route the cellular calls to the home phone number via landlines. If the signal is lost between the wireless handset and the base (out of range), the phone registers with the cellular network. Indicators on the phone let you know which system you're using, cellular or cordless.

Although there is no per-minute charge for using this cellular phone as a cordless phone at your house, usually there is a nominal monthly charge from the carrier for this feature. It can range anywhere from $6.95 to $9.95. This charge offsets the cost of the ACRE and the use of the spectrum while in cordless mode.

The phone will look for the least-cost usage when establishing itself with a system. For example, the phone will try to find your home cordless base before looking for the cellular network. Then, with call follow activated, the cellular network will forward inbound cellular calls to your home phone number so you can answer them in cordless mode on your PPS™ 800 handset. In order to use the PPS™ 800 as a wireless extension at your office, your in-building wireless PBX at work must be IS-94 compliant. Check with your telecommunications manager for more details.

Unfortunately, this one-phone, one-number, anywhere service isn't available everywhere, but only in select markets. BellSouth Cellular and

Southwestern Bell are two companies offering this service in some of their markets.

In February 1998, Panasonic introduced a cellular/cordless model called the Telenium. This model differs from the Motorola PPS™800 system in that it is both an 800 MHz cellular phone and a 900 MHz cordless phone rolled into one device. Therefore, it is not dependent on special infrastructure.

CenturyTel has a one-phone, one-number, anywhere system in some of its Michigan markets. It is using Nortel switching equipment and a tri-mode phone to provide cordless service at home and cellular/PCS coverage elsewhere. The phone is a TDMA digital phone that operates in TDMA mode at both 800 MHz and 1900 MHz, and also functions in AMPS mode at 800 MHz. It operates in cordless mode at 1900 MHz. CenturyTel has segregated the markets offering this service into several areas. Each area spans about three miles in diameter and is called a Zone<sup>SM</sup>. Calls made within your home Zone<sup>SM</sup> are virtually unlimited and designed to compete with your local phone company, or LEC. Calls made outside your Zone<sup>SM</sup> or to areas beyond your Zone<sup>SM</sup> border are treated as wireless calls and billed accordingly. The monthly access fee includes voice mail, caller ID, and other custom calling features.

## Enhanced 9-1-1

Enhanced 9-1-1 (E 9-1-1) services will take the 9-1-1 service currently available on wireless services a step further. Today, when you call 9-1-1 from a wireless phone, your call is transferred to the public safety answering point (PSAP) to report your emergency. The difference between calling from your wireless phone and calling from your home phone is that your home phone is at a fixed address. Your address can be readily identified by the PSAP because it is linked to your home phone number. On the other hand, your wireless phone does not have a fixed address (because you move around with it). Also, when you call 9-1-1 from a wireless phone, the wireless phone companies don't forward your mobile number to the PSAP. This is where the enhanced part comes in.

In July 1996, the FCC mandated wireless phone companies to meet certain requirements and a schedule of implementation for enhanced 9-1-1 services. April 1, 1998 was the deadline set for wireless phone companies to begin transmitting the automatic number identification (ANI) to the PSAP. ANI will allow the PSAP to see your mobile number the way it sees your home phone number when you call 9-1-1. This is helpful if you get disconnected for some reason. The 9-1-1 operator can call you back if need be. Transmission of the automatic location identification (ALI) is to be implemented by October 1, 2001. The ALI information requires the carrier to identify your location by latitude and longitude within a radius of 125 meters, but they don't have to do it every time, only two-thirds of the time.

Ideally, E 9-1-1 will be available nationwide, and there is a big push for just such a deployment. However, if the PSAP can't handle the E 9-1-1 information or doesn't request the information from the carrier, the FCC mandate doesn't apply. Remember, there are places in the U.S. that don't even have 9-1-1 service for landline calls.

How the ALI will actually work is still being discussed. Some feel that a triangulation technique is best. Others want to put a GPS-type device into each phone. The latter has the potential to provide extra benefits to you, such as directions when you're lost. Regardless, the FCC's mandate includes cost recovery for the PSAPs and the wireless carriers, the same way that 9-1-1 service is surcharged on our home phone bill. When you see that 25¢ charge on your wireless phone bill for E 9-1-1 service, take comfort in knowing that if you ever need to call, emergency services will have a better chance of locating you. Just remember, everyone involved with providing E 9-1-1 service is held harmless from liability, in the same fashion as the 9-1-1 service providers. Resolving liability issues in each state may cause delays in implementation.

You can find out what progress is being made with E 9-1-1 at CTIA's Web site (*www.wow-com.com*).

## CALEA

The Communications Assistance for Law Enforcement Act (CALEA) was enacted in 1994 to allow law enforcement surveillance access to wireless telecommunications. Tapping a wireless phone is more complicated than tapping a landline phone. With a landline phone, location of the tapped phone is known. If the call is to another landline phone, the address of the connection is also known. With wireless, the locations of the person being tapped and the connecting call are often difficult to pinpoint. The intention of the Act was to delineate the compliance requirements for the wireless carriers. The Act mandated implementation, and after much deliberation, the attorney general assigned the task to the FBI. The CALEA has generated a great deal of discussion and dispute due to the FBI's continuous requests for increased surveillance capabilities. Legal analysts for the wireless industry argue that Congress didn't authorize the requests being made by the FBI. The deadline for compliance has been extended to June 30, 2000. For news updates, check CTIA's Web site (*www.wow-com.com*).

For more information, contact:

**CALEA Implementation Section**
14800 Conference Center Drive
Suite 300
Chantilly, VA 20151-0450
800-551-0336

# Equal Access For Long Distance

On your home phone service, you have the ability to choose a "dial-1" (or "1+") long-distance carrier. The deregulation in the late 1970s required the regional Bell operating companies to offer equal access, which allows all the long-distance service providers access to you as a customer, and vice versa. Wireless carriers are not required to offer equal access; however, many do. When you subscribe to your wireless carrier, you may also be asked to choose the carrier you want to provide you with long-distance service when making long-distance calls from your wireless phone in your home market.

In addition to 1+ dialing, equal access also includes the ability to dial 101-XXXX to access a long-distance company. (The Xs represent the numeric code assigned to a long-distance carrier. Preceding the phone number you are dialing with the code from the long-distance carrier directs the charges to that specific carrier.) Bear in mind that, even though you can't control your dial-1 privileges while roaming, sometimes your home market dial-1 selection is honored, but it depends on whether the roaming carrier offers equal access. However, if the roaming carrier supports 101-XXXX, you can direct your long-distance charges to the long-distance carrier of your choice. If your long-distance charges are an important issue for you, ask your carrier whether equal access is available.

# North American Numbering Plan

In 1947, AT&T and Bell Laboratories invented the North American Numbering Plan (NANP) for the public switched telephone network (PSTN) to cover the United States, Canada, Bermuda, and most of the Caribbean countries. The numbering scheme conforms to international numbering plan standards set by E.164 of the International Telecommunications Union (ITU).

The numbers are ten digits long and follow a specific format: NXX-NXX-XXXX. The N represents any number from two to nine, and the X represents any number from zero to nine. The first set of three digits is considered the numbering plan area code or NPA, commonly referred to as the area code. The next set is considered a prefix, central office code, or exchange. The last four digits are considered the line numbers.

The North American Numbering Council (NANC), an advisory group of the FCC, governs the North American Numbering Plan. The NANC has appointed Lockheed Martin IMS to be the North American Numbering Plan Administrator (NANPA).

New area code assignments and new local exchange numbers are issued and administered by the NANPA. More information, plus the latest updates on area code changes, can be found at NANPA's Web site *(www.nanpa.com)*.

# Local Number Portability

The Telecommunications Act of 1996 laid the groundwork for increased competition in the local phone service industry. The new competing companies didn't want any disadvantages, such as making you change your phone number if you went with the new guy offering you service. So part of the

Telecommunications Act of 1996 requires the local exchange carriers (LECs—your local phone company) to figure out how to let you keep your existing phone number when you change local phone companies or move across town.

This concept, called local number portability (LNP), is being extended into the wireless telephone arena, so that you won't have to change your phone number if you want to change wireless carriers. LNP is expected to be available in wireless telephony by the fall of 2002. Implementation of local number portability is quite a bit more complicated in the wireless environment than with landline service.

With a wireless phone, your mobile number is programmed into the phone. In the wireless industry, this mobile number is referred to as the mobile identification number (MIN). This is the number that is transmitted to the carrier to identify your phone and used to bill your calls. However, a carrier "buys" NXXs from its local landline company, and these NXXs are then associated with that specific carrier. Currently, your phone has the ability to contain only one mobile phone number per NAM. This is where LNP gets sticky. Let's use a specific example to make it less confusing.

You live in Houston and subscribe to the 800 MHz A carrier. Your phone number is 713-822-XXXX. You want to switch to the 800 MHz B carrier, but you want to keep the same phone number. The Houston A carrier can't sell the number to the Houston B carrier; it doesn't work that way. What happens is that the Houston B carrier assigns you a new MIN, 713-823-XXXX, but your mobile directory number (MDN—the number you wanted to keep) continues to be the number people use to call you. Now you have two numbers: the MIN, which is in the phone, and the MDN, which is the number you give to your friends and relatives. The problem is that if you look at the number programmed into your wireless phone, it is the MIN. Do not give out the MIN as your mobile phone number. It is very important to remember your MDN, especially if you are calling customer service with a problem.

There is a slew of other challenges facing wireless providers when it comes to LNP. For instance, caller ID currently transmits the MIN in your phone. However, you'll want it to transmit the MDN so people can see it's you calling. Public safety answering points (PSAPs), the call centers that answer 9-1-1 calls, use the MIN to call you back if your wireless phone call is disconnected for some reason. Fraudmongers will have a field day thinking up new ways to scam carriers. As for roaming... Well, let's let the carriers work on all this. There are many fine minds at work developing solutions, among which might be phone designs that store both the MIN and the MDN.

You can get the latest information on local number portability at CTIA's Web site *(www.wow-com.com)*.

# Frequently Asked Questions—FAQs

**9**

**Chapter**

## Are cellular phones safe to use (for my health)?

All wireless phones transmit and receive radio frequency signals while turned on. Portable phones use the topmost part of their antennas for sending and receiving signals, so never put the antenna in your mouth, especially during a phone call. Always extend the antenna all the way, and give it an extra tug to be sure. For instance, the Motorola StarTAC™ phone antenna clicks when you pull it out. Although it feels as if it is fully extended, pulling a little more on the antenna often clicks it into another stop.

Wireless phones manufactured today comply with guidelines adopted by the FCC in August, 1996, which delineate safety levels of RF exposure with regard to handheld wireless phones. In fact, most wireless phone manuals include the following under their sections on safety or exposure to RF energy:

*In August, 1996, the Federal Communications Commission (FCC) adopted RF exposure guidelines with safety levels for handheld wireless phones. Those guidelines are consistent with the safety standards previously set by both U.S. and international standards bodies:*

*ANSI (American National Standards Institute) C95.1 (1992)*

*NCRP (National Council on Radiation Protection and Measurements) Report 86 (1986)*

*ICNIRP (International Commission on Non-Ionizing Radiation Protection) (1996)*

*Those standards were based on comprehensive and periodic evaluations of the relevant scientific literature. For example, over 120 scientists, engineers, and physicians from universities, government health agencies, and industry reviewed the available body of research to develop the ANSI Standard (C95.1).*

*The design of your phone complies with the FCC guidelines (and those standards).*

One way to minimize health and safety concerns is to limit the duration of calls made on handheld portables. Install a hands-free kit in your vehicle if you use a phone a lot while driving. If this isn't practical, try to get some sort of headset or cigarette lighter hands-free setup. If you use a bag phone, keep the antenna three feet away from you and your loved ones. In other words, don't put a bag phone on your console while you and your kids are in the front seat of the car. Best of all, get an external antenna: magnetic-mount, window-clip, or even a permanent-mount antenna.

More information can be found at the CTIA's Web site (*www.wow-com.com/consumer/faqs/faq_health.cfm*) and at CNN's news archives (*cnnfn.com/digitaljam/ 9611/ 12/cell_pkg/index.htm*).

# How can I prevent my wireless phone number from being read on caller ID devices?

Most carriers offer permanent caller ID block at no charge. This blocks the information each time you make a phone call, and you appear as "private" or "anonymous" on the caller ID box. In most markets, you can lift the permanent block on a per-call basis by preceding the number you dial with *82 (example: *82-1-312-555-1212 for long distance; *82-555-1212 for local). Check with your carrier, though. Sprint PCS uses *68 instead of *82. Temporarily lifting the permanent block allows your wireless phone number to be transmitted to the caller ID box for that call only. This is handy if you want to block your number all the time, except when you call home, for instance. Then, you want your family to see it's you calling. If you don't elect the permanent caller ID block, you can block on a per-call basis by dialing *67 preceding the number you dial.

# What is a NAM (number assignment module)?

Your phone needs certain information to work on a wireless system. The carrier assigns the wireless phone number, or mobile identification number (MIN), and provides information for use on its network, such as the system ID (SID), the access overload class, the group ID, and the initial paging channel. As the user of the phone, you decide what your unlock code and security code will be. All this information is stored in a special place in your phone called the NAM.

## What information should I know about my wireless phone, and why?

The following pieces of information are found either on or in the phone:

**Mobile phone number** You need to know this so that 1) other people can call you and 2) you can report it to the police and the carrier if the phone is lost or stolen.

**ESN** The electronic serial number is unique to your phone. Do not share this number with anyone but your service provider. No one else needs to know this piece of information. If your phone is lost or stolen, you will need to report your mobile number to your carrier. They will already have the ESN and put it on restriction so that whoever finds the phone will be unable to obtain service from any carrier.

**MSN** The mechanical serial number is the actual hardware serial number. This number is usually what the police need to complete a police report.

**Unlock code** This is often found on your service agreement if assigned by the carrier's dealer, or it is in your user manual as the manufacturer's default. If your phone has the capability, it is recommended that you change your unlock code from the factory default. Be sure you remember what you change it to, though.

**Security code** This number code, usually four to six digits, allows you to change your unlock code, reprogram your wireless phone, and change other security features of your phone. This number should be changed from the factory default, which is usually in the manual. Check your agreement. Dealers usually make a note on the contract if they change the security code at the time of purchase. In PCS, this is sometimes referred to as a subsidy lock code.

## What should I do if I lose my phone?

The moment you realize you don't have possession of your phone (or don't know where it is), **call your airtime service provider** and have your number suspended. Whether you have lost your phone or it was stolen, a prompt report to your carrier will minimize your liability for charges to your phone bill. Next, report the loss or theft to the police department. Check with your local police department to see if you need to file the police report where you live or where the phone was lost or stolen.

## What is a SID?

A system identification, or SID, is a unique identification code transmitted by the carrier in its overhead signal. This SID number is also programmed into the wireless phone to designate your home market. The phone compares the numbers to determine if you are roaming or not. In 800 MHz cellular, an even-numbered SID indicates a B system while an odd-numbered SID indicates an A system.

## How does my phone know that I am in my home market?

When you turn on your phone, it listens for information being broadcast by the carrier on what is called an overhead signal. Part of this information contains the identity or system ID of the carrier. Your phone compares the SID from the carrier to the SID programmed into the NAM of the phone. If the SIDs match, the phone indicates it is in its home market. If they don't match, the phone turns its ROAM indicator on. If the phone can't find a system at all, it turns its NO SERVICE indicator on. For more details, refer to Chapter 2.

## Why does my phone say NO SERVICE when I first turn it on?

When a phone is turned on, it listens for information from the carrier, which is constantly broadcasting a signal. It uses this information to determine whether your phone is in its home market or not in order to give you feedback about the network. This process takes a few seconds. If the NO SERVICE indicator stays lit, there is either no service where you are or your phone is unable to connect to any of the networks.

## Why do my calls drop?

Dropped calls usually occur when you are on the move. Wireless telephony is a dynamic process. The cell site continually measures the phone's signal strength. As you move within the cell site and then from cell to cell, your phone's signal strength can vary, and your phone can be handed off to different channels. Sometimes, as you are about to move into a new cell, the system tries to hand off your call to a new channel. If there are none available at that moment for you to use, your call has no where to go, so it gets dropped by the system. Placing the call again will usually result in a successful connection.

## Why doesn't my phone retain the feature changes I made?

Wireless phones will usually retain repertory numbers stored into them whether the phone is turned off or loses power, such as when a battery goes dead. However, some feature changes require you to "lock" them in by powering off your phone. If you make a feature change and then, without turning your phone off, you replace your battery or otherwise interrupt or change the power source of the phone, the feature changes you made will probably be lost. I had a habit of unplugging my phone from the cigarette lighter adapter without turning the phone off. Any feature changes I had made would always revert to their previous settings until I figured out what I was doing wrong.

## Why do I lose my signal when I go into a building or drive into a garage or valley?

Wireless telephony signals are based on line-of-sight signals. That means that if your phone can't "see" the signal, your phone won't work. Because signals can bounce and reflect, your phone doesn't always have to be in direct line of sight with the wireless tower. However, some buildings have metal in their internal or external walls that shields the signal from the phone and makes it inaccessible to you. The same concept occurs when you go into a parking garage or drive into a valley. Your phone loses "sight" of the signal and is unable to hear the overhead signal from the carrier. Your phone will indicate NO SERVICE, and any call attempts will be met with a system-busy signal.

## Why do I get a system-busy indication when I should have service (or have had service in the same area before)?

A system-busy signal is your phone's way of telling you that you can't access the system at the moment. Check to see if your NO SERVICE indicator is lit. If you are in hilly terrain, you may have driven into a valley or dip where the signal is temporarily unavailable. As you continue to move out of the low-lying area to higher ground, your NO SERVICE indicator will go out, and you should be able to place your call. Sometimes, during peak calling periods when channels are at a premium, you may have to wait your turn for a voice channel. When this occurs, your phone alerts you by providing a system-busy signal. Try again in a few minutes. If your phone has a system-busy redial feature, press the SEND key instead of the END key, and let the phone do the redialing.

## Sometimes my call gets very staticky, and then it clears up. What happened here?

This is an analog problem that is related to the paragraph above on why calls drop. Sometimes, as you get to the edge of a cell, your phone tries its best to maintain its connection by transmitting at maximum power, but it's just not enough. Eventually, as the signal gets weaker and weaker, the system will try to hand off the call to another cell site. Meanwhile, you hear hisses, pops, crackles, and sometimes even silence. Then, all of a sudden, your call is crystal clear because the system successfully handed off your call.

## How can I have a digital phone on an analog system?

Almost all 800 MHz digital phones are dual mode phones. They can access both the digital network and the analog network offered by the carrier. In fact, when most analog carriers implement a digital network, the geographic coverage area, or footprint, of the digital network is smaller than the analog service area. The carrier has had 16 years to build out its analog network and develop a customer base that uses it. Digital networks are only two or three years old, and the footprint of the digital network will expand as the digital customer base develops. Meanwhile, if you opted for digital service and your service area is reduced just because you chose the newer technology, you won't be happy. By using a dual mode phone, your phone will function in digital mode when you are within the digital footprint. However, if you venture beyond the digital footprint, but remain within your home market service area, your phone will fall back to analog mode. This way, you still have the use of your phone.

If you travel and the market you are visiting has incompatible digital technology, your phone will also revert to the analog mode. Check the section on roaming for more details.

## How does cellular compare to the new PCS services available?

Let's dissect this question. PCS advertises digital services, but many of the cellular carriers are making the transition to digital switching equipment as well. Therefore, you either need to compare analog cellular with digital cellular, or compare digital cellular (800 MHz) with digital PCS (1900 MHz). Comparing analog cellular call quality with digital cellular call quality is like comparing a cassette tape to a compact disc. Digital brings signal clarity and adds security to wireless. Cellular offers digital service at 800 MHz, and PCS does this at 1900 MHz. It is better to compare cellular 800 MHz digital to PCS 1900 MHz digital. For instance, when you compare CDMA 800 MHz to CDMA 1900 MHz, the PCS service may seem a bit clearer, but consider that the PCS customer base is a fraction of the cellular carrier's customer base. If the two systems achieved the same level of users, you probably couldn't tell them apart. The same comparison holds true for TDMA technology at 800 MHz and 1900 MHz. GSM-NA at 1900 MHz may also sound clearer than 800 MHz digital technologies due to its recent entry into the U.S. wireless telephony market.

Among the many benefits of digital are short messaging service (SMS), security of transmissions, clarity of voice conversations, and increased capacity. At some point in the next few years, new analog-only phones will no longer be manufactured. However, most dual mode 800 MHz digital phones or dual frequency 1900 MHz/800 MHz digital phones will be capable of accessing analog networks simply because AMPS provides a common thread for wireless telephony in the United States.

## Why can't I use my phone out of town?

There are several reasons you would be unable to use your phone out of town. Following are some possible reasons and potential solutions:

**Problem**: Your carrier doesn't have a roaming agreement with the market that you are visiting.

**Solution**: If this is the case, try changing your network selection. For example, if you are an A system subscriber, try scanning B systems. Sometimes, your home market carrier has a relationship with the opposing carrier, rather than the "like" carrier in the market you're visiting. Check your manual for instructions on changing networks.

**Problem**: Your carrier has implemented a "brownout" for your NPA-NXX (or possibly all its numbers) roaming into the market you are visiting. This means that excessive fraud has taken place in the market you are visiting, and your subscribing carrier is refusing to accept any charges billed from that roaming market. The blockage is usually temporary, ranging from days to six months.

**Solution**: Ask the visiting market carrier if you can make calls and have them billed to a major credit card. (See the end of this answer regarding FCC regulations and access.)

**Problem**: You purchased a phone that works only on a specific frequency or specific technology, and the carrier has no roaming agreements in place or has subsidy locks on the phone. For example, if you purchased a 1900 MHz CDMA phone to use on the PrimeCo network, you won't be able to use that phone on a Sprint PCS network (until they establish a roaming agreement).

**Solution**: None.

**Problem**: You locked the system registration of your phone on HOME only and forgot to change the setting when you left town.

**Solution**: Change your system registration to standard or automatic.

**Problem**: Your phone isn't registering properly, so the system doesn't know if you are a legitimate user.

**Solution**: Contact customer service in either the roaming market or your home market **while you are still roaming!** If you wait until you get back home to see what went wrong, you may find that no one can help you until you roam again.

**Problem**: You need to use a PIN code to let the roaming market know you are a legitimate user.

**Solution**: Usually, you will receive an intercept message asking you for your PIN code.

> If you know it, enter the PIN code when prompted. Otherwise, contact your home market carrier to set up your PIN code.

On August 27, 1996, the Code of Federal Regulations was amended to add the following paragraph (C) to 47CFR20.12 regarding roaming. It reads as follows:

"(c) Roaming. Each licensee subject to this section must provide mobile radio service upon request to all subscribers in good standing to the services on any carrier subject to this Section, including roamers, while such subscribers are located within any portion of the licensee's licensed service area where facilities have been constructed and service to subscribers has commenced, if such subscribers are using mobile equipment that is technically compatible with the licensee's base stations.

"The licensees governed by this paragraph are providers of Broadband Personal Communications Services (1.9 GHz carriers), providers of Cellular Radio Telephone Service (800 MHz carriers), providers of Specialized Mobile Radio Services in the 800 MHz and 900 MHz bands that hold area licenses and offer real-time two-way voice service that is interconnected with the public switched network, as delineated in paragraph (a) of 47CFR20.12."[3]

POINTER

What this means to you is that the carrier must allow you to roam, providing your equipment is compatible and the carrier is offering service. You may need a major credit card to handle the charges if there is no roaming agreement in place. However, this probably won't work if the carrier you subscribe to has a subsidy lock on the phone.

[3]Code of Federal Regulations 47CFR20.12, page 12, revised as of October 1, 1996

# What is dual NAM?

Dual NAM (number assignment module) is a feature in a wireless phone that allows a user to subscribe to two different carriers concurrently. There are actually two NAMs in the phone. Each NAM is programmed with a SID, a phone number, a station class mark, an access overload class, a group ID, an initial paging channel, and a MIN mark. The unlock code and security code are usually only programmed into the first NAM. There are some phones available with as many as eight NAMs. Check the manual for your phone on how to toggle between phone numbers. Dual NAM is not the same as a two-line phone. You can only use one wireless phone number at a time. The second number remains unavailable until you toggle over to it, which renders the first number unavailable. You pay a monthly access fee for each number subscription.

# Subscribing to more than one system—why would I want to?

Your wireless phone bill is enormous. You're on the best rate plan locally, but you travel all the time, and your roaming charges are out of sight. What can you do to control them? Dual registration, dual NAM, two-system registration—whatever you want to call it, subscribing to more than one system may save you money. How can you tell? Plug your usage into the following blanks, and get out your calculator.

Look at your bills for at least the last three months. Do you see one or two markets you have visited regularly? Did you talk a lot while there? Let's use these for calculations. Before you complete this, you'll need to do some homework about the markets you're evaluating. On your next visit, stop to see a couple of wireless providers and pick up their rate plans. Now, let's run some numbers.

### Roaming Analysis

| | | Roaming Market 1 | Roaming Market 2 | Example |
|---|---|---|---|---|
| Number of roaming minutes | (A) | _____ | _____ | 120 |
| Roaming minute charge | (B) | _____ | _____ | 99¢ |
| Multiply: A x B | (C) | _____ | _____ | $118.80 |
| Daily access fee | (D) | _____ | _____ | $3.00 |
| Number of days in market | (E) | _____ | _____ | 8 |
| Multiply: D x E | (F) | _____ | _____ | $24.00 |
| Add: C+F (total roaming costs) | (G) | _____ | _____ | $142.80 |
| Local monthly access fee | (H) | _____ | _____ | $19.95 |
| Local per-minute rate | (I) | _____ | _____ | 25¢ |
| Multiply: A x I | (J) | _____ | _____ | $30.00 |
| Add: H + J (total local costs) | (K) | _____ | _____ | $49.95 |
| Subtract: G - K (savings) | | _____ | _____ | $92.85 |

Here's another reason for dual registration. You live in a mountainous area. The wireless carriers offer service, but none can give you 100 percent coverage. If you register on two systems in your home market, you can maximize your coverage. Usually you select one of the two numbers to be your primary number and the other to be your secondary number. Unfortunately, you will pay two monthly access fees for this convenience.

It is possible to subscribe to a digital carrier and an AMPS carrier if you have a dual mode or dual mode/dual frequency phone.

Two-system registration for roaming becomes virtually unnecessary with plans such as AT&T's Digital One-Rate[SM]. Since its introduction, other companies are following AT&T's lead and are offering their own one-rate roaming and long-distance programs.

## Which carrier is offering dual NAM in my market?

This is not a valid question. Dual NAM, by its definition, means one phone (ESN) subscribing to two different carriers. Therefore, no single carrier in a market could offer or provide dual NAM. The question is probably, "Which carrier is offering one-number-on-two-phones capability in my market?"

## Can I have one number on two phones?

Yes, but your carrier has to support the ability to register two ESNs to one mobile number. The old way of having the same number in two phones required cloning or duplicating the ESN into a second phone to fool the wireless switch. Because cloning is the method selected by thieves to perpetrate wireless phone fraud, carriers have implemented measures to detect cloning and restrict the ESN until the problem is corrected. Cellular service was originally designed to have only one ESN per mobile number as a means to detect fraud. However, some carriers now have software that can support assigning two ESNs to one mobile number. There is usually a nominal monthly charge for this benefit, perhaps $9.95. You can't use both phones at the same time, so one phone can't call the other. In addition, only the primary phone can be used to roam.

## How do I erase a stored number?

If you are unable to find instructions in your manual, try this. Press and hold the CLEAR key until the display is clear, then, without entering anything, store "nothing" into the memory location you are trying to erase. Follow your instruction manual for storing new numbers.

## My car kit drains my car's battery. Why? What can I do about it?

It is likely your car kit was not installed properly. Car kits are usually installed to turn on, or activate, with your car's ignition. For example, if your charger stays on even when the car's ignition is off, then the installation was done incorrectly. A quick way to address this problem is to see if there is a separate, detachable cord to the charger. If there is, just unplug this cord when you get out of your car. There are two drawbacks to this remedy. First, you have to remember to unplug it every time you get out of your car, and second, you have to remember to plug it back in every time you get into your car. As you are also plugging and unplugging your phone each time you get in and out of your car, this may not be a problem. If it is, however, have your car kit reinstalled correctly.

## What about cellular in other countries?

Two elements that make wireless telephony in other countries compatible with wireless telephony in the United States are the operating frequency and the technology used by the system. North, Central, and South America, the Caribbean, parts of Southern Asia and Russia, as well as Australia and New Zealand all use AMPS technology at the same 800 MHz frequencies. Hence, their systems are all compatible with U.S. AMPS networks. However, some of these countries, such as Australia, restrict the use of phones to those made in their country, and your wireless phone will be appropriated by customs for the duration of your visit. Rentals are available. Be sure to check before you travel. Roaming agreements are in place with

Canadian networks, but wireless service south of the U.S. border needs to be set up in advance.

On the Continent, roaming among European countries in the 1980s was all but impossible because there were nine different types of systems, none compatible with the other, and several different frequencies. Europeans became accustomed to renting phones when they traveled to the different countries on the Continent. In the early 1990s, GSM digital technology was adopted and used on a standard frequency of 900 MHz. In the U.S., this 900 MHz frequency was allocated for other uses such as two-way radio, but in most other parts of the world, it was available. GSM technology at 900 MHz has become extremely widespread and is now available in more than 60 countries.

If you travel abroad and want a phone you can take with you rather than endure the hassle of establishing service once you arrive, check with your carrier for available rental programs. Also, check out "Where can I rent a wireless phone?" at the end of this section. Companies such as AT&T Wireless, GTE Wireless, and Motorola Cellular Service, Inc. have GSM 900 MHz phones for use abroad that are available for purchase domestically. This is ideal for international travelers.

## Can I use a wireless phone on an airplane?

Yes, and no.

No, you aren't allowed to use your terrestrial wireless phone system in an airborne airplane. Contrary to popular belief, this is not an FAA rule, but rather an FCC regulation[4]. Using your wireless phone in

[4] 47CFR22.925: "The use of cellular telephones while the aircraft is airborne is prohibited by FCC rules, and the violation of this rule could result in suspension of service and/or fine. The use of cellular telephones while the aircraft is on the ground is subject to FAA regulations."

the air can scramble the terrestrial wireless networks. The FAA regulates the use of a wireless phone while the plane is still on the ground, as it may interfere with avionics equipment.

And yes. The FCC has designated a specific set of channels in the 450 MHz range for wireless telephony in aircraft. The phones currently in use in commercial aircraft and available for general aviation operate at this frequency.

A company called AirCell is offering a new alternative. AirCell offers airtime service as a reseller through arrangements it has made with rural cellular companies. Aircell reuses underutilized frequencies in the rural carriers' systems by collocating a proprietary antenna on one of the carriers' cell sites. AirCell's network of 150 specialized antennas provides cones of coverage that are 120 to 130 miles in diameter and two degrees above the horizon. In addition to airtime service, AirCell offers the TrimConnect 3100D Flight Telephone System manufactured by Trimble Avionics. The phone is an 800 MHz Motorola bag phone, outfitted with a proprietary antenna and modified into an avionics box with proprietarily modified power levels. The Trimble phone transmits at 10 milliwatts, whereas most portables transmit at a maximum of 600 milliwatts, and standard bag phones transmit at a maximum of 3,000 milliwatts. By using different control channels than terrestrial systems, AirCell system's users are invisible to terrestrial networks. The result is that you can use this 800 MHz cellular phone on your private plane.

There are two models of phones. One model can only be used in the air and costs $3,995. The other model can be used both in the air and on the ground and costs $6,995. The phones need to be installed by a certified avionics shop, requiring an estimated 40 hours of shop time. The airtime is a flat $1.75 per minute, but this includes roaming and long-distance charges. The monthly access fee is $39.95 for calls from the air and an additional $19.95 if calling while on the ground.

AirCell's setup is great for keeping in touch with your office, sending or receiving faxes, transferring data, or connecting to the Internet. Future phone models may include GPS and weather data interfaces. Coverage and purchasing information is available by contacting:

**AirCell, Inc.**
1172 Century Drive
Suite 280
Building B
Louisville, CO  80027
303-379-0200 VOICE
303-379-0201 FAX
*www.aircell.com*

**Trimble Avionics**
2105 Donley Drive
Austin, TX  78758
888-FLY-TRIMB
512-432-0400 VOICE
512-836-9413 FAX
*www.trimble.com*

## Where can I rent a wireless phone?

Renting a wireless phone is an expensive proposition, the way renting a car is. Just as you wouldn't rent a car for a year at a time, you also wouldn't rent a phone for very long. So why rent one at all? Some possible reasons follow:

- **Pregnancy**  The last month or two can get hairy. Renting a wireless phone can provide some peace of mind, knowing you'll be in touch. This way you don't have to obligate yourself for a year or two for something you don't want to keep—especially with all your baby expenses.

- **Local number**  It would be great to have a local number when you get where you're going because callers often have difficulty reaching you while you are traveling on trips or on vacation. Sometimes your phone doesn't work at all due to roaming restrictions. Renting a phone can provide you with a local wireless number, local calling, etc.

- **Global traveler**   Set up your wireless phone service even before you get on the plane to leave the U.S. There's no hassle when you arrive at your foreign destination. You'll start making calls the minute you land.

## Action Cellular Rent-a-Phone International
99 Osgood Place
Penthouse
San Francisco, CA  94133
415-929-0400 VOICE
415-346-1080 FAX
800-RENT-PHONES or 800-727-0600
e-mail: *hello@rentaphone.com*
*www.rentaphone.com*

## InTouch USA
4100 Westfax Drive
Chantilly, VA  20151
703-222-7161 VOICE
703-222-9597 FAX
800-USA-ROAM
e-mail: *info@intouchusa.com*
*www.intouchusa.com*

## National Cellular Rentals, Inc.
50 Lindsey Avenue
Nashville, TN  37210
615-322-5365 VOICE
615-322-5363 FAX
800-779-3785
e-mail: *ncrnash@edge.net*
*allwirelessrentals.com*

# Equipment Manufacturers

## Audiovox Communications Corp.
555 Wireless Boulevard
Hauppauge, NY 11788
516-233-3300
800-229-1235 CUSTOMER SERVICE
*www.audiovox.com*

## Ericsson Mobile Phones & Terminals
7001 Development Drive
P.O. Box 13969
Research Triangle Park, NC 27709
800-Ericsson
*www.ericsson.com/us/phones*

## Fujitsu Microelectronics, Inc.
3545 North First Street
San Jose, CA 95134-1804
800-866-8608
*www.fujitsumicro.com*

## Mitsubishi Personal Mobile Communications Division
1050 East Arques Avenue
Sunnyvale, CA 94086
408-523-6900 VOICE
408-736-5912 FAX
*www.mobileaccessphone.com*

## Mitsubishi Wireless Communications, Inc.
3805 Crestwood Parkway
Suite 350
Duluth, GA 30096
770-638-2100 VOICE
770-921-4522 FAX
*www.mitsubishiwireless.com*

## Motorola, Inc.
Cellular Subscriber Sector
600 North U.S. Highway 45
Libertyville, IL 60048
800-331-6456
*www.mot.com*

## NEC Wireless Communications
1621 West Walnut Hill Lane
Irving TX 75038
800-421-2141 SALES
800-637-5917 SERVICE
*www.nec.com*

## Nokia Mobile Phones
6200 Courtney Campbell Causeway
Suite 900
Tampa, FL 33607
888-NOKIA2U (888-665-4228)
*www.nokia.com*

## OKI Telecom, Inc.
437 Old Peachtree Road
Suwanee, GA 30174
800-554-3112
*www.okitele.com*

## Panasonic
Matsushita Electric Corporation of America
One Panasonic Way
Secaucus, NJ 07094
800-414-4408 CUSTOMER SERVICE
800-441-7262 SALES
*www.panasonic.com*

## Philips Consumer Communications
5 Woodhollow Road
Parsippany, NJ 07054
973-581-3600
*www.philipsconsumer.com*

## QUALCOMM Incorporated
6455 Lusk Boulevard
San Diego, CA 92121-2779
619-587-1121 VOICE
619-658-2100 FAX
*www.qualcomm.com*

## Samsung Telecommunications America, Inc.
1130 East Arapaho Road
Richardson, TX 75081
972-761-7000 VOICE
972-761-7001 FAX
*samsungelectronics.com*

## Sony Personal Mobile Communications America
16450 West Bernardo Drive
San Diego, CA 92127
800-578-SONY
*www.sony.com/wireless*

## Uniden America Corp.
4700 Amon Carter Boulevard
Fort Worth, TX 76155
817-858-3470 CUSTOMER SERVICE
*www.uniden.com*

# Resources

## Satellite Companies

### Comsat Corporation (Intelsat GEO)
6560 Rock Spring Drive
Bethesda, MD 20817
888-PLANET1
301-214-3000 VOICE
301-214-7100 FAX
*www.comsat.com*

### Globalstar (Big LEO)
3200 Zanker Road
P. O. Box 640670
San Jose, CA 95164-0670
408-933-4000 VOICE
408-933-4100 FAX
*www.globalstar.com*

### ICO Global Communications Services, Inc. (MEO)
1101 Connecticut Avenue NW
Suite 250
Washington, DC 20036
202-887-8111 VOICE
202-887-0889 FAX
*www.i-co.co.uk*

### Inmarsat Communication Systems (GEO)
99 City Road
London, England LC1Y 1AX
44-171-728-1000 VOICE
44-171-728-1044 FAX
*www.inmarsat.org*

**Iridium, Inc.** (Big LEO)
8440 South River Parkway
Tempe, AZ 85284
888-IRIDIUM (888-474-3486)
*www.iridium.com*

**Intelsat** (GEO)
3400 International Drive NW
Washington, DC 20008-3098
202-944-6800 VOICE
202-944-7898 FAX
*www.intelsat.int*

**LandSea Communications** (Inmarsat GEO)
849 Sea Hawk Circle
Suite 103
Virginia Beach, VA 23452
757-468-0448 VOICE
757-468-0625 FAX
*www.landseasystems.com*

**O'Gara Satellite Networks** (Inmarsat GEO)
1 Brandywine Drive
Dear Park, NY 11729
310-547-0021 VOICE
310-547-3888 FAX
*www.ogarasat.com*

**Teledesic Corp.** (Broadband LEO)
2300 Carillon Point
Kirkland, WA 98033
415-602-0000 VOICE
415-602-0001 FAX
*www.teledesic.com*

# Phone Rental Companies

### Action Cellular Rent-a-Phone International

99 Osgood Place
Penthouse
San Francisco, CA  94133
415-929-0400 VOICE
415-346-1080 FAX
e-mail: *hello@rentaphone.com*
800-RENT-PHONES (800-727-0600)
*www.rentaphone.com*

### InTouch USA

4100 Westfax Drive
Chantilly, VA  20151
703-222-7161 VOICE
703-222-9597 FAX
e-mail: *info@intouchusa.com*
*www.intouchusa.com*

### National Cellular Rentals, Inc.

50 Lindsey Avenue
Nashville, TN  37210
800-779-3785
615-322-5365 VOICE
615-322-5363 FAX
e-mail: *ncrnash@edge.net*
*allwirelessrentals.com*

# Miscellaneous Companies

### 3Com Corporation

Great America Site
5400 Bayfront Plaza
Santa Clara, CA  95052
408-326-5000 VOICE
408-326-5001 FAX
*palmpilot.3com.com*

## Belkin Components
501 West Walnut Street
Compton, CA 90220
800-2BELKIN (800-223-5546)
800-BATTERIES (800-228-8374)
*www.belkin.com*

## Diamond Multimedia Systems, Inc.
San Jose, California
408-325-7000
800-468-5846

## GoAmerica Communications Corp.
401 Hackensack Avenue
Hackensack, NJ 07601
888-462-4600
*www.goamerica.net*

## GTE Telecommunications Services
201 North Franklin Street
7th Floor
Tampa, FL 33602
888-724-3579
*www.tsi.gte.com*

## ILLUMINET
800-486-4636
*www.illuminetSS7.com*

## Nextel Communications, Inc.
1505 Farm Credit Drive
McLean, VA 22102
703-394-3000
800-Nextel9 (800-639-8349)
*www.nextel.com*

## Novatel Wireless, Inc.
San Diego, California
888-888-9231
*www.novatelwireless.com*

## Siemens Security & Chip Card ICs

3050 Democracy Way
MS 500
Santa Clara, CA 95054
408-492-3271

## SRS Technologies

1811 Quail Street
Newport Beach, CA  92660
949-852-6900 VOICE
949-852-6901 FAX
*www.srs.com*

## Technocel

800-843-5600
*www.technocel.com*

## Telular Corporation

647 North Lakeview Parkway
Vernon Hills, IL  60061
847-247-9400 VOICE
847-247-0021 FAX
*www.telular.com*

## Wireless Dimension

Nth Dimension Corporation
19015 North Creek Parkway, Suite 105
Bothell, Washington 98011
425-951-4400 VOICE
425-951-4401 FAX
*www.wirelessdimension.com*

# Wireless Organizations

## CNP – Cellular Networking Perspectives

*www.cnp-wireless.com*

## Cellular Telephone Industry of America (CTIA)

*www.wow-com.com*

## Federal Communications Commission (FCC)

*www.fcc.gov*

## North American Cellular Network (NACN)

P.O. Box 97060
Kirkland, WA 98083-9760
*www.nacn.com*

## North American Numbering Plan Administrator (NANPA)

1133 15th Street NW
12th Floor
Washington, DC 20005
*www.nanpa.com*

## Personal Communications Industry Association (PCIA)

*www.pcia.com*

## Wireless Now

*www.commnow.com*
(Wireless & Cable industry information online)

## The World of Wireless Communications

*www.wow-com.com/consumer*

# Wireless Publications

## Cellular & Mobile International

Intertec Publishing Corp.
9800 Metcalf
Overlook Park, KS  66212
913-341-1300
(Industry professionals' magazine)

## Cellular Travel Guide

Communications Publishing
P. O. Box 500
Mercer Island, WA  98040
206-232-8800
800 927-8800

**RCR Weekly** (magazine)
Subscriber Services
965 East Jefferson
Detroit, MI 48207
800-678-9595
(RCR Weekly, RCR Cellular Handbook, RCR PCS
  Handbook)

**RCR Global Wireless**
*www.rcrnews.com*

**Spread Spectrum Scene Online**
*www.sss-mag.com*

**Wireless Review**
Intertec Publishing Corp.
9800 Metcalf
Overlook Park, KS 66212
913-341-1300
(Industry professionals' magazine)

**Wireless Week**
Fast Fourward
600 South Cherry Street
Suite 400
Denver, CO 80246-1702
212-887-8467
*www.wirelessweek.com*

## Mail Order Companies

### Everything Wireless
888-EVERY99 (888-383-7999)
*www.everythingwireless.com*

### Hello Direct
800-HI-HELLO (800-444-3556)
800-456-2566 fax
e-mail: *xpressit@hihello.com*
*www.hello-direct.com*

### 1-800-Batteries
2301 Robb Drive
Reno, NV 89523
800-228-8374
e-mail: *orders@1800Batteries.com*
*www.1800Batteries.com*

## National Resellers

### MCI WorldCom
515 East Amite Street
Jackson, MS 39201-2702
601-360-8600
800-844-1009
800-444-3333 HOME SALES
800-539-2000 BUSINESS SALES
800-727-5555 SMALL BUSINESS SALES
*www.mciworldcom.com*

### Motorola Cellular Service, Inc.
2440 Commerce Drive
Libertyville, IL 60048
800-232-MCSI (800-232-6274)
*www.mot.com/GSS/CSG/WhereToBuy/*
  *MotorolaDirect/vip.html*

# Cellular Market Areas

Appendix C

## Metropolitan Service Areas (MSAs) Numerical Market Listing for Cellular 800 MHz

| MSA# | Market Name | State |
|------|-------------|-------|
| 0001 | New York | NY |
| 0002 | Los Angeles | CA |
| 0003 | Chicago | IL |
| 0004 | Philadelphia | PA |
| 0005 | Detroit | MI |
| 0006 | Boston | MA |
| 0007 | San Francisco | CA |
| 0008 | Washington | DC |
| 0009 | Dallas | TX |
| 0010 | Houston | TX |
| 0011 | St. Louis | MO/IL |
| 0012 | Miami | FL |
| 0013 | Pittsburgh | PA |
| 0014 | Baltimore | MD |
| 0015 | Minneapolis-St. Paul | MN/WI |
| 0016 | Cleveland | OH |
| 0017 | Atlanta | GA |
| 0018 | San Diego | CA |
| 0019 | Denver | CO |
| 0020 | Seattle-Everett | WA |
| 0021 | Milwaukee | WI |
| 0022 | Tampa | FL |
| 0023 | Cincinnati | OH |
| 0024 | Kansas City | MO/KS |
| 0025 | Buffalo | NY |
| 0026 | Phoenix | AZ |

*continued on page 190*

A resizable, interactive portable document file (.pdf) version of this map is available at the FCC Web site (*www.fcc.gov/wtb/auctions/maps/rsamsa.pdf*).

# Metropolitan Statistic

# as and Rural Service Areas

MSAs
RSAs

RSA's not shown
730-731 U.S. Virgin Islands
732 Guam
733 American Samoa
734 Northern Mariana Isl.

Note: Due to the size and the quantity of RSA's and MSA's not all numbers appear

*continued from page 187*

| MSA# | Market Name | State |
|------|-------------|-------|
| 0027 | San Jose | CA |
| 0028 | Indianapolis | IN |
| 0029 | New Orleans | LA |
| 0030 | Portland | OR/WA |
| 0031 | Columbus | OH |
| 0032 | Hartford | CT |
| 0033 | San Antonio | TX |
| 0034 | Rochester | NY |
| 0035 | Sacramento | CA |
| 0036 | Memphis | TN/AR/MS |
| 0037 | Louisville | KY/IN |
| 0038 | Providence-Warwick-Pawtucket | RI/MA |
| 0039 | Salt Lake City-Ogden | UT |
| 0040 | Dayton | OH |
| 0041 | Birmingham | AL |
| 0042 | Bridgeport | CT |
| 0043 | Norfolk-VA Beach-Portsmouth | VA/NC |
| 0044 | Albany-Schenectady-Troy | NY |
| 0045 | Oklahoma City | OK |
| 0046 | Nashville-Davidson | TN |
| 0047 | Greensboro-Winston Salem-High Point | NC |
| 0048 | Toledo | OH/MI |
| 0049 | New Haven | CT |
| 0050 | Honolulu | HI |
| 0051 | Jacksonville | FL |
| 0052 | Akron | OH |
| 0053 | Syracuse | NY |
| 0054 | Gary-Hammond-East Chicago | IN |
| 0055 | Worcester | MA |
| 0056 | Northeast Pennsylvania | PA |
| 0057 | Tulsa | OK |
| 0058 | Allentown-Bethlehem-Easton | PA/NJ |
| 0059 | Richmond | VA |
| 0060 | Orlando | FL |
| 0061 | Charlotte-Gastonia-Rock Hill | NC |
| 0062 | New Brunswick-Perth Amboy-Sayreville | NJ |
| 0063 | Springfield-Chicopee-Holyoke | MA |
| 0064 | Grand Rapids | MI |
| 0065 | Omaha | NE/IA |
| 0066 | Youngstown-Warren | OH |
| 0067 | Greenville-Spartanburg | SC |
| 0068 | Flint | MI |

| MSA# | Market Name | State |
|------|-------------|-------|
| 0069 | Wilmington | DE/NJ/MD |
| 0070 | Long Branch-Asbury Park | NJ |
| 0071 | Raleigh-Durham | NC |
| 0072 | West Palm Beach-Boca Raton | FL |
| 0073 | Oxnard-Simi Valley-Ventura | CA |
| 0074 | Fresno | CA |
| 0075 | Austin | TX |
| 0076 | New Bedford | MA |
| 0077 | Tucson | AZ |
| 0078 | Lansing-East Lansing | MI |
| 0079 | Knoxville | TN |
| 0080 | Baton Rouge | LA |
| 0081 | El Paso | TX |
| 0082 | Tacoma | WA |
| 0083 | Mobile | AL |
| 0084 | Harrisburg | PA |
| 0085 | Johnson City-Kingsport-Bristol | TN/VA |
| 0086 | Albuquerque | NM |
| 0087 | Canton | OH |
| 0088 | Chattanooga | TN/GA |
| 0089 | Wichita | KS |
| 0090 | Charleston-North Charleston | SC |
| 0091 | San Juan-Caguas | PR |
| 0092 | Little Rock-North Little Rock | AR |
| 0093 | Las Vegas | NV |
| 0094 | Saginaw-Bay City-Midland | MI |
| 0095 | Columbia | SC |
| 0096 | Fort Wayne | IN |
| 0097 | Bakersfield | CA |
| 0098 | Davenport-Rock Island-Moline | IA/IL |
| 0099 | York | PA |
| 0100 | Shreveport | LA |
| 0101 | Beaumont-Port Arthur | TX |
| 0102 | Des Moines | IA |
| 0103 | Peoria | IL |
| 0104 | Newport News-Hampton | VA |
| 0105 | Lancaster | PA |
| 0106 | Jackson | MS |
| 0107 | Stockton | CA |
| 0108 | Augusta | GA/SC |
| 0109 | Spokane | WA |
| 0110 | Huntington-Ashland | WV/KY/OH |
| 0111 | Vallejo-Fairfield-Napa | CA |
| 0112 | Corpus Christi | TX |

| MSA# | Market Name | State |
|------|-------------|-------|
| 0113 | Madison | WI |
| 0114 | Lakeland-Winter Haven | FL |
| 0115 | Utica-Rome | NY |
| 0116 | Lexington-Fayette | KY |
| 0117 | Colorado Springs | CO |
| 0118 | Reading | PA |
| 0119 | Evansville | IN/KY |
| 0120 | Huntsville | AL |
| 0121 | Trenton | NJ |
| 0122 | Binghamton | NY |
| 0123 | Santa Rosa-Petaluma | CA |
| 0124 | Santa Barbara-Santa Maria-Lompoc | CA |
| 0125 | Appleton-Oshkosh-Neenah | WI |
| 0126 | Salinas-Seaside-Monterey | CA |
| 0127 | Pensacola | FL |
| 0128 | Mcallen-Edinburg-Mission | TX |
| 0129 | South Bend-Mishawaka | IN |
| 0130 | Erie | PA |
| 0131 | Rockford | IL |
| 0132 | Kalamazoo | MI |
| 0133 | Manchester-Nashua | NH |
| 0134 | Atlantic City | NJ |
| 0135 | Eugene-Springfield | OR |
| 0136 | Lorain-Elyria | OH |
| 0137 | Melbourne-Titusville-Palm Bay | FL |
| 0138 | Macon-Warner Robins | GA |
| 0139 | Montgomery | AL |
| 0140 | Charleston | WV |
| 0141 | Duluth | MN/WI |
| 0142 | Modesto | CA |
| 0143 | Johnstown | PA |
| 0144 | Orange County | NY |
| 0145 | Hamilton-Middletown | OH |
| 0146 | Daytona Beach | FL |
| 0147 | Ponce | PR |
| 0148 | Salem | OR |
| 0149 | Fayetteville | NC |
| 0150 | Visalia-Tulare-Porterville | CA |
| 0151 | Poughkeepsie | NY |
| 0152 | Portland | ME |
| 0153 | Columbus | GA/AL |
| 0154 | New London-Norwich | CT/RI |
| 0155 | Savannah | GA |
| 0156 | Portsmouth-Dover-Rochester | NH |

| MSA# | Market Name | State |
|------|-------------|-------|
| 0157 | Roanoke | VA |
| 0158 | Lima | OH |
| 0159 | Provo-Orem | UT |
| 0160 | Killeen-Temple | TX |
| 0161 | Lubbock | TX |
| 0162 | Brownsville-Harlingen | TX |
| 0163 | Springfield | MO |
| 0164 | Fort Myers | FL |
| 0165 | Fort Smith | AR/OK |
| 0166 | Hickory | NC |
| 0167 | Sarasota | FL |
| 0168 | Tallahassee | FL |
| 0169 | Mayaguez | PR |
| 0170 | Galveston-Texas City | TX |
| 0171 | Reno | NV |
| 0172 | Lincoln | NE |
| 0173 | Biloxi-Gulfport | MS |
| 0174 | Lafayette | LA |
| 0175 | Santa Cruz | CA |
| 0176 | Springfield | IL |
| 0177 | Battle Creek | MI |
| 0178 | Wheeling | WV/OH |
| 0179 | Topeka | KS |
| 0180 | Springfield | OH |
| 0181 | Muskegon | MI |
| 0182 | Fayetteville-Springdale | AR |
| 0183 | Asheville | NC |
| 0184 | Houma-Thibodaux | LA |
| 0185 | Terre Haute | IN |
| 0186 | Green Bay | WI |
| 0187 | Anchorage | AK |
| 0188 | Amarillo | TX |
| 0189 | Racine | WI |
| 0190 | Boise City | ID |
| 0191 | Yakima | WA |
| 0192 | Gainesville | FL |
| 0193 | Benton Harbor | MI |
| 0194 | Waco | TX |
| 0195 | Cedar Rapids | IA |
| 0196 | Champaign-Urbana-Rantoul | IL |
| 0197 | Lake Charles | LA |
| 0198 | St. Cloud | MN |
| 0199 | Steubenville-Weirton | OH/WV |
| 0200 | Parkersburg-Marietta | OH/WV |

| MSA# | Market Name | State |
|------|-------------|-------|
| 0201 | Waterloo-Cedar Falls | IA |
| 0202 | Arecibo | PR |
| 0203 | Lynchburg | VA |
| 0204 | Aguadilla | PR |
| 0205 | Alexandria | LA |
| 0206 | Longview-Marshall | TX |
| 0207 | Jackson | MI |
| 0208 | Fort Pierce | FL |
| 0209 | Clarksville-Hopkinsville | TN/KY |
| 0210 | Fort Collins-Loveland | CO |
| 0211 | Bradenton | FL |
| 0212 | Bremerton | WA |
| 0213 | Pittsfield | MA |
| 0214 | Richland-Kennewick-Pasco | WA |
| 0215 | Chico | CA |
| 0216 | Janesville-Beloit | WI |
| 0217 | Anderson | IN |
| 0218 | Wilmington | NC |
| 0219 | Monroe | LA |
| 0220 | Abilene | TX |
| 0221 | Fargo-Moorehead | ND/MN |
| 0222 | Tuscaloosa | AL |
| 0223 | Elkhart-Goshen | IN |
| 0224 | Bangor | ME |
| 0225 | Altoona | PA |
| 0226 | Florence | AL |
| 0227 | Anderson | SC |
| 0228 | Vineland-Millville-Bridgeton | NJ |
| 0229 | Medford | OR |
| 0230 | Decatur | IL |
| 0231 | Mansfield | OH |
| 0232 | Eau Claire | WI |
| 0233 | Wichita Falls | TX |
| 0234 | Athens | GA |
| 0235 | Petersburg-Colonial Heights-Hopewell | VA |
| 0236 | Muncie | IN |
| 0237 | Tyler | TX |
| 0238 | Sharon | PA |
| 0239 | Joplin | MO |
| 0240 | Texarkana | TX/AR |
| 0241 | Pueblo | CO |
| 0242 | Olympia | WA |
| 0243 | Greeley | CO |
| 0244 | Kenosha | WI |

| MSA# | Market Name | State |
|------|-------------|-------|
| 0245 | Ocala | FL |
| 0246 | Dothan | AL |
| 0247 | Lafayette | IN |
| 0248 | Burlington | VT |
| 0249 | Anniston | AL |
| 0250 | Bloomington-Normal | IL |
| 0251 | Williamsport | PA |
| 0252 | Pascagoula | MS |
| 0253 | Sioux City | IA/NE |
| 0254 | Redding | CA |
| 0255 | Odessa | TX |
| 0256 | Charlottesville | VA |
| 0257 | Hagerstown | MD |
| 0258 | Jacksonville | NC |
| 0259 | State College | PA |
| 0260 | Lawton | OK |
| 0261 | Albany | GA |
| 0262 | Danville | VA |
| 0263 | Wausau | WI |
| 0264 | Florence | SC |
| 0265 | Fort Walton Beach | FL |
| 0266 | Glens Falls | NY |
| 0267 | Sioux Falls | SD |
| 0268 | Billings | MT |
| 0269 | Cumberland | MD/WV |
| 0270 | Bellingham | WA |
| 0271 | Kokomo | IN |
| 0272 | Gadsden | AL |
| 0273 | Kankakee | IL |
| 0274 | Yuba City | CA |
| 0275 | St. Joseph | MO |
| 0276 | Grand Forks | ND |
| 0277 | Sheboygan | WI |
| 0278 | Columbia | MO |
| 0279 | Lewiston-Auburn | ME |
| 0280 | Burlington | NC |
| 0281 | Laredo | TX |
| 0282 | Bloomington | IN |
| 0283 | Panama City | FL |
| 0284 | Elmira | NY |
| 0285 | Las Cruces | NM |
| 0286 | Dubuque | IA |
| 0287 | Bryan-College Station | TX |
| 0288 | Rochester | MN |

| MSA# | Market Name | State |
|------|-------------|-------|
| 0289 | Rapid City | SD |
| 0290 | La Crosse | WI |
| 0291 | Pine Bluff | AR |
| 0292 | Sherman-Denison | TX |
| 0293 | Owensboro | KY |
| 0294 | San Angelo | TX |
| 0295 | Midland | TX |
| 0296 | Iowa City | IA |
| 0297 | Great Falls | MT |
| 0298 | Bismarck | ND |
| 0299 | Casper | WY |
| 0300 | Victoria | TX |
| 0301 | Lawrence | KS |
| 0302 | Enid | OK |
| 0303 | Aurora-Elgin | IL |
| 0304 | Joliet | IL |
| 0305 | Alton-Granite City | IL |
| 0306 | Gulf of Mexico | |

# Rural Service Areas (RSAs) Numerical Market Listing for Cellular 800 MHz

| RSA# | State | Market |
|------|-------|--------|
| 0307 | Alabama | 1 - Franklin |
| 0308 | Alabama | 2 - Jackson |
| 0309 | Alabama | 3 - Lamar |
| 0310 | Alabama | 4 - Bibb |
| 0311 | Alabama | 5 - Cleburne |
| 0312 | Alabama | 6 - Washington |
| 0313 | Alabama | 7 - Butler |
| 0314 | Alabama | 8 - Lee |
| 0315 | Alaska | 1 - Wade Hampton |
| 0316 | Alaska | 2 - Bethel |
| 0317 | Alaska | 3 - Haines |
| 0318 | Arizona | 1 - Mohave |
| 0319 | Arizona | 2 - Coconino |
| 0320 | Arizona | 3 - Navajo |
| 0321 | Arizona | 4 - Yuma |
| 0322 | Arizona | 5 - Gila |
| 0323 | Arizona | 6 - Graham |
| 0324 | Arkansas | 1 - Madison |
| 0325 | Arkansas | 2 - Marion |

| RSA# | State | Market |
|------|-------|--------|
| 0326 | Arkansas | 3 - Sharp |
| 0327 | Arkansas | 4 - Clay |
| 0328 | Arkansas | 5 - Cross |
| 0329 | Arkansas | 6 - Cleburne |
| 0330 | Arkansas | 7 - Pope |
| 0331 | Arkansas | 8 - Franklin |
| 0332 | Arkansas | 9 - Polk |
| 0333 | Arkansas | 10 - Garland |
| 0334 | Arkansas | 11 - Hempstead |
| 0335 | Arkansas | 12 - Ouchita |
| 0336 | California | 1 - Del Norte |
| 0337 | California | 2 - Modoc |
| 0338 | California | 3 - Alpine |
| 0339 | California | 4 - Madera |
| 0340 | California | 5 - San Luis Obispo |
| 0341 | California | 6 - Mono |
| 0342 | California | 7 - Imperial |
| 0343 | California | 8 - Tehama |
| 0344 | California | 9 - Mendocino |
| 0345 | California | 10 - Sierra |
| 0346 | California | 11 - El Dorado |
| 0347 | California | 12 - Kings |
| 0348 | Colorado | 1 - Moffat |
| 0349 | Colorado | 2 - Logan |
| 0350 | Colorado | 3 - Garfield |
| 0351 | Colorado | 4 - Park |
| 0352 | Colorado | 5 - Elbert |
| 0353 | Colorado | 6 - San Miguel |
| 0354 | Colorado | 7 - Saguache |
| 0355 | Colorado | 8 - Kiowa |
| 0356 | Colorado | 9 - Costilla |
| 0357 | Connecticut | 1 - Litchfield |
| 0358 | Connecticut | 2 - Windham |
| 0359 | Delaware | 1 - Kent |
| 0360 | Florida | 1 - Collier |
| 0361 | Florida | 2 - Glades |
| 0362 | Florida | 3 - Hardee |
| 0363 | Florida | 4 - Citrus |
| 0364 | Florida | 5 - Putnam |
| 0365 | Florida | 6 - Dixie |
| 0366 | Florida | 7 - Hamilton |
| 0367 | Florida | 8 - Jefferson |
| 0368 | Florida | 9 - Calhoun |
| 0369 | Florida | 10 -Walton |

| RSA# | State | Market |
|------|-------|--------|
| 0370 | Florida | 11 - Monroe |
| 0371 | Georgia | 1 - Whitfield |
| 0372 | Georgia | 2 - Dawson |
| 0373 | Georgia | 3 - Chattooga |
| 0374 | Georgia | 4 - Jasper |
| 0375 | Georgia | 5 - Haralson |
| 0376 | Georgia | 6 - Spalding |
| 0377 | Georgia | 7 - Hancock |
| 0378 | Georgia | 8 - Warren |
| 0379 | Georgia | 9 - Marion |
| 0380 | Georgia | 10 - Bleckley |
| 0381 | Georgia | 11 - Toombs |
| 0382 | Georgia | 12 - Liberty |
| 0383 | Georgia | 13 - Early |
| 0384 | Georgia | 14 - Worth |
| 0385 | Hawaii | 1 - Kauai |
| 0386 | Hawaii | 2 - Maui |
| 0387 | Hawaii | 3 - Hawaii |
| 0388 | Idaho | 1 - Boundary |
| 0389 | Idaho | 2 - Idaho |
| 0390 | Idaho | 3 - Lemhi |
| 0391 | Idaho | 4 - Elmore |
| 0392 | Idaho | 5 - Butte |
| 0393 | Idaho | 6 - Clark |
| 0394 | Illinois | 1 - Jo Daviess |
| 0395 | Illinois | 2 - Bureau |
| 0396 | Illinois | 3 - Mercer |
| 0397 | Illinois | 4 - Adams |
| 0398 | Illinois | 5 - Mason |
| 0399 | Illinois | 6 - Montgomery |
| 0400 | Illinois | 7 - Vermilion |
| 0401 | Illinois | 8 - Washington |
| 0402 | Illinois | 9 - Clay |
| 0403 | Indiana | 1 - Newton |
| 0404 | Indiana | 2 - Kosciusko |
| 0405 | Indiana | 3 - Huntington |
| 0406 | Indiana | 4 - Miami |
| 0407 | Indiana | 5 - Warren |
| 0408 | Indiana | 6 - Randolph |
| 0409 | Indiana | 7 - Owen |
| 0410 | Indiana | 8 - Brown |
| 0411 | Indiana | 9 - Decatur |
| 0412 | Iowa | 1 - Mills |
| 0413 | Iowa | 2 - Union |

| RSA# | State | Market |
|------|-------|--------|
| 0414 | Iowa | 3 - Monroe |
| 0415 | Iowa | 4 - Muscatine |
| 0416 | Iowa | 5 - Jackson |
| 0417 | Iowa | 6 - Iowa |
| 0418 | Iowa | 7 - Audubon |
| 0419 | Iowa | 8 - Monona |
| 0420 | Iowa | 9 - Ida |
| 0421 | Iowa | 10 - Humboldt |
| 0422 | Iowa | 11 - Hardin |
| 0423 | Iowa | 12 - Winneshiek |
| 0424 | Iowa | 13 - Mitchell |
| 0425 | Iowa | 14 - Kossuth |
| 0426 | Iowa | 15 - Dickinson |
| 0427 | Iowa | 16 - Lyon |
| 0428 | Kansas | 1 - Cheyenne |
| 0429 | Kansas | 2 - Norton |
| 0430 | Kansas | 3 - Jewell |
| 0431 | Kansas | 4 - Marshall |
| 0432 | Kansas | 5 - Brown |
| 0433 | Kansas | 6 - Wallace |
| 0434 | Kansas | 7 - Trego |
| 0435 | Kansas | 8 - Ellsworth |
| 0436 | Kansas | 9 - Morris |
| 0437 | Kansas | 10 - Franklin |
| 0438 | Kansas | 11 - Hamilton |
| 0439 | Kansas | 12 - Hodgeman |
| 0440 | Kansas | 13 - Edwards |
| 0441 | Kansas | 14 - Reno |
| 0442 | Kansas | 15 - Elk |
| 0443 | Kentucky | 1 - Fulton |
| 0444 | Kentucky | 2 - Union |
| 0445 | Kentucky | 3 - Meade |
| 0446 | Kentucky | 4 - Spencer |
| 0447 | Kentucky | 5 - Barren |
| 0448 | Kentucky | 6 - Madison |
| 0449 | Kentucky | 7 - Trimble |
| 0450 | Kentucky | 8 - Mason |
| 0451 | Kentucky | 9 - Elliott |
| 0452 | Kentucky | 10 - Powell |
| 0453 | Kentucky | 11 - Clay |
| 0454 | Louisiana | 1 - Claiborne |
| 0455 | Louisiana | 2 - Morehouse |
| 0456 | Louisiana | 3 - De Soto |
| 0457 | Louisiana | 4 - Caldwell |

| RSA# | State | Market |
|------|-------|--------|
| 0458 | Louisiana | 5 - Beauregard |
| 0459 | Louisiana | 6 - Iberville |
| 0460 | Louisiana | 7 - West Feliciana |
| 0461 | Louisiana | 8 - St. James |
| 0462 | Louisiana | 9 - Plaquemines |
| 0463 | Maine | 1 - Oxford |
| 0464 | Maine | 2 - Somerset |
| 0465 | Maine | 3 - Kennebec |
| 0466 | Maine | 4 - Washington |
| 0467 | Maryland | 1 - Garrett |
| 0468 | Maryland | 2 - Kent |
| 0469 | Maryland | 3 - Frederick |
| 0470 | Massachusetts | 1 - Franklin |
| 0471 | Massachusetts | 2 - Barnstable |
| 0472 | Michigan | 1 - Gogebic |
| 0473 | Michigan | 2 - Alger |
| 0474 | Michigan | 3 - Emmet |
| 0475 | Michigan | 4 - Cheboygan |
| 0476 | Michigan | 5 - Manistee |
| 0477 | Michigan | 6 - Roscommon |
| 0478 | Michigan | 7 - Newaygo |
| 0479 | Michigan | 8 - Allegan |
| 0480 | Michigan | 9 - Cass |
| 0481 | Michigan | 10 - Tuscola |
| 0482 | Minnesota | 1 - Kittson |
| 0483 | Minnesota | 2 - Lake Of The Woods |
| 0484 | Minnesota | 3 - Koochiching |
| 0485 | Minnesota | 4 - Lake |
| 0486 | Minnesota | 5 - Wilkin |
| 0487 | Minnesota | 6 - Hubbard |
| 0488 | Minnesota | 7 - Chippewa |
| 0489 | Minnesota | 8 - Lac Qui Parle |
| 0490 | Minnesota | 9 - Pipestone |
| 0491 | Minnesota | 10 - Le Sueur |
| 0492 | Minnesota | 11 - Goodhue |
| 0493 | Mississippi | 1 - Tunica |
| 0494 | Mississippi | 2 - Benton |
| 0495 | Mississippi | 3 - Bolivar |
| 0496 | Mississippi | 4 - Yalobusha |
| 0497 | Mississippi | 5 - Washington |
| 0498 | Mississippi | 6 - Montgomery |
| 0499 | Mississippi | 7 - Leake |
| 0500 | Mississippi | 8 - Claiborne |
| 0501 | Mississippi | 9 - Copiah |

| RSA# | State | Market |
|------|-------|--------|
| 0502 | Mississippi | 10 - Smith |
| 0503 | Mississippi | 11 - Lamar |
| 0504 | Missouri | 1 - Atchison |
| 0505 | Missouri | 2 - Harrison |
| 0506 | Missouri | 3 - Schuyler |
| 0507 | Missouri | 4 - De Kalb |
| 0508 | Missouri | 5 - Linn |
| 0509 | Missouri | 6 - Marion |
| 0510 | Missouri | 7 - Saline |
| 0511 | Missouri | 8 - Callaway |
| 0512 | Missouri | 9 - Bates |
| 0513 | Missouri | 10 - Benton |
| 0514 | Missouri | 11 - Moniteau |
| 0515 | Missouri | 12 - Maries |
| 0516 | Missouri | 13 - Washington |
| 0517 | Missouri | 14 - Barton |
| 0518 | Missouri | 15 - Stone |
| 0519 | Missouri | 16 - Laclede |
| 0520 | Missouri | 17 - Shannon |
| 0521 | Missouri | 18 - Perry |
| 0522 | Missouri | 19 - Stoddard |
| 0523 | Montana | 1 - Lincoln |
| 0524 | Montana | 2 - Toole |
| 0525 | Montana | 3 - Phillips |
| 0526 | Montana | 4 - Daniels |
| 0527 | Montana | 5 - Mineral |
| 0528 | Montana | 6 - Deer Lodge |
| 0529 | Montana | 7 - Fergus |
| 0530 | Montana | 8 - Beaverhead |
| 0531 | Montana | 9 - Carbon |
| 0532 | Montana | 10 - Prairie |
| 0533 | Nebraska | 1 - Sioux |
| 0534 | Nebraska | 2 - Cherry |
| 0535 | Nebraska | 3 - Knox |
| 0536 | Nebraska | 4 - Grant |
| 0537 | Nebraska | 5 - Boone |
| 0538 | Nebraska | 6 - Keith |
| 0539 | Nebraska | 7 - Hall |
| 0540 | Nebraska | 8 - Chase |
| 0541 | Nebraska | 9 - Adams |
| 0542 | Nebraska | 10 - Cass |
| 0543 | Nevada | 1 - Humboldt |
| 0544 | Nevada | 2 - Lander |
| 0545 | Nevada | 3 - Storey |

| RSA# | State | Market |
|------|-------|--------|
| 0546 | Nevada | 4 - Mineral |
| 0547 | Nevada | 5 - White Pine |
| 0548 | New Hampshire | 1 - Coos |
| 0549 | New Hampshire | 2 - Carroll |
| 0550 | New Jersey | 1 - Hunterdon |
| 0551 | New Jersey | 2 - Ocean |
| 0552 | New Jersey | 3 - Sussex |
| 0553 | New Mexico | 1 - San Juan |
| 0554 | New Mexico | 2 - Colfax |
| 0555 | New Mexico | 3 - Catron |
| 0556 | New Mexico | 4 - Santa Fe |
| 0557 | New Mexico | 5 - Grant |
| 0558 | New Mexico | 6 - Lincoln |
| 0559 | New York | 1 - Jefferson |
| 0560 | New York | 2 - Franklin |
| 0561 | New York | 3 - Chautauqua |
| 0562 | New York | 4 - Yates |
| 0563 | New York | 5 - Otsego |
| 0564 | New York | 6 - Columbia |
| 0565 | North Carolina | 1 - Cherokee |
| 0566 | North Carolina | 2 - Yancey |
| 0567 | North Carolina | 3 - Ashe |
| 0568 | North Carolina | 4 - Henderson |
| 0569 | North Carolina | 5 - Anson |
| 0570 | North Carolina | 6 - Chatham |
| 0571 | North Carolina | 7 - Rockingham |
| 0572 | North Carolina | 8 - Northampton |
| 0573 | North Carolina | 9 - Camden |
| 0574 | North Carolina | 10 - Harnett |
| 0575 | North Carolina | 11 - Hoke |
| 0576 | North Carolina | 12 - Sampson |
| 0577 | North Carolina | 13 - Greene |
| 0578 | North Carolina | 14 - Pitt |
| 0579 | North Carolina | 15 - Cabarrus |
| 0580 | North Dakota | 1 - Divide |
| 0581 | North Dakota | 2 - Bottineau |
| 0582 | North Dakota | 3 - Barnes |
| 0583 | North Dakota | 4 - Mckenzie |
| 0584 | North Dakota | 5 - Kidder |
| 0585 | Ohio | 1 - Williams |
| 0586 | Ohio | 2 - Sandusky |
| 0587 | Ohio | 3 - Ashtabula |
| 0588 | Ohio | 4 - Mercer |
| 0589 | Ohio | 5 - Hancock |

| RSA# | State | Market |
|------|-------|--------|
| 0590 | Ohio | 6 - Morrow |
| 0591 | Ohio | 7 - Tuscarawas |
| 0592 | Ohio | 8 - Clinton |
| 0593 | Ohio | 9 - Ross |
| 0594 | Ohio | 10 - Perry |
| 0595 | Ohio | 11 - Columbiana |
| 0596 | Oklahoma | 1 - Cimarron |
| 0597 | Oklahoma | 2 - Harper |
| 0598 | Oklahoma | 3 - Grant |
| 0599 | Oklahoma | 4 - Nowata |
| 0600 | Oklahoma | 5 - Roger Mills |
| 0601 | Oklahoma | 6 - Seminole |
| 0602 | Oklahoma | 7 - Beckham |
| 0603 | Oklahoma | 8 - Jackson |
| 0604 | Oklahoma | 9 - Garvin |
| 0605 | Oklahoma | 10 - Haskell |
| 0606 | Oregon | 1 - Clatsop |
| 0607 | Oregon | 2 - Hood River |
| 0608 | Oregon | 3 - Umatilla |
| 0609 | Oregon | 4 - Lincoln |
| 0610 | Oregon | 5 - Coos |
| 0611 | Oregon | 6 - Crook |
| 0612 | Pennsylvania | 1 - Crawford |
| 0613 | Pennsylvania | 2 - McKean |
| 0614 | Pennsylvania | 3 - Potter |
| 0615 | Pennsylvania | 4 - Bradford |
| 0616 | Pennsylvania | 5 - Wayne |
| 0617 | Pennsylvania | 6 - Lawrence |
| 0618 | Pennsylvania | 7 - Jefferson |
| 0619 | Pennsylvania | 8 - Union |
| 0620 | Pennsylvania | 9 - Greene |
| 0621 | Pennsylvania | 10 - Bedford |
| 0622 | Pennsylvania | 11 - Huntingdon |
| 0623 | Pennsylvania | 12 - Lebanon |
| 0624 | Rhode Island | 1 - Newport |
| 0625 | South Carolina | 1 - Oconee |
| 0626 | South Carolina | 2 - Laurens |
| 0627 | South Carolina | 3 - Cherokee |
| 0628 | South Carolina | 4 - Chesterfield |
| 0629 | South Carolina | 5 - Georgetown |
| 0630 | South Carolina | 6 - Clarendon |
| 0631 | South Carolina | 7 - Calhoun |
| 0632 | South Carolina | 8 - Hampton |
| 0633 | South Carolina | 9 - Lancaster |

| RSA# | State | Market |
|------|-------|--------|
| 0634 | South Dakota | 1 - Harding |
| 0635 | South Dakota | 2 - Corson |
| 0636 | South Dakota | 3 - Mcpherson |
| 0637 | South Dakota | 4 - Marshall |
| 0638 | South Dakota | 5 - Custer |
| 0639 | South Dakota | 6 - Haakon |
| 0640 | South Dakota | 7 - Sully |
| 0641 | South Dakota | 8 - Kingsbury |
| 0642 | South Dakota | 9 - Hanson |
| 0643 | Tennessee | 1 - Lake |
| 0644 | Tennessee | 2 - Cannon |
| 0645 | Tennessee | 3 - Macon |
| 0646 | Tennessee | 4 - Hamblen |
| 0647 | Tennessee | 5 - Fayette |
| 0648 | Tennessee | 6 - Giles |
| 0649 | Tennessee | 7 - Bledsoe |
| 0650 | Tennessee | 8 - Johnson |
| 0651 | Tennessee | 9 - Maury |
| 0652 | Texas | 1 - Dallam |
| 0653 | Texas | 2 - Hansford |
| 0654 | Texas | 3 - Parmer |
| 0655 | Texas | 4 - Briscoe |
| 0656 | Texas | 5 - Hardeman |
| 0657 | Texas | 6 - Jack |
| 0658 | Texas | 7 - Fannin |
| 0659 | Texas | 8 - Gaines |
| 0660 | Texas | 9 - Runnels |
| 0661 | Texas | 10 - Navarro |
| 0662 | Texas | 11 - Cherokee |
| 0663 | Texas | 12 - Hudspeth |
| 0664 | Texas | 13 - Reeves |
| 0665 | Texas | 14 - Loving |
| 0666 | Texas | 15 - Concho |
| 0667 | Texas | 16 - Burleson |
| 0668 | Texas | 17 - Newton |
| 0669 | Texas | 18 - Edwards |
| 0670 | Texas | 19 - Atascosa |
| 0671 | Texas | 20 - Wilson |
| 0672 | Texas | 21 - Chambers |
| 0673 | Utah | 1 - Box Elder |
| 0674 | Utah | 2 - Morgan |
| 0675 | Utah | 3 - Juab |
| 0676 | Utah | 4 - Beaver |
| 0677 | Utah | 5 - Carbon |

| RSA# | State | Market |
|------|-------|--------|
| 0678 | Utah | 6 - Piute |
| 0679 | Vermont | 1 - Franklin |
| 0680 | Vermont | 2 - Addison |
| 0681 | Virginia | 1 - Lee |
| 0682 | Virginia | 2 - Tazewell |
| 0683 | Virginia | 3 - Giles |
| 0684 | Virginia | 4 - Bedford |
| 0685 | Virginia | 5 - Bath |
| 0686 | Virginia | 6 - Highland |
| 0687 | Virginia | 7 - Buckingham |
| 0688 | Virginia | 8 - Amelia |
| 0689 | Virginia | 9 - Greensville |
| 0690 | Virginia | 10 - Frederick |
| 0691 | Virginia | 11 - Madison |
| 0692 | Virginia | 12 - Caroline |
| 0693 | Washington | 1 - Clallam |
| 0694 | Washington | 2 - Okanogan |
| 0695 | Washington | 3 - Ferry |
| 0696 | Washington | 4 - Grays Harbor |
| 0697 | Washington | 5 - Kittitas |
| 0698 | Washington | 6 - Pacific |
| 0699 | Washington | 7 - Skamania |
| 0700 | Washington | 8 - Whitman |
| 0701 | West Virginia | 1 - Mason |
| 0702 | West Virginia | 2 - Wetzel |
| 0703 | West Virginia | 3 - Monongalia |
| 0704 | West Virginia | 4 - Grant |
| 0705 | West Virginia | 5 - Tucker |
| 0706 | West Virginia | 6 - Lincoln |
| 0707 | West Virginia | 7 - Raleigh |
| 0708 | Wisconsin | 1 - Burnett |
| 0709 | Wisconsin | 2 - Bayfield |
| 0710 | Wisconsin | 3 - Vilas |
| 0711 | Wisconsin | 4 - Marinette |
| 0712 | Wisconsin | 5 - Pierce |
| 0713 | Wisconsin | 6 - Trempealeau |
| 0714 | Wisconsin | 7 - Wood |
| 0715 | Wisconsin | 8 - Vernon |
| 0716 | Wisconsin | 9 - Columbia |
| 0717 | Wisconsin | 10 - Door |
| 0718 | Wyoming | 1 - Park |
| 0719 | Wyoming | 2 - Sheridan |
| 0720 | Wyoming | 3 - Lincoln |
| 0721 | Wyoming | 4 - Niobrara |

| RSA# | State | Market |
|------|-------|--------|
| 0722 | Wyoming | 5 - Converse |
| 0723 | Puerto Rico | 1 - Rincon |
| 0724 | Puerto Rico | 2 - Adjuntas |
| 0725 | Puerto Rico | 3 - Ciales |
| 0726 | Puerto Rico | 4 - Aibonito |
| 0727 | Puerto Rico | 5 - Ceiba |
| 0728 | Puerto Rico | 6 - Vieques |
| 0729 | Puerto Rico | 7 - Culebra |
| 0730 | Virgin Islands | 1 - St. Thomas Island |
| 0731 | Virgin Islands | 2 - St. Croix Island |
| 0732 | Guam | |
| 0733 | American Samoa | |
| 0734 | Northern Mariana Islands | |

# PCS Market Areas

## Major Trading Areas Numerical Market Listing

This list of the 51 Major Trading Areas (MTAs) is used to identify the geographic boundaries assigned to the 1900 MHz PCS carriers operating channel blocks A and B. Cross-reference the MTA map for locations.

| Mkt # | Market Name |
|---|---|
| M1 | New York |
| M2 | Los Angeles-San Diego |
| M3 | Chicago |
| M4 | San Francisco-Oakland-San Jose |
| M5 | Detroit |
| M6 | Charlotte-Greensboro-Greenville-Raleigh, NC |
| M7 | Dallas-Fort Worth |
| M8 | Boston, MA-Providence, RI |
| M9 | Philadelphia |
| M10 | Washington, DC-Baltimore, MD |
| M11 | Atlanta |
| M12 | Minneapolis-St. Paul |
| M13 | Tampa-St. Petersburg-Orlando, FL |
| M14 | Houston |
| M15 | Miami-Fort Lauderdale |
| M16 | Cleveland |
| M17 | New Orleans-Baton Rouge |
| M18 | Cincinnati-Dayton |
| M19 | St. Louis |
| M20 | Milwaukee |
| M21 | Pittsburgh |
| M22 | Denver |

*continued on page 210*

A resizable, interactive portable document file (.pdf) version of this map is available at the FCC Web site (*www.fcc.gov/wtb/auctions/maps/mtamap.pdf*).

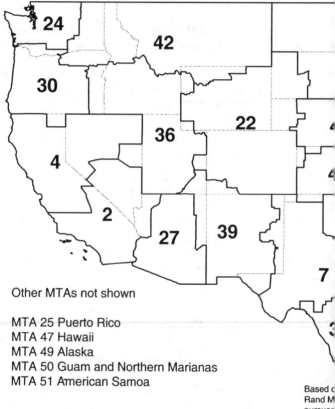

# Broadband Personal
# FCC Licenses b

Other MTAs not shown

MTA 25 Puerto Rico
MTA 47 Hawaii
MTA 49 Alaska
MTA 50 Guam and Northern Marianas
MTA 51 American Samoa

Based ⊙
Rand M
pursuar
Compan
the Pers
Associa

# munications Services
# or Trading Areas

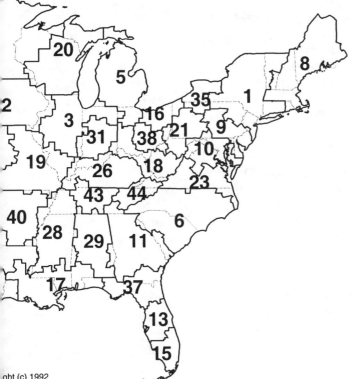

*continued from page 207*

| Mkt # | Market Name |
|-------|-------------|
| M23 | Richmond-Norfolk, VA |
| M24 | Seattle |
| M25 | Puerto Rico & U.S. Virgin Islands |
| M26 | Louisville-Lexington-Evansville, KY |
| M27 | Phoenix |
| M28 | Memphis-Jackson, TN |
| M29 | Birmingham, AL |
| M30 | Portland, OR |
| M31 | Indianapolis |
| M32 | Des Moines, IA-Quad Cities |
| M33 | San Antonio |
| M34 | Kansas City |
| M35 | Buffalo-Rochester, NY |
| M36 | Salt Lake City |
| M37 | Jacksonville, FL |
| M38 | Columbus, OH |
| M39 | El Paso-Albuquerque, NM |
| M40 | Little Rock, AR |
| M41 | Oklahoma City |
| M42 | Spokane, WA-Billings, MT |
| M43 | Nashville, TN |
| M44 | Knoxville, TN |
| M45 | Omaha, NE |
| M46 | Wichita, KS |
| M47 | Honolulu |
| M48 | Tulsa, OK |
| M49 | Alaska |
| M50 | Guam & Northern Mariana Islands |
| M51 | American Samoa |

# Basic Trading Areas
## Numerical Market Listing

This list of 493 Basic Trading Areas (BTAs) is used to define the geographic boundaries assigned to the 1900 MHz PCS carriers operating blocks C, D, E, and F. Check the BTA map for locations. (This list is cross-referenced with the Major Trading Areas.)

| Mkt # | Market Name | State | MTA |
|---|---|---|---|
| B1 | Aberdeen | SD | M12 |
| B2 | Aberdeen | WA | M24 |
| B3 | Abilene | TX | M7 |
| B4 | Ada | OK | M41 |
| B5 | Adrian | MI | M5 |
| B6 | Albany-Tifton | GA | M11 |
| B7 | Albany-Schenectady | NY | M1 |
| B8 | Albuquerque | NM | M39 |
| B9 | Alexandria | LA | M17 |
| B10 | Allentown-Bethlehem-Easton | PA | M1 |
| B11 | Alpena | MI | M5 |
| B12 | Altoona | PA | M21 |
| B13 | Amarillo | TX | M7 |
| B14 | Anchorage | AK | M49 |
| B15 | Anderson | IN | M31 |
| B16 | Anderson | SC | M6 |
| B17 | Anniston | AL | M29 |
| B18 | Appleton-Oshkosh | WI | M20 |
| B19 | Ardmore | OK | M41 |
| B20 | Asheville-Hendersonville | NC | M6 |
| B21 | Ashtabula | OH | M16 |
| B22 | Athens | GA | M11 |
| B23 | Athens | OH | M38 |
| B24 | Atlanta | GA | M11 |
| B25 | Atlantic City | NJ | M9 |
| B26 | Augusta | GA | M11 |
| B27 | Austin | TX | M7 |
| B28 | Bakersfield | CA | M2 |
| B29 | Baltimore | MD | M10 |
| B30 | Bangor | ME | M8 |
| B31 | Bartlesville | OK | M48 |
| B32 | Baton Rouge | LA | M17 |

*continued on page 214*

A resizable, interactive portable document file (.pdf) version of this map is available at the FCC Web site (*www.fcc.gov/wtb/auctions/maps/btamap.pdf*).

Basic Tr

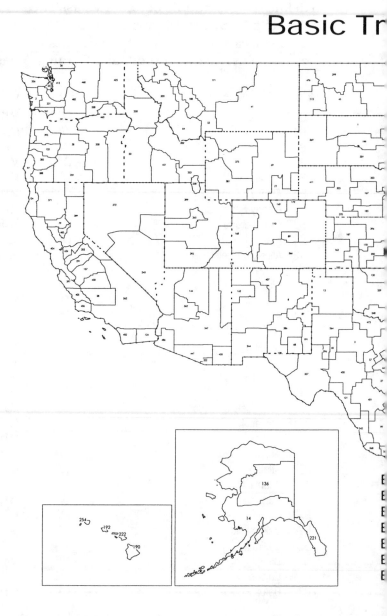

g Areas

reas not shown:
Juan, PR
guez, PR
n
irgin Islands
rican Samoa
ern Mariana Islands

Based on Material Copyright (c) 1992
Rand McNally & Company.  Rights granted
pursuant to a license from Rand McNally &
Company through an arrangement with
the Personal Communications Industry
Association.

*continued from page 211*

| Mkt # | Market Name | State | MTA |
|-------|-------------|-------|-----|
| B33 | Battle Creek | MI | M5 |
| B34 | Beaumont-Port Arthur | TX | M14 |
| B35 | Beckley | WV | M18 |
| B36 | Bellingham | WA | M24 |
| B37 | Bemidji | MN | M12 |
| B38 | Bend | OR | M30 |
| B39 | Benton Harbor | MI | M3 |
| B40 | Big Spring | TX | M7 |
| B41 | Billings | MT | M42 |
| B42 | Biloxi-Gulfport-Pascagoula | MS | M17 |
| B43 | Binghamton | NY | M1 |
| B44 | Birmingham | AL | M29 |
| B45 | Bismarck | ND | M12 |
| B46 | Bloomington | IL | M3 |
| B47 | Bloomington-Bedford | IN | M31 |
| B48 | Bluefield | WV | M18 |
| B49 | Blytheville | AR | M28 |
| B50 | Boise-Nampa | ID | M36 |
| B51 | Boston | MA | M8 |
| B52 | Bowling Green-Glasgow | KY | M26 |
| B53 | Bozeman | MT | M42 |
| B54 | Brainerd | MN | M12 |
| B55 | Bremerton | WA | M24 |
| B56 | Brownsville-Harlingen | TX | M33 |
| B57 | Brownwood | TX | M7 |
| B58 | Brunswick | GA | M37 |
| B59 | Bryan-College Station | TX | M14 |
| B60 | Buffalo-Niagara Falls | NY | M35 |
| B61 | Burlington | IA | M32 |
| B62 | Burlington | NC | M6 |
| B63 | Burlington | VT | M1 |
| B64 | Butte | MT | M42 |
| B65 | Canton-New Philadelphia | OH | M16 |
| B66 | Cape Girardeau-Sikeston | MO | M19 |
| B67 | Carbondale-Marion | IL | M19 |
| B68 | Carlsbad | NM | M39 |
| B69 | Casper-Gillette | WY | M22 |
| B70 | Cedar Rapids | IA | M32 |
| B71 | Champaign-Urbana | IL | M3 |
| B72 | Charleston | SC | M6 |
| B73 | Charleston | WV | M18 |
| B74 | Charlotte-Gastonia | NC | M6 |

| Mkt # | Market Name | State | MTA |
|-------|-------------|-------|-----|
| B75 | Charlottesville | VA | M10 |
| B76 | Chattanooga | TN | M11 |
| B77 | Cheyenne | WY | M22 |
| B78 | Chicago | IL | M3 |
| B79 | Chico-Oroville | CA | M4 |
| B80 | Chillicothe | OH | M38 |
| B81 | Cincinnati | OH | M18 |
| B82 | Clarksburg-Elkins | WV | M21 |
| B83 | Clarksville, TN-Hopkinsville, KY | TN | M43 |
| B84 | Cleveland-Akron | OH | M16 |
| B85 | Cleveland | TN | M11 |
| B86 | Clinton, IA-Sterling, IL | IA | M32 |
| B87 | Clovis | NM | M7 |
| B88 | Coffeyville | KS | M48 |
| B89 | Colorado Springs | CO | M22 |
| B90 | Columbia | MO | M19 |
| B91 | Columbia | SC | M6 |
| B92 | Columbus | GA | M11 |
| B93 | Columbus | IN | M31 |
| B94 | Columbus -Starkville | MS | M28 |
| B95 | Columbus | OH | M38 |
| B96 | Cookeville | TN | M43 |
| B97 | Coos Bay-North Bend | OR | M30 |
| B98 | Corbin | KY | M26 |
| B99 | Corpus Christi | TX | M33 |
| B100 | Cumberland | MD | M10 |
| B101 | Dallas-Fort Worth | TX | M7 |
| B102 | Dalton | GA | M11 |
| B103 | Danville | IL | M3 |
| B104 | Danville | VA | M23 |
| B105 | Davenport, IA-Moline, IL | IA | M32 |
| B106 | Dayton-Springfield | OH | M18 |
| B107 | Daytona Beach | FL | M13 |
| B108 | Decatur | AL | M29 |
| B109 | Decatur-Effingham | IL | M3 |
| B110 | Denver | CO | M22 |
| B111 | Des Moines | IA | M32 |
| B112 | Detroit | MI | M5 |
| B113 | Dickinson | ND | M12 |
| B114 | Dodge City | KS | M46 |
| B115 | Dothan-Enterprise | AL | M29 |
| B116 | Dover | DE | M9 |
| B117 | Du Bois-Clearfield | PA | M21 |

| Mkt # | Market Name | State | MTA |
|-------|-------------|-------|-----|
| B118 | Dubuque | IA | M32 |
| B119 | Duluth | MN | M12 |
| B120 | Dyersburg-Union City | TN | M28 |
| B121 | Eagle Pass-Del Rio | TX | M33 |
| B122 | East Liverpool-Salem | OH | M16 |
| B123 | Eau Claire | WI | M12 |
| B124 | El Centro-Calexico | CA | M2 |
| B125 | El Dorado-Magnolia-Camden | AR | M40 |
| B126 | Elkhart | IN | M3 |
| B127 | Elmira-Corning-Hornell | NY | M1 |
| B128 | El Paso | TX | M39 |
| B129 | Emporia | KS | M34 |
| B130 | Enid | OK | M41 |
| B131 | Erie | PA | M16 |
| B132 | Escanaba | MI | M20 |
| B133 | Eugene-Springfield | OR | M30 |
| B134 | Eureka | CA | M4 |
| B135 | Evansville | IN | M26 |
| B136 | Fairbanks | AK | M49 |
| B137 | Fairmont | WV | M21 |
| B138 | Fargo | ND | M12 |
| B139 | Durango | CO | M39 |
| B139 | Farmington | NM | M39 |
| B140 | Fayetteville-Springdale-Rogers | AR | M40 |
| B141 | Fayetteville-Lumberton | NC | M6 |
| B142 | Fergus Falls | MN | M12 |
| B143 | Findlay-Tiffin | OH | M5 |
| B144 | Flagstaff | AZ | M27 |
| B145 | Flint | MI | M5 |
| B146 | Florence | AL | M29 |
| B147 | Florence | SC | M6 |
| B148 | Fond du Lac | WI | M20 |
| B149 | Fort Collins-Loveland | CO | M22 |
| B150 | Fort Dodge | IA | M32 |
| B151 | Fort Myers | FL | M15 |
| B152 | Fort Pierce, Vero Beach, Stuart | FL | M15 |
| B153 | Fort Smith | AR | M40 |
| B154 | Fort Walton Beach | FL | M17 |
| B155 | Fort Wayne | IN | M3 |
| B156 | Fredericksburg | VA | M10 |
| B157 | Fresno | CA | M4 |
| B158 | Gadsden | AL | M29 |
| B159 | Gainesville | FL | M37 |

| Mkt # | Market Name | State | MTA |
|-------|-------------|-------|-----|
| B160 | Gainesville | GA | M11 |
| B161 | Galesburg | IL | M3 |
| B162 | Gallup | NM | M39 |
| B163 | Garden City | KS | M46 |
| B164 | Glens Falls | NY | M1 |
| B165 | Goldsboro-Kinston | NC | M6 |
| B166 | Grand Forks | ND | M12 |
| B167 | Grand Island-Kearney | NE | M45 |
| B168 | Grand Junction | CO | M22 |
| B169 | Grand Rapids | MI | M5 |
| B170 | Great Bend | KS | M46 |
| B171 | Great Falls | MT | M42 |
| B172 | Greeley | CO | M22 |
| B173 | Green Bay | WI | M20 |
| B174 | Greensboro-Winston Salem-High Point | NC | M6 |
| B175 | Greenville-Greenwood | MS | M28 |
| B176 | Greenville-Washington | NC | M6 |
| B177 | Greenville-Spartanburg | SC | M6 |
| B178 | Greenwood | SC | M6 |
| B179 | Hagerstown, MD-Chambersburg, PA | MD | M10 |
| B180 | Hammond | LA | M17 |
| B181 | Harrisburg | PA | M9 |
| B182 | Harrison | AR | M40 |
| B183 | Harrisonburg | VA | M10 |
| B184 | Hartford | CT | M1 |
| B185 | Hastings | NE | M45 |
| B186 | Hattiesburg | MS | M17 |
| B187 | Hays | KS | M46 |
| B188 | Helena | MT | M42 |
| B189 | Hickory-Lenoir-Morganton | NC | M6 |
| B190 | Hilo | HI | M47 |
| B191 | Hobbs | NM | M7 |
| B192 | Honolulu | HI | M47 |
| B193 | Hot Springs | AR | M40 |
| B194 | Houghton | MI | M20 |
| B195 | Houma-Thibodaux | LA | M17 |
| B196 | Houston | TX | M14 |
| B197 | Huntington, WV-Ashland, KY | WV | M18 |
| B198 | Huntsville | AL | M29 |
| B199 | Huron | SD | M12 |
| B200 | Hutchinson | KS | M46 |
| B201 | Hyannis | MA | M8 |
| B202 | Idaho Falls | ID | M36 |

| Mkt # | Market Name | State | MTA |
|-------|-------------|-------|-----|
| B203 | Indiana | PA | M21 |
| B204 | Indianapolis | IN | M31 |
| B205 | Iowa City | IA | M32 |
| B206 | Iron Mountain | MI | M20 |
| B207 | Ironwood | MI | M12 |
| B208 | Ithaca | NY | M1 |
| B209 | Jackson | MI | M5 |
| B210 | Jackson | MS | M28 |
| B211 | Jackson | TN | M28 |
| B212 | Jacksonville | FL | M37 |
| B213 | Jacksonville | IL | M3 |
| B214 | Jacksonville | NC | M6 |
| B215 | Jamestown-Dunkirk, NY-Warren, PA | NY | M35 |
| B216 | Janesville-Beloit | WI | M20 |
| B217 | Jefferson City | MO | M19 |
| B218 | Johnstown | PA | M21 |
| B219 | Jonesboro-Paragould | AR | M40 |
| B220 | Joplin | MO | M19 |
| B220 | Miami | OK | M34 |
| B221 | Juneau-Ketchikan | AK | M49 |
| B222 | Kahului-Wailuku-Lahaina | HI | M47 |
| B223 | Kalamazoo | MI | M5 |
| B224 | Kalispell | MT | M42 |
| B225 | Kankakee | IL | M3 |
| B226 | Kansas City | MO | M34 |
| B227 | Keene | NH | M8 |
| B228 | Kennewick-Pasco-Richland | WA | M42 |
| B229 | Kingsport-Johnson City | TN | M44 |
| B230 | Kirksville | MO | M19 |
| B231 | Klamath Falls | OR | M30 |
| B232 | Knoxville | TN | M44 |
| B233 | Kokomo-Logansport | IN | M31 |
| B234 | La Crosse, WI-Winona, MN | WI | M20 |
| B235 | Lafayette | IN | M31 |
| B236 | Lafayette-New Iberia | LA | M17 |
| B237 | La Grange | GA | M11 |
| B238 | Lake Charles | LA | M14 |
| B239 | Lakeland-Winter Haven | FL | M13 |
| B240 | Lancaster | PA | M9 |
| B241 | Lansing | MI | M5 |
| B242 | Laredo | TX | M33 |
| B243 | LaSalle-Peru-Ottawa-Streator | IL | M3 |
| B244 | Las Cruces | NM | M39 |

| Mkt # | Market Name | State | MTA |
|-------|-------------|-------|-----|
| B245 | Las Vegas | NV | M2 |
| B246 | Laurel | MS | M17 |
| B247 | Lawrence | KS | M34 |
| B248 | Lawton-Duncan | OK | M41 |
| B249 | Lebanon-Claremont | NH | M8 |
| B250 | Lewiston-Moscow | ID | M42 |
| B251 | Lewiston-Auburn | ME | M8 |
| B252 | Lexington | KY | M26 |
| B253 | Liberal | KS | M46 |
| B254 | Lihue | HI | M47 |
| B255 | Lima | OH | M5 |
| B256 | Lincoln | NE | M45 |
| B257 | Little Rock | AR | M40 |
| B258 | Logan | UT | M36 |
| B259 | Logan | WV | M18 |
| B260 | Longview-Marshall | TX | M7 |
| B261 | Longview | WA | M30 |
| B262 | Los Angeles | CA | M2 |
| B263 | Louisville | KY | M26 |
| B264 | Lubbock | TX | M7 |
| B265 | Lufkin-Nacogdoches | TX | M14 |
| B266 | Lynchburg | VA | M23 |
| B267 | McAlester | OK | M41 |
| B268 | McAllen | TX | M33 |
| B269 | McComb-Brookhaven | MS | M17 |
| B270 | McCook | NE | M45 |
| B271 | Macon-Warner Robins | GA | M11 |
| B272 | Madison | WI | M20 |
| B273 | Madisonville | KY | M26 |
| B274 | Manchester-Nashua-Concord | NH | M8 |
| B275 | Manhattan-Junction City | KS | M34 |
| B276 | Manitowoc | WI | M20 |
| B277 | Mankato-Fairmont | MN | M12 |
| B278 | Mansfield | OH | M16 |
| B279 | Menominee | MI | M20 |
| B279 | Marinette | WI | M20 |
| B280 | Marion | IN | M31 |
| B281 | Marion | OH | M38 |
| B282 | Marquette | MI | M20 |
| B283 | Marshalltown | IA | M32 |
| B284 | Martinsville | VA | M23 |
| B285 | Mason City | IA | M32 |
| B286 | Mattoon | IL | M3 |

| Mkt # | Market Name | State | MTA |
|-------|-------------|-------|-----|
| B287 | Meadville | PA | M16 |
| B288 | Medford-Grants Pass | OR | M30 |
| B289 | Melbourne-Titusville | FL | M13 |
| B290 | Memphis | TN | M28 |
| B291 | Merced | CA | M4 |
| B292 | Meridian | MS | M28 |
| B293 | Miami-Fort Lauderdale | FL | M15 |
| B294 | Michigan City-LaPorte | IN | M3 |
| B295 | Middlesboro-Harlan | KY | M44 |
| B296 | Midland | TX | M7 |
| B297 | Milwaukee | WI | M20 |
| B298 | Minneapolis-St. Paul | MN | M12 |
| B299 | Minot | ND | M12 |
| B300 | Missoula | MT | M42 |
| B301 | Mitchell | SD | M12 |
| B302 | Mobile | AL | M17 |
| B303 | Modesto | CA | M4 |
| B304 | Monroe | LA | M7 |
| B305 | Montgomery | AL | M29 |
| B306 | Morgantown | WV | M21 |
| B307 | Mount Pleasant | MI | M5 |
| B308 | Mount Vernon-Centralia | IL | M19 |
| B309 | Muncie | IN | M31 |
| B310 | Muskegon | MI | M5 |
| B311 | Muskogee | OK | M48 |
| B312 | Myrtle Beach | SC | M6 |
| B313 | Naples | FL | M15 |
| B314 | Nashville | TN | M43 |
| B315 | Natchez | MS | M28 |
| B316 | New Bern | NC | M6 |
| B317 | New Castle | PA | M21 |
| B318 | New Haven-Waterbury-Meriden | CT | M1 |
| B319 | New London-Norwich | CT | M1 |
| B320 | New Orleans | LA | M17 |
| B321 | New York | NY | M1 |
| B322 | Nogales | AZ | M27 |
| B323 | Norfolk | NE | M45 |
| B324 | Norfolk-Va Beach-Newport News | VA | M23 |
| B325 | North Platte | NE | M45 |
| B326 | Ocala | FL | M13 |
| B327 | Odessa | TX | M7 |
| B328 | Oil City-Franklin | PA | M21 |
| B329 | Oklahoma City | OK | M41 |

| Mkt # | Market Name | State | MTA |
|---|---|---|---|
| B330 | Olean, NY-Bradford, PA | NY | M35 |
| B331 | Olympia-Centralia | WA | M24 |
| B332 | Omaha | NE | M45 |
| B333 | Oneonta | NY | M1 |
| B334 | Opelika-Auburn | AL | M11 |
| B335 | Orangeburg | SC | M6 |
| B336 | Orlando | FL | M13 |
| B337 | Ottumwa | IA | M32 |
| B338 | Owensboro | KY | M26 |
| B339 | Paducah-Murray-Mayfield | KY | M26 |
| B340 | Panama City | FL | M37 |
| B341 | Paris | TX | M7 |
| B342 | Parkersburg, WV-Marietta, OH | wv | M38 |
| B342 | Parkersburg | WV | M38 |
| B343 | Pensacola | FL | M17 |
| B344 | Peoria | IL | M3 |
| B345 | Petoskey | MI | M5 |
| B346 | Philadelphia-Wilmington, DE-Trenton, NJ | PA | M9 |
| B347 | Phoenix | AZ | M27 |
| B348 | Pine Bluff | AR | M40 |
| B349 | Pittsburg-Parsons | KS | M34 |
| B350 | Pittsburgh | PA | M21 |
| B351 | Pittsfield | MA | M8 |
| B352 | Plattsburgh | NY | M1 |
| B353 | Pocatello | ID | M36 |
| B354 | Ponca City | OK | M41 |
| B355 | Poplar Bluff | MO | M19 |
| B356 | Port Angeles | WA | M24 |
| B357 | Portland-Brunswick | ME | M8 |
| B358 | Portland | OR | M30 |
| B359 | Portsmouth | OH | M18 |
| B360 | Pottsville | PA | M9 |
| B361 | Poughkeepsie-Kingston | NY | M1 |
| B362 | Prescott | AZ | M27 |
| B363 | Presque Isle | ME | M8 |
| B364 | Providence, RI-New Bedford, MA | RI | M8 |
| B365 | Provo-Orem | UT | M36 |
| B366 | Pueblo | CO | M22 |
| B367 | Quincy, IL-Hannibal, MO | IL | M19 |
| B368 | Raleigh-Durham | NC | M6 |
| B369 | Rapid City | SD | M22 |
| B370 | Reading | PA | M9 |
| B371 | Redding | CA | M4 |

| Mkt # | Market Name | State | MTA |
|-------|-------------|-------|-----|
| B372 | Reno | NV | M4 |
| B373 | Richmond | IN | M31 |
| B374 | Richmond-Petersburg | VA | M23 |
| B375 | Riverton | WY | M22 |
| B376 | Roanoke | VA | M23 |
| B377 | Roanoke Rapids | NC | M6 |
| B378 | Rochester-Austin-Albert Lea | MN | M12 |
| B379 | Rochester | NY | M35 |
| B380 | Rockford | IL | M3 |
| B381 | Rock Springs | WY | M22 |
| B382 | Rocky Mount-Wilson | NC | M6 |
| B383 | Rolla | MO | M19 |
| B384 | Rome | GA | M11 |
| B385 | Roseburg | OR | M30 |
| B386 | Roswell | NM | M39 |
| B387 | Russellville | AR | M40 |
| B388 | Rutland-Bennington | VT | M1 |
| B389 | Sacramento | CA | M4 |
| B390 | Saginaw-Bay City | MI | M5 |
| B391 | St. Cloud | MN | M12 |
| B392 | St. George | UT | M36 |
| B393 | St. Joseph | MO | M34 |
| B394 | St. Louis | MO | M19 |
| B395 | Salem-Albany-Corvallis | OR | M30 |
| B396 | Salina | KS | M46 |
| B397 | Salinas-Monterey | CA | M4 |
| B398 | Salisbury | MD | M10 |
| B399 | Salt Lake City-Ogden | UT | M36 |
| B400 | San Angelo | TX | M7 |
| B401 | San Antonio | TX | M33 |
| B402 | San Diego | CA | M2 |
| B403 | Sandusky | OH | M16 |
| B404 | San Francisco-Oakland-San Jose | CA | M4 |
| B405 | San Luis Obispo | CA | M2 |
| B406 | Santa Barbara-Santa Maria | CA | M2 |
| B407 | Santa Fe | NM | M39 |
| B408 | Sarasota-Bradenton | FL | M13 |
| B409 | Sault Ste. Marie | MI | M5 |
| B410 | Savannah | GA | M11 |
| B411 | Scottsbluff | NE | M22 |
| B412 | Scranton-Wilkes-Barre-Hazelton | PA | M1 |
| B413 | Seattle-Tacoma | WA | M24 |
| B414 | Sedalia | MO | M34 |

| Mkt # | Market Name | State | MTA |
|-------|-------------|-------|-----|
| B415 | Selma | AL | M29 |
| B416 | Sharon | PA | M16 |
| B417 | Sheboygan | WI | M20 |
| B418 | Sherman-Denison | TX | M7 |
| B419 | Shreveport | LA | M7 |
| B420 | Sierra Vista-Douglas | AZ | M27 |
| B421 | Sioux City | IA | M32 |
| B422 | Sioux Falls | SD | M12 |
| B423 | Somerset | KY | M26 |
| B424 | South Bend-Mishawaka | IN | M3 |
| B425 | Spokane | WA | M42 |
| B426 | Springfield | IL | M3 |
| B427 | Springfield-Holyoke | MA | M8 |
| B428 | Springfield | MO | M19 |
| B429 | State College | PA | M9 |
| B430 | Staunton-Waynesboro | VA | M23 |
| B431 | Steubenville | OH | M21 |
| B431 | Weirton | WV | M21 |
| B432 | Stevens Point-Marshfield | WI | M20 |
| B433 | Stillwater | OK | M41 |
| B434 | Stockton | CA | M4 |
| B435 | Stroudsburg | PA | M1 |
| B436 | Sumter | SC | M6 |
| B437 | Sunbury-Shamokin | PA | M9 |
| B438 | Syracuse | NY | M1 |
| B439 | Tallahassee | FL | M37 |
| B440 | Tampa-St. Petersburg-Clearwater | FL | M13 |
| B441 | Temple-Killeen | TX | M7 |
| B442 | Terre Haute | IN | M31 |
| B443 | Texarkana | AR | M7 |
| B443 | Texarkana | TX | M7 |
| B444 | Toledo | OH | M5 |
| B445 | Topeka | KS | M34 |
| B446 | Traverse City | MI | M5 |
| B447 | Tucson | AZ | M27 |
| B448 | Tulsa | OK | M48 |
| B449 | Tupelo-Corinth | MS | M28 |
| B450 | Tuscaloosa | AL | M29 |
| B451 | Twin Falls | ID | M36 |
| B452 | Tyler | TX | M7 |
| B453 | Utica-Rome | NY | M1 |
| B454 | Valdosta | GA | M37 |
| B455 | Vicksburg | MS | M28 |

| Mkt # | Market Name | State | MTA |
|-------|-------------|-------|-----|
| B456 | Victoria | TX | M14 |
| B457 | Vincennes-Washington | IN | M31 |
| B458 | Visalia-Porterville-Hanford | CA | M4 |
| B459 | Waco | TX | M7 |
| B460 | Walla Walla, WA-Pendleton, OR | WA | M42 |
| B461 | Washington, DC | DC | M10 |
| B462 | Waterloo-Cedar Falls | IA | M32 |
| B463 | Watertown | NY | M1 |
| B464 | Watertown | SD | M12 |
| B465 | Waterville-Augusta | ME | M8 |
| B466 | Wausau-Rhinelander | WI | M20 |
| B467 | Waycross | GA | M37 |
| B468 | Wenatchee | WA | M24 |
| B469 | West Palm Beach-Boca Raton | FL | M15 |
| B470 | West Plains | MO | M19 |
| B471 | Wheeling | WV | M21 |
| B472 | Wichita | KS | M46 |
| B473 | Wichita Falls | TX | M7 |
| B474 | Williamson, WV-Pikeville, KY | WV | M18 |
| B475 | Williamsport | PA | M9 |
| B476 | Williston | ND | M12 |
| B477 | Willmar-Marshall | MN | M12 |
| B478 | Wilmington | NC | M6 |
| B479 | Winchester | VA | M10 |
| B480 | Worcester-Fitchburg-Leominster | MA | M8 |
| B481 | Worthington | MN | M12 |
| B482 | Yakima | WA | M24 |
| B483 | York-Hanover | PA | M9 |
| B484 | Youngstown-Warren | OH | M16 |
| B485 | Yuba City-Marysville | CA | M4 |
| B486 | Yuma | AZ | M27 |
| B487 | Zanesville-Cambridge | OH | M38 |
| B488 | San Juan, Puerto Rico | PR | M25 |
| B489 | Mayaguez, Puerto Rico | PR | M25 |
| B490 | Guam | GU | M50 |
| B491 | U.S. Virgin Islands | VI | M25 |
| B492 | American Samoa | AS | M51 |
| B493 | Northern Mariana Islands | MP | M50 |

# Nextel Market Areas

## Nextel Market Listing

Nextel Communications, Inc.
1505 Farm Credit Drive
McLean, VA 22102
703-394-3000
800-Nextel9 (800-639-8349)
*www.nextel.com*

### New England Area

Boston, MA
Brockton, MA
Fall River, MA
Falmouth, MA
Fitchburg, MA
Framingham, MA
Hyannis, MA
Leominster, MA
Lowell, MA
New Bedford, MA
Plymouth, MA
Quincy, MA
Worcester, MA
Concord, NH
Manchester, NH
Nashua, NH
Portsmouth, NH
Cranston, RI
East Greenwich, RI
Newport, RI
Pawtucket, RI
Providence, RI
Warwick, RI
Woonsocket, RI

### New York/ New Jersey/ Connecticut/ W. Massachusetts

Bridgeport, CT
Danbury, CT
Hartford, CT
Madison, CT
Manchester, CT
Meriden, CT
Milford, CT
Mohegan, CT
New Britain, CT
New Haven, CT
Norwich, CT
Poquonock, CT
Stamford, CT
Waterbury, CT
Holland, Ct
Merrick, CT
Springfield, MA
Basking Ridge, NJ
Brighton Beach, NJ
Edison, NJ
Elizabeth, NJ
Jersey City, NJ
Long Branch, NJ

Littleton, NJ
Morriston, NJ
Newark, NJ
Parsipanny, NJ
Paterson, NJ
Piscataway, NJ
Toms River, NJ
Babylon, NY
Beekman, NY
Hempstead, NY
Hicksville, NY
Levittown, NY
Mahopac, NY
Montauk Pt., NY
New York, NY
Newburgh, NY
Nyack, NY
Poughkeepsie, NY
Spring Vally, NY
Staten Island, NY
Tarrytown, NY
White Plains, NY

### Philadelphia Area

Dover, DE
Wilmington, DE

*continued on page 228*

# Nextel

# Coverage

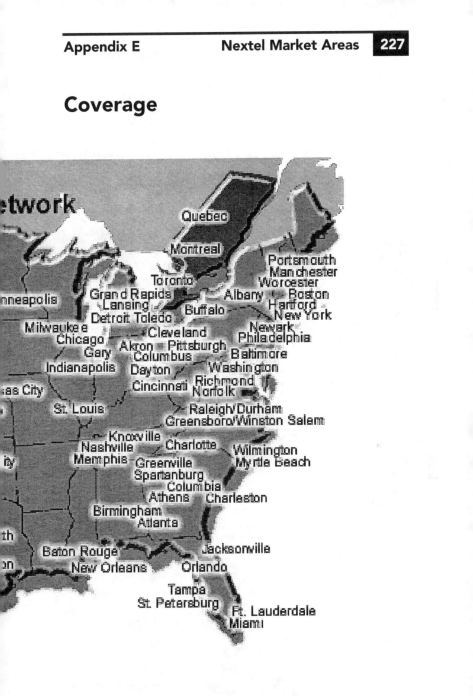

*continued from page 225*

Atlantic City, NJ
Camden, NJ
Princeton, NJ
Trenton, NJ
Vineland, NJ
Allentown, PA
Bethlehem, PA
Easton, PA
Philadelphia, PA
Reading, PA

## Baltimore/ Washington DC Area

Washington DC
Baltimore, MD
Frederick, MD
Rockville, MD
Silver Spring, MD
Alexandria, VA
Arlington, VA
Fredericksburg, VA
Annapolis, MD
Leesburg, VA
Towson, MD
Chevy Chase, MD

## Richmond/ Norfolk Area

Ashland, VA
Chesapeake, VA
Chester, VA
Colonial Heights, VA
Glen Allen, VA
Gloucester, VA
Hickory, VA
Hopewell, VA
Mechanicsville, VA
Midlothian, VA
Newport News, VA
Norfolk, VA
Petersburg, VA
Poquoson, VA
Portsmouth, VA
Providence Forge, VA
Suffolk, VA
Varina, VA
Virginia Beach, VA

Williamsburg, VA
Yorkton, VA

## North Carolina/ Greenville / Spartanburg Area

Apex, NC
Burlington, NC
Cary, NC
Chapel Hill, NC
Charlotte, NC
Clayton, NC
Cleveland, NC
Concord, NC
Durham, NC
Fuquay Varina, NC
Garner, NC
Gastonia, NC
Greensboro, NC
Harrisburg, NC
Hickory, NC
High Point, NC
Hillsborough, NC
Jamestown, NC
Kannapolis, NC
King, NC
Knightdate, NC
Lenior, NC
Lexington, NC
Matthews, NC
Morresville, NC
Morganton, NC
Morrisville, NC
Mount Mourne, NC
Raliegh, NC
Reidsville, NC
Rural Hall, NC
Salisbury, NC
Statesville, NC
Thomasville, NC
Wake Forest, NC
Walnut Cove, NC
Winston-Salem, NC
Anderson, SC
Blacksburg, SC
Clemson, SC
Converse, SC

Drayton, SC
Easley, SC
Fort Mill, SC
Gaffney, SC
Glendale, SC
Greenville, SC
Greer, SC
Mauldin, SC
Peidmont, SC
Rock Hill, SC
Simpsonville, SC
Spartansburg, SC
Taylors, SC
White Stone, SC

## Georgia Area

Alpharetta, GA
Athens, GA
Atlanta, GA
Buford, GA
Cartersville, GA
Clarkston, GA
College Park, GA
Conyers, GA
Covington, GA
Decatur, GA
Doraville, GA
Douglasville, GA
Duluth, GA
East Point, GA
Fayetteville, GA
Jonesboro, GA
Lavonia, GA
Macon, GA
Marietta, GA
Newnan, GA
Peachtree City, GA
Roswell, GA
Sand Springs, GA

## North Florida Area

Alachua, FL
Amelia Island, FL
Baldwin, Fl
Bushnell, FL
Callahan, FL
Durbin, FL
Fernandina Beach, FL

Gross, FL
Highland, FL
Jacksonville, FL
Jacksonville Beach, FL
Lacrosse, FL
Lake City, FL
Olustee, FL
Ortega, FL
St. Augustine, FL
Starke, FL
Waldo, FL
White Springs, FL

## Central Florida Area

Altamonte Springs, FL
Apopka, FL
Cocoa Beach, FL
Daytona Beach, FL
Deland, FL
Kissimmee/St. Cloud, FL
Leesburg, FL
Maitland, FL
Melbourne, FL
Merritt Island, FL
Orlando, FL
Ormond Beach, FL
Oviedo, FL
Port Orange, FL
Sanford, FL
Titusville, FL
Winter Park, FL

## West Florida Area

Bradenton, FL
Brandon, FL
Brooksville, FL
Clearwater, FL
Ft. Myers, FL
Lakeland, FL
Naples, FL
New Port Richey, FL
Ocala, FL
Port Charlotte, FL
Sarasota, FL
St. Petersburg, FL
Tampa, FL
Venice, FL

## South Florida Area

Boca Raton, FL
Boynton Beach, FL
Coral Gables, FL
Coral Springs, FL
Deerfield Beach, FL
Delray Beach, FL
Florida Keys, FL
Ft. Lauderdale, FL
Ft. Pierce, FL
Hollywood, FL
Jupiter, FL
Miami, FL
Plantation, FL
Pompano Beach, FL
Vero Beach, FL
West Palm Beach, FL

## Nashville/ Knoxville Area

Alcoa, TN
Andersonville, TN
Antioch, TN
Brentwood, TN
Clarksville, TN
Clinton, TN
Dandridge, TN
Franklin, TN
Friendsville, TN
Gallatin, TN
Gatlinburg, TN
Goodlettsville, TN
Hendersonville, TN
Hermitage, TN
Joelton, TN
Knoxville, TN
La Vergne, TN
Lebanon, TN
Lenior City, TN
Louisville, TN
Madison, TN
Maryville, TN
Mount Juliet, TN
Murfreesboro, TN
Nashville, TN
Nolensville, TN
Oak Ridge, TN
Old Hickory, TN

Powell, TN
Sevierville, TN
Seymour, TN
Smyrna, TN
Spring Hill, TN
Springfield, TN
Strawberry Plains., TN

## Alabama Area

Abernathy, AL
Annison, AL
Bessemer, AL
Birmingham, AL
Calera, AL
Childersburg, AL
Echo Lake, AL
Gadsden, AL
Hyatt Gap, AL
Morris, AL
Springville, AL
Sylacauga, AL
Talladega, AL
Tuscaloosa, AL
Westover, AL
Woodstock Junction, AL

## Columbia, SC Area

Ballentine, SC
Blythewood, SC
Cayce, SC
Chapin, SC
Columbia, SC
Gaston, SC
Gilbert, SC
Irmo, SC
Lexington, SC
Monticello, SC
Peak, SC
White Rock, SC

## Houston Area

Addicks, TX
Almeda, TX
Baytown, TX
Bellaire, TX
Brookshire, TX
Cannelview, TX
Conroe, TX
Conroe, TX

Galveston, TX
Houston, TX
Kingwood, TX
La Marque, TX
League City, TX
Missouri City, TX
Mont Belvieu, TX
Pasadena, TX
Port of Houston, TX
Richmond, TX
Rosenberg, TX
Rosenberg, TX
Spring, TX
Sugar Land, TX
Texas City, TX
The Woodlands, TX
W. University Place, TX

## Austin/San Antonio Area
Alamo Heights, TX
Austin, TX
Buda, TX
Gruene, TX
Kelly AFB, TX
Kyle, TX
Lackland AFB, TX
New Braunfels, TX
Round Rock, TX
San Antonio, TX
San Marcos, TX
Selma, TX
West Lake Hills, TX

## Dallas/Ft. Worth Area
Allen, TX
Argyle, TX
Arlington, TX
Benbrook, TX
Burleson, TX
Carrolton, TX
Dallas, TX
Denton, TX
Ducanville, TX
Fort Worth, TX
Garland, TX
Grand Prairie, TX
Keller, TX
Lewisville, TX

McKinney, TX
Palmer, TX
Plano, TX
Red Oak, TX
Richardson, TX
Roanoke, TX
Rowlett, TX
Seagoville, TX
Wasahachie, TX
White Settlement, TX

## Oklahoma City and Tulsa Area
Bethany, OK
Broken Arrow, OK
Del City, OK
Edmond, OK
El Reno, OK
Guthrie, OK
Jenks, OK
Midwest City, OK
Moore, OK
Mustang, OK
Nichols Hills, OK
Noble, OK
Norman, OK
Oklahoma City, OK
Sandy Springs, OK
Sapulpa, OK
Shawnee, OK
The Village, OK
Tulsa, OK
Warr Acres, OK
Glen Pool, TX

## Wichita Area
Arthur Heights, KS
Bellaire, KS
Child Acres, KS
Derby, KS
Eastborough, KS
Glenville, KS
Haysville, KS
Meadownview, KS
Murray Gill, KS
Oaklawn, KS
Park City, KS
Prospect Park, KS
Rolling Hills, KS
Spasticville, KS

Valley Center, KS
Wego-Waco, KS
Wichita, KS
Wichita Heights, KS

## Kansas City Area
Elwood, KS
Kansas City, KS
Lawrence, KS
Leavenworth, KS
Lenexa, KS
Olathe, KS
Overland Park, KS
Shawnee, KS
Topeka, KS
Belton, MO
Blue Springs, MO
Harrisonville, MO
Independence, MO
Kansas City, MO
Liberty, MO
Raytown, MO
St. Joseph, MO

## Minnesota Area
Afton, MN
Apple Valley, MN
Bayport, MN
Blaine, MN
Bloomington, MN
Brooklyn Center, MN
Brooklyn Park, MN
Burnsville, MN
Champlin, MN
Chanhassen, MN
Columbia, MN
Coon Rapids, MN
Cottage Grove, MN
Crystal Bay, MN
Dayton, MN
Dellwood, MN
Eagan, MN
Eden Prarie, MN
Edina, MN
Excelsior, MN
Farmington, MN
Forest Lake, MN
Golden Valley, MN
Hamel, MN

Hopkins, MN
Hugo, MN
Inver Grove Heights, MN
Lake Elmo, MN
Lakeland, MN
Lakeville, MN
Little Canada, MN
Long Lake, MN
Loretto, MN
Maple Grove, MN
Maplewood, MN
Mendota, MN
Mendota Heights, MN
Minneapolis, MN
Minnetonka, MN
Minnetonka Beach, MN
Mound, MN
New Hope, MN
Newport, MN
North Oaks, MN
Oakdale, MN
Osseo, MN
Plymouth, MN
Prior Lake, MN
Ramsey, MN
Richfield, MN
Rogers, MN
Rosemont, MN
Savage, MN
Shakopee, MN
Shoreview, MN
South St. Paul, MN
Spring Park, MN
St. Louis Park, MN
St. Paul, MN
St. Paul Park, MN
Stillwater, MN
Wayzata, MN
West St. Paul, MN
White Bear Lake, MN
Woodbury, MN
Hudson, WI
Roberts, WI

## Michigan/ Northwest Ohio Area

Ann Arbor, MI
Battle Creek, MI

Bay City, MI
Dearborn, MI
Detriot, MI
Flint, MI
Grand Rapids, MI
Holland, MI
Jackson, MI
Kalamazoo, MI
Lansing, MI
Livonia, MI
Midland, MI
Mt. Pleasant, MI
Muskegon, MI
Pontiac, MI
Port Huron, MI
Saginaw, MI
South Haven, MI
Southfield, MI
St. Clair Shores, MI
Sterling Heights, MI
Taylor, MI
Warren, MI
Westland, MI
Bowling Green, OH
Findlay, OH
Lima, OH
Toledo, OH

## Tri-State Area

Aurora, IL
Chicago, IL
DeKalb, IL
Elgin, IL
Joliet, IL
Kankakee, IL
Naperville, IL
Rockford, IL
Schaumburg, IL
Gary, IN
Michigan City, IN
South Bend, IN
Valparaiso, IN
Beloit, WI
Brookfield, WI
Brown Deer, WI
Butler, WI
Caledonia, WI
Cedarburg, WI
Cudahy, WI
Delafield, WI

Elm Grove, WI
Franklin, WI
Germantown, WI
Glendale, WI
Grafton, WI
Greendale, WI
Greenfield, WI
Hales Corners, WI
Hartland, WI
Jackson, WI
Janesville, WI
Kenosha, WI
Lake Geneva, WI
Lannon, WI
Madison, WI
Menomonee Falls, WI
Mequon, WI
Middleton, WI
Milwaukee, WI
Muskego, WI
Nashota, WI
Oak Creek, WI
Oconomowoc, WI
Okauchee, WI
Pewaukee, WI
Pleasant Prairie, WI
Racine, WI
Richfield, WI
River Hills, WI
Saukville, WI
Slinger, WI
St. Francis, WI
Sturtevant, WI
Sussex, WI
Union Grove, WI
Verona, WI
Wales, WI
Waukesha, WI
Waunankee, WI
Wauwatosa, WI
West Allis, WI
Whitefish Bay, WI

## Ohio Area

Akron, OH
Canton, OH
Cincinnati, OH
Cleveland, OH
Columbus, OH
Dayton, OH

Elyria, OH
Lancaster, OH
Lorain, OH
Mansfield, OH
Marysville, OH
Medina, OH
Sandusky, OH
Springfield, OH
Warren, OH
Youngstown, OH
Zanesville, OH

### Western PA Area

Beaver Falls, PA
Butler, PA
Kittanning, PA
New Castle, PA
Pittsburgh, PA
Portersville, PA
Uniontown, PA
Washington, PA
Wilkingsburg, PA

### Colorado Area

Avon, CO
Boulder, CO
Breckenridge, CO
Carbondale, CO
Colorado City, CO
Colorado Springs, CO
Denver, CO
Dillion, CO
Eagle, CO
Estes Park, CO
Fort Collins, CO
Frisco, CO
Glenwood Springs, CO
Greeley, CO
La Junta, CO
Lamar, CO
Longmont, CO
Loveland, CO
Pueblo, CO
Pueblo West, CO
Vail, CO
Woodland Park, CO
Cheyenne, WY

### Phoenix Area

Carefree, AZ

Casa Grande, AZ
Eloy, AZ
Florence, AZ
Mesa, AZ
Peoria, AZ
Phoenix, AZ
Scottsdale, AZ
Tucson, AZ

### Salt Lake City Area

Brigham City, UT
Grantsville, UT
Logan, UT
Ogden, UT
Park City, UT
Payson, UT
Provo, UT
Salt Lake City, UT
Tooele, UT
Tremonton, UT

### Spokane Area

Clark Fork, ID
Coeur d'Alene, ID
Coolin, ID
Hayden, ID
Lakeview, ID
Naples, ID
Nordman, ID
Post Falls, ID
Sandpoint, ID
Spirit Lake, ID
Cheney, WA
Deer Park, WA
Medical Lake, WA
Newport, WA
Spokane, WA
Usk, WA

### Western Washington Area

Anacortes, WA
Arlington, WA
Auburn, WA
Bellevue, WA
Bellingham, WA
Blaine, WA
Bremerton, WA

Centralia, WA
Chehalis, WA
Enumclaw, WA
Everett, WA
Federal Way, WA
Issaquah, WA
Kent, WA
Kirkland, WA
Monroe, WA
Mt. Vernon, WA
Oak Harbor, WA
Olympia, WA
Port Townsend, WA
Poulsbo, WA
Puyallup, WA
Redmond, WA
Renton, WA
Seattle, WA
Shelton, WA
Tacoma, WA

### Western/SW Washington/ Oregon Area

Albany, OR
Astoria, OR
Beaverton, OR
Bend, OR
Corvallis, OR
Eugene, OR
Forest Grove, OR
Gresham, OR
Hillsboro, OR
Lake Oswego, OR
Lyons, OR
Madras, OR
McMinnville, OR
Oregon City, OR
Portland, OR
Prineville, OR
Redmond, OR
Salem, OR
Springfield, OR
Sweet Home, OR
Tigard, OR
Wilsonville, OR
Woodburn, OR
Longview, WA
Vancouver, WA

### Northern and Central California Area

Auburn, CA
Bakersfield, CA
Coalinga, CA
Fairfield, CA
Fresno, CA
Gilroy, CA
Grapevine, CA
Grass Valley, CA
Hanford, CA
Healdsburg, CA
King City, CA
Lodi, CA
Los Banos, CA
Madera, CA
Marysville, CA
Merced, CA
Modesto, CA
Monterey, CA
Napa, CA
Oakland, CA
Oroville, CA
Placerville, CA
Porterville, CA
Red Bluff, CA
Redding, CA
Roseville, CA
Sacramento, CA
Salinas, CA
San Francisco, CA
San Jose, CA
Santa Cruz, CA
Santa Rosa, CA
South Lake Tahoe, CA
Stockton, CA
Tahoe City, CA
Trucklee, CA
Tulare, CA
Vallejo, CA
Watsonville, CA
Yolo, CA
Yuba City, CA
Carson City, NV
Reno, NV

### Southern California and Las Vegas Area

Bullhead City, AZ
Kingman, AZ
Acton, CA
Alhambra, CA
Anaheim, CA
Avalon, CA
Baldwin Park, CA
Barstow, CA
Beverly Hills, CA
Buena Park, CA
Burbank, CA
Calexico, CA
Carlsbad, CA
Chino, CA
Chula Vista, CA
Compton, CA
Corona, CA
El Cajon, CA
El Monte, CA
Escondido, CA
Fontanta, CA
Fullerton, CA
Garden Grove, CA
Glendale, CA
Hesperia, CA
Huntington Beach, CA
Inglewood, CA
Irvine, CA
La Jolla, CA
Lancaster, CA
Long Beach, CA
Los Angeles, CA
Mission Viejo, CA
Monterey Park, CA
Moreno Valley, CA
National City, CA
Newport Beach, CA
Norwalk, CA
Oceanside, CA
Ontario, CA
Orange, CA
Oxnard, CA
Palm Desert, CA
Palm Springs, CA
Pasadena, CA
Pico Rivera, CA

Pomona, CA
Rancho Cucamonga, CA
Redlands, CA
Redondo Beach, CA
Rialto, CA
Riverside, CA
San Bernadino, CA
San Diego, CA
San Pedro, CA
Santa Ana, CA
Santa Barbara, CA
Santa Clarita, CA
Santa Maria, CA
Santa Monica, CA
Santa Rosa Island, CA
Simi Valley, CA
South Gate, CA
Thousand Oaks, CA
Torrance, CA
Trabuco Canyon, CA
Upland, CA
Ventura, CA
West Covina, CA
Whittier, CA
Boulder City, NV
Henderson, NV
Las Vegas, NV
Mesquite, NV

# Carrier Information

**F**

Appendix

## Carriers

The companies listed are represented in at least ten markets in the Carriers by Market, Channel Block, and Technology table. The company name listed is the managing company if it is cellular, and may operate under a branded name such as Cellular One (block A companies). The names of the PCS companies listed are from licensee information, and the operating company name may differ.

Remember, you won't see GSM technology at 800 MHz. If two technologies are listed, the first is for the 800 MHz operation and the second is for the 1900 MHz operation.

As much information as was obtainable has been included. If there is a Web address, but no street address, it is because the Web site did not have a street address that I could find. Some companies are too new and do not have Web sites available yet. My Web site contains links to companies in the wireless industry (*www.wirelesswhiz.com*).

This list represents 73 percent of the 800 MHz carriers and 86 percent of the 1900 MHz carriers.

| Carrier | Tech-nology | AMPS Mkts | PCS Mkts |
|---|---|---|---|
| **21st Century Telesis** | PACS | — | 28 |

650 Town Center Drive
Suite 1999
Costa Mesa, CA  92626
714-752-2178
*21stcentel.com*

| | | | |
|---|---|---|---|
| **ACC-PCS** | | — | 11 |

| | | | |
|---|---|---|---|
| **Aer Force** | | — | 18 |

| | | | |
|---|---|---|---|
| **Aerial** | GSM | — | 45 |

CS-NOC
P. O. Box 21367
Tampa, FL  33622-1367
888-223-7425 (888-2AERIAL) CUSTOMER SERVICE
888-237-4251 (888-AERIAL1) SALES
*www.aerial1.com*

| | | | |
|---|---|---|---|
| **Airadigm Communications** | GSM | — | 18 |

*www.airadigm.com*
800-745-1818 CUSTOMER SERVICE
888-687-1130 SALES

| | | | |
|---|---|---|---|
| **AirTouch Communications** | CDMA | 79 | — |

One California Street
San Francisco, CA  94111
415-658-2000
*www.airtouch.com*

| | | | |
|---|---|---|---|
| **ALLTEL** | CDMA | 95 | 76 |

*www.alltel.com*

| | | | |
|---|---|---|---|
| **Alpine PCS** | CDMA | — | 12 |
| **Americall** | GSM | — | 15 |

| Carrier | Tech-nology | AMPS Mkts | PCS Mkts |
|---|---|---|---|
| **Ameritech** | **CDMA** | 19 | 23 |

30 South Wacker
34th Floor
Chicago, IL  60606
800-221-0994 CUSTOMER SERVICE
*www.ameritech.com*

| | | | |
|---|---|---|---|
| **AT&T Wireless** | **TDMA** | 86 | 439 |

800-888-7600 CUSTOMER SERVICE
888-290-4613 SALES
*www.attws.com*

| | | | |
|---|---|---|---|
| **Bell Atlantic Mobility** | **CDMA** | 44 | — |

Bedminster, New Jersey
800-416-8434
*www.bam.com*

| | | | |
|---|---|---|---|
| **BellSouth Cellular Corp.** | **TDMA/GSM** | 56 | 54 |

1100 Peachtree Street, NE
Suite 1000
Atlanta, GA  30309-4599
*www.bscc.com*

| | | | |
|---|---|---|---|
| **BRK Wireless Co.** | | — | 13 |
| **Cellular Info** | | 12 | — |
| **Centennial Cellular** | **CDMA** | 13 | 2 |

800-493-3121 CUSTOMER SERVICE
219-750-3880 CUSTOMER SERVICE
*www.toog.com/centennial/home.htm*

| | | | |
|---|---|---|---|
| **Century Tel Wireless** | | 17 | 41 |

100 Century Park Drive
Monroe, LA  71203
318-388-9000
*www.centurytel.com*

| Carrier | Technology | AMPS Mkts | PCS Mkts |
|---|---|---|---|
| **Century Personal Access Network** | | | 12 |
| **Chase Telecommunications** | CDMA | | 12 |
| **ClearComm** | CDMA/GSM | 2 | 15 |
| **Comcast PCS** 480 Swedesford Road Wayne, PA 19087 610-995-5000 *www.comcastcellular.com* | | 5 | 14 |
| **CommNet 2000** *www.commnet2000.com* | | 20 | — |
| **DCC PCS** | | — | 10 |
| **Devon Mobile** | CDMA | — | 35 |
| **GenCell Management** | | 12 | — |
| **General Wireless** | CDMA | — | 15 |
| **GTE Wireless** P. O. Box 105194 Atlanta, GA 30348 770-391-8000 800-333-4004 800-669-5665 *www.gte.com* | CDMA | 103 | 26 |
| **Integrated Communications** | CDMA | — | 10 |
| **Kansas Cellular** 621 Westport Boulevard Salina, KS 67401 800-383-5090 913-823-5049 *www.midusa.net/kscellular* | | 10 | — |

| Carrier | Tech- nology | AMPS Mkts | PCS Mkts |
|---|---|---|---|
| **Magnacom Wireless** | | — | 20 |
| **MCG PCS** | | — | 14 |
| **McLeod USA** | | — | 29 |
| **Mercury Mobile** | | — | 23 |
| **Mercury PCS II** | | — | 33 |
| **Minnesota PCS** | | — | 13 |
| **Montana PCS** | | — | 10 |
| **Mountain Solutions** | GSM | — | 12 |
| **MVI Corp.** | | — | 29 |
| **Nextwave** | CDMA | — | 103 |
| **Northcoast Operating Company** | — | | 52 |

**Omnipoint Communications, Inc.** — GSM — 159
16 Wing Drive
Cedar Knolls, NJ  07927
(888) 784-6664
*www.omnipoint.com*

**PacBel Mobile** — GSM — 18
P.O. Box 1907
San Ramon, CA  94583
800-393-PBMS (7267) CUSTOMER SERVICE
888 ON THE FLY (888-668-4335) SALES
*www.pacbell.com*

| **PCSouth** | | — | 16 |
|---|---|---|---|
| **Pocket** | GSM | — | 44 |

| Carrier | Tech-nology | AMPS Mkts | PCS Mkts |
|---|---|---|---|
| **Poka Lambro** | **CDMA** | 1 | 20 |

WIRELESS               CELLULAR
Poka Lambro Plaza        P.O. Box 1340
7006 University       Tahoka, TX  79373
(University Avenue      800-422-2387
   and Loop 289)
Lubbock, TX  79413
888-765-2526 (888-POKALAM)
*www.poka.com*

| | | | |
|---|---|---|---|
| **Polycell** | **CDMA** | — | 15 |
| **Powertel** | **GSM** | — | 62 |

1233 O. G. Skinner Drive
West Point, GA 31833
*www.powertel.com*

| | | | |
|---|---|---|---|
| **PrimeCo Personal Communications** | **CDMA** | — | 78 |

6 Campus Circle
Westlake, TX  76262
*www.primeco.com*

| | | | |
|---|---|---|---|
| **Redwood Wireless** | | — | 14 |
| **Rivgam** | | — | 14 |
| **Southwestern Bell** | **TDMA** | 43 | 29 |

888-29-GUIDE (PRERECORDED INFO)
*www.swbellwireless.com*

| | | | |
|---|---|---|---|
| **Sprint PCS** | **CDMA** | — | 459 |

4900 Main Street
Kansas City, MO  64112
800-818-0961
*www.sprintpcs.com*

| | | | |
|---|---|---|---|
| **Touch America** | | — | 12 |
| **Triad Cellular** | | — | 23 |

| Carrier | Tech-nology | AMPS Mkts | PCS Mkts |
|---|---|---|---|
| **United States Cellular** | | 77 | — |

8410 W. Bryn Mawr
Suite 700
Chicago, IL  60631
773-399-8900
*www.uscc.com*

| | | | |
|---|---|---|---|
| **U.S. West** | CDMA | — | 56 |

1801 California Street
Denver, CO  80202
800-ACCESS2 (800-222-3772) SALES
*www.uswest.com*

| | | | |
|---|---|---|---|
| **Urban Comm** | CDMA | — | 26 |
| **Vanguard Cellular** | TDMA | 16 | — |

2002 Pisgah Church Road
Greensboro, NC  72455
*www.vcela.com*

| | | | |
|---|---|---|---|
| **Virginia PCS** | CDMA | — | 15 |

Intelos (Managing Partner
    CFW Communications)
1150 Shenandoah Village Drive
P.O. Box 1328
Waynesboro, VA  22980
*www.intelos.com*

| | | | |
|---|---|---|---|
| **Western Wireless** | GSM | — | 194 |

Marketed as VoiceStream Wireless
800-937-8997
*www.voicestream.com*

| | | | |
|---|---|---|---|
| **Wireless One Network** | TDMA/CDMA | 5 | 2 |

2100 Electronics Lane
Ft. Myers, FL 33912
800-782-2808
*www.wirelessonenet.com*

# Appendix F
## Carriers by Market, Channel Block, and Technology

This appendix is listed alphabetically by city within each state. The market names are BTAs. Cross-check with the BTA map and Market List. Where a BTA covers cities in more than one state, the cities covered are listed in their respective states. For example, BTA 346 covers Philadelphia, PA, Wilmington, DE, and Trenton, NJ. If you live in Wilmington, you can look up Wilmington under Delaware instead of looking up Philadelphia under Pennsylvania. U.S. Properties are listed at the end of this section. The table lists the company licensed to operate in the market, not the operating name of the service provider. Some block A cellular carriers operate under the brand name Cellular One. It does not represent that coverage is available. This information is subject to change. At the time of this printing, two of the major C block carriers, Nextwave, Pocket and General Wireless, had filed for reorganization bankruptcy, with their spectrum to be reauctioned in spring of 1999.

Key: $C$ = CDMA; $T$ = TDMA; $G$ = GSM; $P$ = PACS.

| Market Name | Cellular Carriers | | PCS Carriers | | | | | |
|---|---|---|---|---|---|---|---|---|
| | A Block | B Block | A Block | B Block | C Block | D Block | E Block | F Block |
| **Alabama** | | | | | | | | |
| Anniston | GTE Wireless[C] | BellSouth[T] | Sprint PCS[C] | Powertel[G] | Mercury PCS[C] | Public Service PCS | Alltel[C] | Technicom |
| Birmingham | GTE Wireless[C] | BellSouth[T] | Sprint PCS[C] | Powertel[G] | Mercury PCS[C] | Alltel[C] | AT&T Wireless[T] | Omnipoint[G] |
| Decatur | GTE Wireless[C] | BellSouth[T] | Sprint PCS[C] | Powertel[G] | Mercury PCS[C] | Alltel[C] | AT&T Wireless[T] | Omnipoint[G] |
| Dothan-Enterprise | Price Wireless | Alltel[C] | Sprint PCS[C] | Powertel[G] | Enterprise Comm[C] | Alltel[C] | BellSouth[T] | Mercury PCS II |
| Florence | GTE Wireless[C] | BellSouth[T] | Sprint PCS[C] | Powertel[G] | Chase Telecomm[C] | Alltel[C] | AT&T Wireless[T] | Mercury PCS II |
| Gadsden | GTE Wireless[C] | BellSouth[T] | Sprint PCS[C] | Powertel[G] | Mercury PCS[C] | Alltel[C] | BellSouth[G] | Omnipoint[G] |
| Huntsville | GTE Wireless[C] | BellSouth[T] | Sprint PCS[C] | Powertel[G] | Mercury PCS[C] | Alltel[C] | AT&T Wireless[T] | Omnipoint[G] |
| Mobile | BellSouth[T] | GTE Wireless[C] | Sprint PCS[C] | PrimeCo[C] | Mobile Tri-States LP13[C] | Alltel[C] | BellSouth[C] | Mercury PCS II |
| Montgomery | Price Wireless | Alltel[C] | Sprint PCS[C] | Powertel[G] | Central AL Partnership 132 | Alltel[C] | BellSouth[C] | Mercury PCS II |
| Opelika-Auburn | Price Wireless | InterCel | AT&T Wireless[T] | Powertel[G] | Enterprise Comm[C] | Sprint PCS[C] | BellSouth[C] | Technicom |
| Selma | Dominion Cellular | Southeastern Cellular | Sprint PCS[C] | Powertel[G] | Central AL Partnership 132 | Alltel[C] | BellSouth[C] | Mercury PCS II |
| Tuscaloosa | GTE Wireless[C] | BellSouth[T] | Sprint PCS[C] | Powertel[G] | Mercury PCS[C] | Alltel[C] | AT&T Wireless[T] | Mercury Mobility |
| **Alaska** | | | | | | | | |
| Anchorage | AT&T Wireless[T] | MACtel Cellular | PacifiCom | GCI Communications[P] | America1[C] | Sprint PCS[C] | MVI Corp. | PacifiCom Alaska |

| Market Name | Cellular Carriers A Block | Cellular Carriers B Block | PCS Carriers A Block | PCS Carriers B Block | C Block | D Block | E Block | F Block |
|---|---|---|---|---|---|---|---|---|
| Fairbanks | Fairbanks Muni | Cellulink/Pactel | PacifiCom | GCI Communications[P] | Americall[C] | Sprint PCS[C] | MVI Corp. | Americall[C] |
| Juneau-Ketchikan | Mercury Comm | Cellulink/Pactel | PacifiCom | GCI Communications[P] | Loralen[C] | Sprint PCS[C] | MVI Corp | Americall[C] |
| **Arizona** | | | | | | | | |
| Flagstaff | Bell Atlantic[C] | AirTouch[C] | AT&T Wireless[T] | Sprint PCS[C] | CH PCS | U S West[C] | Western Wireless[C] | WebTel Wireless |
| Nogales | Bell Atlantic[C] | Valley Telecom | AT&T Wireless[T] | Sprint PCS[C] | CH PCS | U S West[C] | Western Wireless[C] | Cellutech |
| Phoenix | Bell Atlantic[C] | AirTouch[C] | AT&T Wireless[T] | Sprint PCS[C] | CH PCS | U S West[C] | Western Wireless[C] | Western Wireless[C] |
| Prescott | | | AT&T Wireless[T] | Sprint PCS[C] | CH PCS | U S West[C] | Western Wireless[C] | WebTel Wireless |
| Sierra Vista-Douglas | Bell Atlantic[C] | Valley Telecom | AT&T Wireless[T] | Sprint PCS[C] | CH PCS | U S West[C] | Western Wireless[C] | Poka Lambro[C] |
| Tucson | Bell Atlantic[C] | AirTouch[C] | AT&T Wireless[T] | Sprint PCS[C] | Magnacom Wireless | U S West[C] | Western Wireless[C] | Western Wireless[C] |
| Yuma | Centennial Cellular[C] | GTE Wireless[C] | AT&T Wireless[T] | Sprint PCS[C] | CH PCS | U S West[C] | Western Wireless[C] | Integrated Comm[C] |
| **Arkansas** | | | | | | | | |
| Blytheville | Southwestern Bell[T] | Alltel[C] | Powertel[C] | Southwestern Bell[■] | Eldorado Comm[C] | Sprint PCS[C] | Alltel[C] | PCSouth |
| El Dorado-Magnolia-Camden | Southwestern Bell[T] | Century Tel[T] | Southwestern Bell[■] | Sprint PCS[C] | Eldorado Comm[C] | Alltel[C] | Omnipoint[C] | Mercury Mobility |
| Fayetteville-Springdale-Rogers | Southwestern Bell[T] | Alltel[C] | Southwestern Bell[■] | Sprint PCS[C] | Pocket[C] | Alltel[C] | Western Wireless[C] | Eldorado Comm[C] |
| Fort Smith | Southwestern Bell[T] | Alltel[C] | Southwestern Bell[■] | Sprint PCS[C] | Pocket[C] | Western Wireless[C] | Alltel[C] | Onque[C] |
| Harrison | Southwestern Bell[T] | | Southwestern Bell[■] | Sprint PCS[C] | PCS Plus | Western Wireless[C] | Alltel[C] | PCSouth |
| Hot Springs | Southwestern Bell[T] | Alltel[C] | Southwestern Bell[■] | Sprint PCS[C] | PCS Plus | Western Wireless[C] | Alltel[C] | Eldorado Comm[C] |
| Jonesboro-Paragould | Southwestern Bell[T] | Alltel[C] | Southwestern Bell[■] | Sprint PCS[C] | Pocket[C] | Alltel[C] | Western Wireless[C] | PCSouth |
| Little Rock | Southwestern Bell[T] | Alltel[C] | Southwestern Bell[■] | Sprint PCS[C] | Pocket[C] | Western Wireless[C] | Alltel[C] | Telecorp Holding |
| Pine Bluff | Southwestern Bell[T] | Alltel[C] | Southwestern Bell[■] | Sprint PCS[C] | Omnipoint[C] | Western Wireless[C] | Alltel[C] | Mercury Mobility |
| Russellville | Southwestern Bell[T] | Alltel[C] | Southwestern Bell[■] | Sprint PCS[C] | PCS Plus | Alltel[C] | Western Wireless[C] | Onque[C] |
| Texarkana | Southwestern Bell[T] | Century Cellunet | PrimeCo[C] | Sprint PCS[C] | Pocket[C] | Alltel[C] | AT&T Wireless[T] | Mercury Mobility |

| Market Name | Cellular Carriers | | PCS Carriers ↑ | | | | | |
|---|---|---|---|---|---|---|---|---|
| | A Block | B Block | A Block | B Block | C Block | D Block | E Block | F Block |
| **California** | | | | | | | | |
| Bakersfield | BellSouth[T] | GTE Wireless[C] | Sprint PCS[C] | PacBell Mobile[C] | ClearComm[CG] | AT&T Wireless[T] | Rivgam | Alpine PCS[C] |
| Chico-Oroville | AT&T Wireless[T] | AirTouch[C] | Sprint PCS[C] | PacBell Mobile[C] | General Wireless[C] | AT&T Wireless[T] | AT&T Wireless[T] | Point Enterprises |
| El Centro-Calexico | Centennial Cellular[C] | GTE Wireless[C] | Sprint PCS[C] | PacBell Mobile[C] | CH PCS | Nextwave[C] | AT&T Wireless[T] | Integrated Comm[C] |
| Eureka | U.S. Cellular | Cal-One Cellular | Sprint PCS[C] | PacBell Mobile[C] | ClearComm[CG] | Triad Cellular | AT&T Wireless[T] | Polycell[C] |
| Fresno | AT&T Wireless[T] | GTE Wireless[C] | Sprint PCS[C] | PacBell Mobile[C] | ClearComm[CG] | AT&T Wireless[T] | AT&T Wireless[T] | Central Wireless |
| Los Angeles | AT&T Wireless[T] | AirTouch[C] | Sprint PCS[C] | PacBell Mobile[C] | Nextwave[C] | AT&T Wireless[T] | Rivgam | Aer Force |
| Merced | Cellular 2000 | GTE Wireless[C] | Sprint PCS[C] | PacBell Mobile[C] | ClearComm[CG] | AT&T Wireless[T] | AT&T Wireless[T] | Central Wireless |
| Modesto | AT&T Wireless[T] | AirTouch[C] | Sprint PCS[C] | PacBell Mobile[C] | ClearComm[CG] | AT&T Wireless[T] | West Coast PCS | Central Wireless |
| Redding | AT&T Wireless[T] | AirTouch[C] | Sprint PCS[C] | PacBell Mobile[C] | ClearComm[CG] | AT&T Wireless[T] | Triad Cellular | Point Enterprises |
| Sacramento | AT&T Wireless[T] | GTE Wireless[C] | Sprint PCS[C] | PacBell Mobile[C] | General Wireless[C] | AT&T Wireless[T] | West Coast PCS | Nextwave[C] |
| Salinas-Monterey | CMT Partners[T] | AirTouch[C] | Sprint PCS[C] | PacBell Mobile[C] | General Wireless[C] | Entertainment Unltd | AT&T Wireless[T] | Alpine PCS[C] |
| San Diego | GTE Wireless[C] | AirTouch[C] | Sprint PCS[C] | PacBell Mobile[C] | Nextwave[C] | AT&T Wireless[T] | Rivgam | Central Oregon Cellular |
| San Francisco-Oakland-San Jose | CMT Partners[T] | GTE Wireless[C] | Sprint PCS[C] | PacBell Mobile[C] | General Wireless[C] | AT&T Wireless[T] | Western Wireless[C] | Nextwave[C] |
| San Luis Obispo | AT&T Wireless[T] | GTE Wireless[C] | Sprint PCS[C] | PacBell Mobile[C] | Alpine PCS[C] | Entertainment Unltd | Entertainment Unltd | AT&T Wireless[T] |
| Santa Barbara-Santa Maria | AT&T Wireless[T] | GTE Wireless[C] | Sprint PCS[C] | PacBell Mobile[C] | Alpine PCS[C] | Entertainment Unltd | AT&T Wireless[T] | Aer Force |
| Stockton | AT&T Wireless[T] | AirTouch[C] | Sprint PCS[C] | PacBell Mobile[C] | General Wireless[C] | AT&T Wireless[T] | West Coast PCS | Central Wireless |
| Visalia-Porterville-Hanford | AT&T Wireless[T] | GTE Wireless[C] | Sprint PCS[C] | PacBell Mobile[C] | ClearComm[C] | AT&T Wireless[T] | Entertainment Unltd | Central Wireless |
| Yuba City-Marysville | AT&T Wireless[T] | AirTouch[C] | Sprint PCS[C] | PacBell Mobile[C] | General Wireless[C] | AT&T Wireless[T] | West Coast PCS | Integrated Comm[C] |
| **Colorado** | | | | | | | | |
| Colorado Springs | AT&T Wireless[T] | AirTouch[C] | Sprint PCS[C] | Western Wireless[C] | Mountain Solutions[C] | AT&T Wireless[T] | U S West[C] | Omnipoint[C] |
| Denver | AT&T Wireless[T] | AirTouch[C] | Sprint PCS[C] | Western Wireless[C] | Nextwave[C] | AT&T Wireless[T] | U S West[C] | Radiofone PCS |

| Market Name | Cellular Carriers | | PCS Carriers | | | | | |
| --- | --- | --- | --- | --- | --- | --- | --- | --- |
| | A Block | B Block | A Block | B Block | C Block | D Block | E Block | F Block |
| Durango | Unitel | CommNet 2000 | Western Wireless[C] | AT&T Wireless[T] | PCS Plus | Sprint PCS[C] | Triad Cellular | Lite-Wave |
| Fort Collins-Loveland | AT&T Wireless[T] | AirTouch[C] | Sprint PCS[C] | Western Wireless[C] | Mountain Solutions[C] | AT&T Wireless[T] | U S West[C] | PCSouth |
| Grand Junction | AT&T Wireless[T] | AirTouch[C] | Sprint PCS[C] | Western Wireless[C] | Mountain Solutions[C] | AT&T Wireless[T] | U S West[C] | Lite-Wave |
| Greeley | AT&T Wireless[T] | AirTouch[C] | Sprint PCS[C] | Western Wireless[C] | Mountain Solutions[C] | U S West[C] | AT&T Wireless[T] | PCSouth |
| Pueblo | Western Wireless | CommNet2000 | Sprint PCS[C] | Western Wireless[C] | Mountain Solutions[C] | AT&T Wireless[T] | Century Tel[T] | Mercury Mobility |
| **Connecticut** | | | | | | | | |
| Hartford | Bell Atlantic[C] | SNET[T] | Omnipoint[C] | Sprint PCS[C] | Fortunet Wireless | AT&T Wireless[T] | AT&T Wireless[T] | Northcoast OpCo. |
| New Haven-Waterbury-Meriden | Bell Atlantic[C] | SNET[T] | Omnipoint[C] | Sprint PCS[C] | Nextwave[C] | AT&T Wireless[T] | AT&T Wireless[T] | Northcoast OpCo. |
| New London-Norwich | Bell Atlantic[C] | SNET[T] | Omnipoint[C] | Sprint PCS[C] | Nextwave[C] | AT&T Wireless[T] | AT&T Wireless[T] | Northcoast OpCo. |
| **Delaware** | | | | | | | | |
| Dover | Comcast[C] | Bell Atlantic[C] | AT&T Wireless[T] | Sprint PCS[C] | Omnipoint[C] | AT&T Wireless[T] | Comcast PCS | Nextwave[C] |
| Wilmington | Comcast[C] | Bell Atlantic[C] | AT&T Wireless[T] | Sprint PCS[C] | Omnipoint[C] | Comcast PCS | Rivgam | Nextwave[C] |
| **Florida** | | | | | | | | |
| Daytona Beach | AT&T Wireless[T] | BellSouth[T] | Aerial[C] | PrimeCo[C] | Aer Force | Sprint PCS[C] | AT&T Wireless[T] | Nextwave[C] |
| Fort Myers | Wireless One[C] | GTE Wireless[C] | Sprint PCS[C] | PrimeCo[C] | General Wireless[C] | BellSouth[C] | BellSouth[C] | Wireless One[C] |
| Fort Pierce, Stuart | AT&T Wireless[T] | U.S. Cellular | Sprint PCS[C] | PrimeCo[C] | General Wireless[C] | BellSouth[C] | AT&T Wireless[T] | Devon Mobile[C] |
| Fort Walton Beach | Wireless One[C] | Alltel[C] | Sprint PCS[C] | PrimeCo[C] | Mobile Tri-States[C] | Alltel[C] | BellSouth[C] | Mercury PCS II |
| Gainesville | U.S. Cellular | Alltel[C] | Powertel[C] | PrimeCo[C] | Nextwave[C] | Sprint PCS[C] | BellSouth[C] | Mercury PCS II |
| Jacksonville | AT&T Wireless[T] | BellSouth[T] | Powertel[C] | PrimeCo[C] | Nextwave[C] | Sprint PCS[C] | Alltel[C] | Southern Wireless[C] |
| Lakeland-Winter Haven | AT&T Wireless[T] | GTE Wireless[C] | Aerial[C] | PrimeCo[C] | Nextwave[C] | Sprint PCS[C] | BellSouth[C] | Eldorado Comm[C] |
| Melbourne-Titusville | AT&T Wireless[T] | BellSouth[T] | Aerial[C] | PrimeCo[C] | Nextwave[C] | Sprint PCS[C] | AT&T Wireless[T] | Telecorp Holding |
| Miami-Fort Lauderdale | AT&T Wireless[T] | BellSouth[T] | Sprint PCS[C] | PrimeCo[C] | General Wireless[C] | AT&T Wireless[T] | Omnipoint[C] | Omnipoint[C] |
| Naples | Wireless One[C] | GTE Wireless[C] | Sprint PCS[C] | PrimeCo[C] | General Wireless[C] | Alltel[C] | BellSouth[C] | Wireless One[C] |

| Market Name | Cellular Carriers | | PCS Carriers | | | | | |
|---|---|---|---|---|---|---|---|---|
| | A Block | B Block | A Block | B Block | C Block | D Block | E Block | F Block |
| Ocala | AT&T Wireless[T] | Alltel[C] | Aerial[C] | PrimeCo[C] | Aer Force | Sprint PCS[C] | BellSouth[C] | Nextwave[C] |
| Orlando | AT&T Wireless[T] | BellSouth[T] | Aerial[C] | PrimeCo[C] | Nextwave[C] | Sprint PCS[C] | BellSouth[C] | Telecorp Holding |
| Panama City | Price Wireless | Alltel[C] | Powertel[C] | PrimeCo[C] | Southeast Wireless | BellSouth[C] | AT&T Wireless[T] | Mercury PCS II |
| Pensacola | Wireless One[C] | GTE Wireless[C] | Sprint PCS[C] | PrimeCo[C] | Mobile Tri-States[C] | Alltel[C] | BellSouth[C] | Mercury PCS II |
| Sarasota-Bradenton | AT&T Wireless[T] | GTE Wireless[C] | Aerial[C] | PrimeCo[C] | Nextwave[C] | Sprint PCS[C] | BellSouth[C] | Aer Force |
| Tallahassee | U.S. Cellular | Alltel[C] | Powertel[C] | PrimeCo[C] | Southeast Wireless | Sprint PCS[C] | BellSouth[C] | Mercury PCS II |
| Tampa-Clearwater St. Petersburg | AT&T Wireless[T] | GTE Wireless[C] | Aerial[C] | PrimeCo[C] | Nextwave[C] | Sprint PCS[C] | BellSouth[C] | Telecorp Holding |
| Vero Beach | AT&T Wireless[T] | BellSouth[T] | Sprint PCS[C] | PrimeCo[C] | General Wireless[C] | BellSouth[C] | AT&T Wireless[T] | Devon Mobile[C] |
| West Palm Beach-Boca Raton | AT&T Wireless[T] | BellSouth[T] | Sprint PCS[C] | PrimeCo[C] | General Wireless[C] | AT&T Wireless[T] | Devon Mobile[C] | Omnipoint[C] |

## Georgia

| Market Name | Cellular Carriers | | PCS Carriers | | | | | |
|---|---|---|---|---|---|---|---|---|
| | A Block | B Block | A Block | B Block | C Block | D Block | E Block | F Block |
| Albany | Price Wireless | Alltel[C] | AT&T Wireless[T] | Powertel[C] | Enterprise Comm | Sprint PCS[C] | BellSouth[C] | Omnipoint[C] |
| Tifton | GMD Limited | Alltel[C] | AT&T Wireless[T] | Powertel[C] | Enterprise Comm | Sprint PCS[C] | BellSouth[C] | Omnipoint[C] |
| Athens | AirTouch[C] | BellSouth[T] | AT&T Wireless[T] | Powertel[C] | General Wireless[C] | Sprint PCS[C] | Alltel[C] | Wireless Telecom[C] |
| Atlanta | AirTouch[C] | BellSouth[T] | AT&T Wireless[T] | Powertel[C] | General Wireless[C] | Sprint PCS[C] | Alltel[C] | Nextwave[C] |
| Augusta | Price Wireless | Alltel[C] | AT&T Wireless[T] | Powertel[C] | Savannah Ind. PCS[C] | BellSouth[C] | Sprint PCS[C] | Omnipoint[C] |
| Brunswick | Price Wireless | Alltel[C] | Powertel[C] | PrimeCo[C] | KMTel | BellSouth[C] | Sprint PCS[C] | Mercury PCS II |
| Columbus | Price Wireless | Public Service | AT&T Wireless[T] | Powertel[C] | R & S PCS | BellSouth[C] | Sprint PCS[C] | Public Service PCS |
| Dalton | AirTouch[C] | BellSouth[T] | AT&T Wireless[T] | Powertel[C] | Southeast Wireless | Sprint PCS[C] | Alltel[C] | Troup EMC Comm |
| Gainesville | Bell Atlantic[C]r | BellSouth[T] | AT&T Wireless[T] | Powertel[C] | General Wireless[C] | Sprint PCS[C] | Alltel[C] | Wireless Telecom[C] |
| La Grange | Blackwater Cellular | InterCel | AT&T Wireless[T] | Powertel[C] | Enterprise Comm | BellSouth[C] | Sprint PCS[C] | Technicom |
| Macon-Warner Robins | Price Wireless | BellSouth[T] | AT&T Wireless[T] | Powertel[C] | Georgia Ind PCS[C] | Sprint PCS[C] | Alltel[C] | Omnipoint[C] |
| Rome | AirTouch[C] | BellSouth[T] | AT&T Wireless[T] | Powertel[C] | Southeast Wireless | Sprint PCS[C] | Alltel[C] | Troup EMC Comm |
| Savannah | Price Wireless | Alltel[C] | AT&T Wireless[T] | Powertel[C] | Southern Wireless[C] | Sprint PCS[C] | BellSouth[C] | Omnipoint[C] |

| Market Name | Cellular Carriers | | PCS Carriers | | | | | |
|---|---|---|---|---|---|---|---|---|
| | A Block | B Block | A Block | B Block | C Block | D Block | E Block | F Block |
| Valdosta | GMD Limited | Alltel[C] | Powertel[G] | PrimeCo[C] | Sowega Wireless Comm | Sprint PCS[C] | BellSouth[C] | Mercury PCS II |
| Waycross | U.S. Cellular | Alltel[C] | Powertel[G] | PrimeCo[C] | Savannah Ind. PCS[C] | Sprint PCS[C] | BellSouth[C] | Mercury PCS II |
| **Hawaii** | | | | | | | | |
| Hilo | U.S. Cellular | GTE Wireless[C] | Western Wireless[C] | Sprint PCS[C] | Pocket[C] | AT&T Wireless[T] | Sprint PCS[C] | Magnacom Wireless |
| Honolulu | Honolulu Cellular[T] | GTE Wireless[C] | Western Wireless[C] | Sprint PCS[C] | Pocket[C] | AT&T Wireless[T] | Sprint PCS[C] | Magnacom Wireless |
| Kahului-Wailuku-Lahaina | AT&T Wireless[T] | GTE Wireless[C] | Western Wireless[C] | Sprint PCS[C] | CH PCS | AT&T Wireless[T] | Sprint PCS[C] | Magnacom Wireless |
| Lihue | Ameritech[C] | GTE Wireless[C] | Western Wireless[C] | Sprint PCS[C] | New Wave PCS[C] | AT&T Wireless[T] | Sprint PCS[C] | Magnacom Wireless |
| **Idaho** | | | | | | | | |
| Boise-Nampa | AT&T Wireless[T] | AirTouch[C] | Western Wireless[C] | Sprint PCS[C] | ClearComm[C][C] | AT&T Wireless[T] | U S West[C] | Magnacom Wireless |
| Idaho Falls | U.S. Cellular | Commnet 2000 | Western Wireless[C] | Sprint PCS[C] | High Country | AT&T Wireless[T] | U S West[C] | Valley Wireless |
| Lewiston-Moscow | Blue Mountain | | GTE Wireless[C] | Sprint PCS[C] | ClearComm[C][G] | Touch America | Western Wireless[C] | Magnacom Wireless |
| Pocatello | U.S. Cellular | Commnet 2000 | Western Wireless[C] | Sprint PCS[C] | High Country | U S West[C] | AT&T Wireless[T] | Westel |
| Twin Falls | U.S. Cellular | | Western Wireless[C] | Sprint PCS[C] | High Country | AT&T Wireless[T] | U S West[C] | Westel |
| **Illinois** | | | | | | | | |
| Bloomington | Southwestern Bell[T] | Ameritech[C] | AT&T Wireless[T] | PrimeCo[C] | Pocket[C] | Sprint PCS[C] | McLeod USA | BRK Wireless Co. |
| Carbondale-Marion | Douglas Telecom | GTE Wireless[C] | AT&T Wireless[T] | Sprint PCS[C] | Pocket[C] | AT&T Wireless[T] | Western Wireless[C] | Omnipoint[C] |
| Champaign-Urbana | Southwestern Bell[T] | Ameritech[C] | AT&T Wireless[T] | PrimeCo[C] | Pocket[C] | Sprint PCS[C] | McLeod USA | BRK Wireless Co. |
| Chicago | Southwestern Bell[T] | Ameritech[C] | AT&T Wireless[T] | PrimeCo[C] | Pocket[C] | Sprint PCS[C] | Sprint PCS[C] | Nextwave[C] |
| Danville | Southwestern Bell[T] | Ameritech[C] | AT&T Wireless[T] | PrimeCo[C] | 21st Century Telesis[P] | Sprint PCS[C] | Sprint PCS[C] | Omnipoint[C] |
| Decatur-Effingham | Southwestern Bell[T] | Ameritech[C] | AT&T Wireless[T] | PrimeCo[C] | Pocket[C] | Sprint PCS[C] | McLeod USA | BRK Wireless Co. |
| Galesburg | U.S. Cellular | Alltel[C] | AT&T Wireless[T] | PrimeCo[C] | BRK Wireless Co. | Sprint PCS[C] | Omnipoint[C] | CM-PCS Partners |
| Jacksonville | Southwestern Bell[T] | U.S. Cellular | AT&T Wireless[T] | PrimeCo[C] | Quantum Comm Group[C] | Sprint PCS[C] | Western Wireless[C] | BRK Wireless Co. |
| Kankakee | Southwestern Bell[T] | Ameritech[C] | AT&T Wireless[T] | PrimeCo[C] | Pocket[C] | Sprint PCS[C] | Sprint PCS[C] | Nextwave[C] |
| LaSalle-Peru-Ottawa-Streator | Southwestern Bell[T] | Illinois Valley | AT&T Wireless[T] | PrimeCo[C] | Pocket[C] | Sprint PCS[C] | Sprint PCS[C] | BRK Wireless Co. |

| Market Name | Cellular Carriers — A Block | Cellular Carriers — B Block | PCS Carriers — A Block | PCS Carriers — B Block | PCS Carriers — C Block | PCS Carriers — D Block | PCS Carriers — E Block | PCS Carriers — F Block |
|---|---|---|---|---|---|---|---|---|
| Mattoon | MCMG | Ameritech[C] | AT&T Wireless[T] | PrimeCo[C] | Quantum Comm Group[C] | Sprint PCS[C] | Consolidated Comm | BRK Wireless Co. |
| Moline | U.S. Cellular | GTE Wireless[C] | Western Wireless[C] | Sprint PCS[C] | Aer Force | AT&T Wireless[T] | McLeod USA | Iowa LP 136 |
| Mount Vernon-Centralia | Douglas Telecom | GTE Wireless[C] | AT&T Wireless[T] | Sprint PCS[C] | Pockell[C] | Western Wireless[C] | Omnipoint[C] | Integrated Comm[C] |
| Peoria | U.S. Cellular | Alltel[C] | AT&T Wireless[T] | PrimeCo[C] | R & S PCS | Sprint PCS[C] | McLeod USA | Omnipoint[C] |
| Quincy | Southwestern Bell[T] | U.S. Cellular | AT&T Wireless[T] | Sprint PCS[C] | Roberts-Roberts[C] | Western Wireless[C] | Omnipoint[C] | Polycel[C] |
| Rockford | BellSouth[T] | GTE Wireless[C] | AT&T Wireless[T] | PrimeCo[C] | Pockell[C] | Sprint PCS[C] | McLeod USA | Northcoast OpCo. |
| Springfield | Southwestern Bell[T] | Ameritech[C] | AT&T Wireless[T] | PrimeCo[C] | Pockell[C] | Sprint PCS[C] | McLeod USA | BRK Wireless Co. |
| Sterling | U.S. Cellular | GTE Wireless[C] | Western Wireless[C] | Sprint PCS[C] | Polycel[C] | Western Wireless[C] | McLeod USA | Redwood Wireless |
| **Indiana** | | | | | | | | |
| Anderson | BellSouth[T] | GTE Wireless[C] | Sprint PCS[C] | Ameritech[C] | Comm Venture PC[C] | AT&T Wireless[T] | AT&T Wireless[T] | Omnipoint[C] |
| Bloomington-Bedford | BellSouth[T] | GTE Wireless[C] | Sprint PCS[C] | Ameritech[C] | Nextwave[C] | 21st Century Telesis[P] | Omnipoint[C] | Comm Venture PC[C] |
| Columbus | Alpha Cellular | GTE Wireless[C] | Sprint PCS[C] | Ameritech[C] | Nextwave[C] | AT&T Wireless[T] | Omnipoint[C] | Omnipoint[C] |
| Elkhart | Centennial Cellular[C] | Alltel[C] | AT&T Wireless[T] | PrimeCo[C] | R & S PCS | Sprint PCS[C] | Omnipoint[C] | 21st Century Telesis[P] |
| Evansville | BellSouth[T] | GTE Wireless[C] | AT&T Wireless[T] | Sprint PCS[C] | Nextwave[C] | Powertel[C] | Powertel[C] | Comm Venture PC[C] |
| Fort Wayne | Centennial Cellular[C] | GTE Wireless[C] | AT&T Wireless[T] | PrimeCo[C] | Comm Venture PC[C] | Sprint PCS[C] | Omnipoint[C] | Omnipoint[C] |
| Indianapolis | BellSouth[T] | GTE Wireless[C] | Sprint PCS[C] | Ameritech[C] | Nextwave[C] | AT&T Wireless[T] | AT&T Wireless[T] | 21st Century Telesis[P] |
| Kokomo | BellSouth[T] | GTE Wireless[C] | Sprint PCS[C] | Ameritech[C] | 21st Century Telesis[P] | Omnipoint[C] | Omnipoint[C] | 21st Century Telesis[P] |
| Lafayette | BellSouth[T] | GTE Wireless[C] | Sprint PCS[C] | Ameritech[C] | Nextwave[C] | AT&T Wireless[T] | AT&T Wireless[T] | 21st Century Telesis[P] |
| Logansport | Centennial Cellular[C] | U.S. Cellular | Sprint PCS[C] | Ameritech[C] | 21st Century Telesis[P] | Omnipoint[C] | Omnipoint[C] | 21st Century Telesis[P] |
| Marion | Centennial Cellular[C] | GTE Wireless[C] | Sprint PCS[C] | Ameritech[C] | 21st Century Telesis[P] | AT&T Wireless[T] | Omnipoint[C] | Comm Venture PC[C] |
| Michigan City-LaPorte | Centennial Cellular[C] | Ameritech[C] | AT&T Wireless[T] | PrimeCo[C] | Pockell[C] | Sprint PCS[C] | AT&T Wireless[T] | 21st Century Telesis[P] |
| Muncie | BellSouth[T] | GTE Wireless[C] | Sprint PCS[C] | Ameritech[C] | Comm Venture PC[C] | 21st Century Telesis[P] | AT&T Wireless[T] | Omnipoint[C] |
| Richmond | Centennial Cellular[C] | GTE Wireless[C] | Sprint PCS[C] | Ameritech[C] | Wireless Ventures[C] | AT&T Wireless[T] | AT&T Wireless[T] | Omnipoint[C] |

| Market Name | Cellular Carriers | | PCS Carriers ↑ | | | | | |
|---|---|---|---|---|---|---|---|---|
| | A Block | B Block | A Block | B Block | C Block | D Block | E Block | F Block |
| South Bend-Mishawaka | Centennial Cellular(C) | Alltel(C) | AT&T Wireless(T) | PrimeCo(C) | 21st Century Telesis(P) | Sprint PCS(C) | AT&T Wireless(T) | Omnipoint(C) |
| Terre Haute | BellSouth(T) | GTE Wireless(C) | Sprint PCS(C) | Ameritech(C) | 21st Century Telesis(P) | AT&T Wireless(T) | Omnipoint(C) | Omnipoint(C) |
| Vincennes-Washington | Cellular of Indiana | GTE Wireless(C) | Sprint PCS(C) | Ameritech(C) | 21st Century Telesis(P) | AT&T Wireless(T) | Omnipoint(C) | Omnipoint(C) |
| **Iowa** | | | | | | | | |
| Burlington | Cellular Plus | GTE Wireless(C) | Western Wireless(C) | Sprint PCS(C) | BRK Wireless Co. | Western Wireless(C) | McLeod USA | Polycell(C) |
| Cedar Rapids | U.S. Cellular | Alltel(C) | Western Wireless(C) | Sprint PCS(C) | Airadigm(C) | McLeod USA | McLeod USA | Iowa LP 136 |
| Clinton | Iowa East Cellular | GTE Wireless(C) | Western Wireless(C) | Sprint PCS(C) | Polycell(C) | Western Wireless(C) | McLeod USA | Redwood Wireless |
| Davenport | U.S. Cellular | GTE Wireless(C) | Western Wireless(C) | Sprint PCS(C) | Aer Force | AT&T Wireless(T) | McLeod USA | Iowa LP 136 |
| Des Moines | U.S. Cellular | AirTouch(C) | Western Wireless(C) | Sprint PCS(C) | Aer Force | McLeod USA | AT&T Wireless(T) | Omnipoint(C) |
| Dubuque | U.S. Cellular | Alltel(C) | Western Wireless(C) | Sprint PCS(C) | Aer Force | McLeod USA | Century Tel(T) | Airadigm(C) |
| Fort Dodge | U.S. Cellular | AirTouch(C) | Western Wireless(C) | Sprint PCS(C) | BRK Wireless Co. | AT&T Wireless(T) | McLeod USA | Redwood Wireless |
| Iowa City | U.S. Cellular | Alltel(C) | Western Wireless(C) | Sprint PCS(C) | Aer Force | McLeod USA | McLeod USA | Iowa LP 136 |
| Marshalltown | Cellular Plus | AirTouch(C) | Western Wireless(C) | Sprint PCS(C) | BRK Wireless Co. | Western Wireless(C) | McLeod USA | Redwood Wireless |
| Mason City | U.S. Cellular | CommNet 2000 | Western Wireless(C) | Sprint PCS(C) | BRK Wireless Co. | Western Wireless(C) | McLeod USA | Redwood Wireless |
| Ottumwa | U.S. Cellular | U.S. Cellular | Western Wireless(C) | Sprint PCS(C) | BRK Wireless Co. | RLV-PCS I Ptshp(C) | McLeod USA | Redwood Wireless |
| Sioux City | Western Wireless | CommNet 2000 | Western Wireless(C) | Sprint PCS(C) | Polycell(C) | McLeod USA | U S West(C) | NE Nebraska TelCo. |
| Waterloo-Cedar Falls | U.S. Cellular | Alltel(C) | Western Wireless(C) | Sprint PCS(C) | Airadigm(C) | McLeod USA | AT&T Wireless(T) | Redwood Wireless |
| **Kansas** | | | | | | | | |
| Coffeyville | Kansas Cellular | U.S. Cellular | Southwestern Bell(T) | Sprint PCS(C) | Western Wireless(C) | Western Wireless(C) | AT&T Wireless(T) | Mercury Mobility |
| Dodge City | Miscellco Comm | Kansas Cellular | AT&T Wireless(T) | Sprint PCS(C) | Cellutech | Pioneer Tel | Pioneer Tel | Global Info Tech |
| Emporia | Western Wireless | Kansas Cellular | Sprint PCS(C) | Aerial(C) | Kansas PCS(C) | Mercury Mobility | AT&T Wireless(T) | Cellutech |
| Garden City | Mercury Cellular | Kansas Cellular | AT&T Wireless(T) | Sprint PCS(C) | TWS | Pioneer Tel | Pioneer Tel | Global Info Tech |
| Great Bend | Miscellco Comm | Kansas Cellular | AT&T Wireless(T) | Sprint PCS(C) | FAMS & Associates | Pioneer Tel | Pioneer Tel | Global Info Tech |

| Market Name | Cellular Carriers A Block | Cellular Carriers B Block | PCS Carriers A Block | PCS Carriers B Block | PCS Carriers C Block | PCS Carriers D Block | PCS Carriers E Block | PCS Carriers F Block |
|---|---|---|---|---|---|---|---|---|
| Hays | Miscellco Comm | Kansas Cellular | AT&T Wireless[T] | Sprint PCS[C] | Mountain Solutions[C] | Pioneer Tel | Pioneer Tel | Global Info Tech |
| Hutchinson | Western Wireless | Kansas Cellular | AT&T Wireless[T] | Sprint PCS[C] | Kansas PCS[C] | Western Wireless[C] | Omnipoint[C] | Mercury Mobility |
| Lawrence | AT&T Wireless[T] | Southwestern Bell[T] | Sprint PCS[C] | Aerial[C] | Mountain Solutions[C] | AT&T Wireless[T] | Allte[C] | DCC PCS[C] |
| Liberal | Mercury Cellular | | AT&T Wireless[T] | Sprint PCS[C] | Global Info Tech | Panhandle Telecom | Panhandle Telecom | Triad Cellular |
| Manhattan-Junction City | Western Wireless | Kansas Cellular | Sprint PCS[C] | Aerial[C] | Mountain Solutions[C] | Western Wireless[C] | Mercury Mobility | DCC PCS[C] |
| Pittsburg-Parsons | Kansas Cellular | U.S. Cellular | Sprint PCS[C] | Aerial[C] | Pocket[C] | AT&T Wireless[T] | Southwestern Bell[T] | Western Wireless[C] |
| Salina | Western Wireless | Kansas Cellular | AT&T Wireless[T] | Sprint PCS[C] | Aer Force | Western Wireless[C] | Omnipoint[C] | Mercury Mobility |
| Topeka | AT&T Wireless[T] | Southwestern Bell[T] | Sprint PCS[C] | Aerial[C] | Kansas PCS[C] | Mercury Mobility | AT&T Wireless[T] | DCC PCS[C] |
| Wichita | AT&T Wireless[T] | Southwestern Bell[T] | AT&T Wireless[T] | Sprint PCS[C] | Omnipoint[C] | Western Wireless[C] | Mercury Mobility | Omnipoint[C] |
| **Kentucky** | | | | | | | | |
| Ashland | AT&T Wireless[T] | | AT&T Wireless[T] | GTE Wireless[T] | Horizon Personal Comm[C] | Sprint PCS[C] | Sprint PCS[C] | Northcoast OpCo. |
| Bowling Green | BellSouth[T] | Bluegrass Cellular | AT&T Wireless[T] | Sprint PCS[C] | SouthEast Telephone[G] | Powertel[G] | Powertel[G] | Mercury PCS II |
| Corbin | U.S. Cellular | GTE Wireless[C] | AT&T Wireless[T] | Sprint PCS[C] | Third Kentucky Cell[G] | Powertel[G] | Powertel[G] | Third Kentucky Cell[G] |
| Glasgow | American Cellular | Bluegrass Cellular | AT&T Wireless[T] | Sprint PCS[C] | SouthEast Telephone[G] | Powertel[G] | Powertel[G] | Mercury PCS II |
| Hopkinsville | GTE Wireless[C] | BellSouth[T] | AT&T Wireless[T] | Sprint PCS[C] | Chase Telecomm[G] | Powertel[G] | Powertel[G] | Tennessee LP 121 |
| Lexington | GTE Wireless[C] | BellSouth[T] | AT&T Wireless[T] | Sprint PCS[C] | Nextwave[C] | Powertel[G] | Powertel[G] | Northcoast OpCo. |
| Louisville | GTE Wireless[C] | BellSouth[T] | AT&T Wireless[T] | Sprint PCS[C] | Nextwave[C] | Powertel[G] | Powertel[G] | Mercury PCS II |
| Madisonville | BellSouth[T] | GTE Wireless[C] | AT&T Wireless[T] | Sprint PCS[C] | SouthEast Telephone[G] | Sprint PCS[C] | Sprint PCS[C] | Troup EMC Comm |
| Middlesboro-Harlan | BellSouth[T] | | AT&T Wireless[T] | BellSouth[C] | Chase Telecomm[G] | Powertel[G] | Powertel[G] | Third Kentucky Cell[G] |
| Murray-Mayfield | BellSouth[T] | GTE Wireless[C] | AT&T Wireless[T] | Sprint PCS[C] | SouthEast Telephone[G] | Powertel[G] | Powertel[G] | Troup EMC Comm |
| Owensboro | BellSouth[T] | GTE Wireless[C] | AT&T Wireless[T] | Sprint PCS[C] | SouthEast Telephone[G] | Powertel[G] | Powertel[G] | Troup EMC Comm |
| Paducah | U.S. Cellular | GTE Wireless[C] | AT&T Wireless[T] | Sprint PCS[C] | SouthEast Telephone[G] | Powertel[G] | Powertel[G] | Troup EMC Comm |
| Pikeville | BellSouth[T] | Appalachian Cellular | AT&T Wireless[T] | GTE Wireless[C] | SouthEast Telephone[G] | Sprint PCS[C] | Sprint PCS[C] | |
| Somerset | American Cellular | Cellular Phone of KY | AT&T Wireless[T] | Sprint PCS[C] | SouthEast Telephone[G] | Powertel[G] | Powertel[G] | Third Kentucky Cell[G] |

| Market Name | Cellular Carriers A Block | Cellular Carriers B Block | PCS Carriers A Block | PCS B Block | PCS C Block | PCS D Block | PCS E Block | PCS F Block |
|---|---|---|---|---|---|---|---|---|
| **Louisiana** | | | | | | | | |
| Alexandria | Centennial Cellular[C] | Century Tel[T] | Sprint PCS[G][C] | PrimeCo[C] | Wireless 2000[C] | AT&T Wireless[T] | BellSouth[C] | Mercury Mobility |
| Baton Rouge | C-1 Baton Rouge | BellSouth[T] | Meretel | AT&T Wireless[T] | AT&T Wireless[T] | Mercury PCS II | | Mercury PCS II |
| Hammond | Radiofone | BellSouth[T] | Sprint PCS[C] | PrimeCo[C] | Meretel | AT&T Wireless[T] | Radiofone PCS | Mercury PCS II |
| Houma-Thibodaux | Radiofone | Mobile Tel | Sprint PCS[C] | PrimeCo[C] | Pocket[C] | SJI Inc. | BellSouth[C] | Mercury PCS II |
| Lafayette | AT&T Wireless[T] | BellSouth[T] | Sprint PCS[C] | PrimeCo[C] | Meretel | AT&T Wireless[C] | AT&T Wireless[T] | Mercury Mobility |
| Lake Charles | Lake Charles Cellular | Cameron Comm | Aerial[C] | PrimeCo[C] | Wireless 2000[C] | Sprint PCS[C] | BellSouth[C] | Mercury Mobility |
| Monroe | AT&T Wireless[T] | Century Tel[T] | PrimeCo[C] | Sprint PCS[C] | Wireless 2000[C] | BellSouth[C] | BellSouth[C] | Mercury PCS II |
| New Iberia | Centennial Cellular[C] | BellSouth[T] | Sprint PCS[C] | PrimeCo[C] | Meretel | AT&T Wireless[T] | AT&T Wireless[T] | Telecorp Holding |
| New Orleans | Radiofone | BellSouth[T] | Sprint PCS[C] | PrimeCo[C] | Pocket[C] | AT&T Wireless[T] | AT&T Wireless[T] | Mercury Mobility |
| Shreveport | AT&T Wireless[T] | Century Tel[T] | PrimeCo[C] | Sprint PCS[C] | Pocket[C] | BellSouth[C] | AT&T Wireless[T] | |
| **Maine** | | | | | | | | |
| Bangor | U.S. Cellular | UNICEL | AT&T Wireless[T] | Sprint PCS[C] | Personal Comm Ntwk[C] | Mid-Maine Wireless | Omnipoint[C] | Northcoast OpCo. |
| Lewiston-Auburn | U.S. Cellular | Maine Cellular | AT&T Wireless[T] | Sprint PCS[C] | Personal Comm Ntwk[C] | Mid-Maine Wireless | Omnipoint[C] | Northcoast OpCo. |
| Portland-Brunswick | Alltel[C] | Maine Cellular | AT&T Wireless[T] | Sprint PCS[C] | Nextwave[C] | Omnipoint[C] | Northcoast OpCo. | NH Wireless |
| Presque Isle | U.S. Cellular | UNICEL | AT&T Wireless[T] | Sprint PCS[C] | Quantum Comm Group[C] | Omnipoint[C] | Omnipoint[C] | Omnipoint[C] |
| Waterville-Augusta | U.S. Cellular | UNICEL | AT&T Wireless[T] | Sprint PCS[C] | Personal Comm Ntwk[C] | ACC-PCS | Omnipoint[C] | Northcoast OpCo. |
| **Maryland** | | | | | | | | |
| Baltimore | Southwestern Bell[C] | Bell Atlantic[C] | Sprint PCS[G][C] | AT&T Wireless[T] | Nextwave[C] | Rivgam | Rivgam | Omnipoint[C] |
| Cumberland | Dobson Cellular | GenCell Mngmt | Sprint PCS[G][C] | AT&T Wireless[T] | Aer Force | Virginia PCS[C] | Omnipoint[C] | Polycel[C] |
| Hagerstown | Dobson Cellular | Atlantic Cellular | Sprint PCS[G][C] | AT&T Wireless[T] | Nextwave[C] | Omnipoint[C] | Virginia PCS[C] | Virginia PCS[C] |
| Salisbury | Southwestern Bell[T] | Bell Atlantic[C] | Sprint PCS[G][C] | AT&T Wireless[T] | Aer Force, | Omnipoint[C] | Omnipoint[C] | Nextwave[C] |
| **Massachusetts** | | | | | | | | |
| Boston | Southwestern Bell[C] | Bell Atlantic[C] | AT&T Wireless[T] | Sprint PCS[C] | Nextwave[C] | Omnipoint[C] | Omnipoint[C] | Northcoast OpCo. |
| Hyannis | Southwestern Bell[C] | Bell Atlantic[C] | AT&T Wireless[T] | Sprint PCS[C] | Alpine PCS[C] | Omnipoint[C] | Northcoast OpCo. | Alpine PCS[C] |
| New Bedford | SNET[T] | Bell Atlantic[C] | AT&T Wireless[T] | Sprint PCS[C] | Nextwave[C] | ACC-PCS | Northcoast OpCo. | Omnipoint[C] |

| Market Name | Cellular Carriers | | PCS Carriers | | | | | |
|---|---|---|---|---|---|---|---|---|
| | A Block | B Block | A Block | B Block | C Block | D Block | E Block | F Block |
| Pittsfield | Bell Atlantic© | SNET[T] | AT&T Wireless[T] | Sprint PCS© | Omnipoint© | Nextwave© | ACC-PCS | Northcoast OpCo. |
| Springfield-Holyoke | Bell Atlantic© | SNET[T] | AT&T Wireless[T] | Sprint PCS© | Omnipoint© | ACC-PCS | Nextwave© | Northcoast OpCo. |
| Worcester-Fitchburg-Leominster | Southwestern Bell[T] | Bell Atlantic© | AT&T Wireless[T] | Sprint PCS© | Nextwave© | Omnipoint© | ACC-PCS | Northcoast OpCo. |
| **Michigan** | | | | | | | | |
| Adrian | | | AT&T Wireless[T] | Sprint PCS© | Pocket© | Century Tel© | Omnipoint© | Omnipoint© |
| Alpena | RFB Cellular | U.S. Cellular | AT&T Wireless[T] | Sprint PCS© | Northern Michigan PCS© | AT&T Wireless[T] | Lite-Wave | Alpine PCS© |
| Battle Creek | Centennial Cellular© | Century Tel[T] | AT&T Wireless[T] | Sprint PCS© | Pocket© | Century Tel[T] | Message Express Co. | Omnipoint© |
| Benton Harbor | Centennial Cellular© | Century Tel[T] | AT&T Wireless[T] | PrimeCo© | R & S PCS | Sprint PCS© | AT&T Wireless[T] | Omnipoint© |
| Detroit | AirTouch© | Ameritech© | AT&T Wireless[T] | Sprint PCS© | Pocket© | Nextwave© | Omnipoint© | Omnipoint© |
| Escanaba | Mackinac Cellular | AirTouch© | Sprint PCS© | PrimeCo© | Northern Michigan PCS© | AT&T Wireless[T] | Century Tel[T] | Alpine PCS© |
| Flint | AirTouch© | Ameritech© | AT&T Wireless[T] | Sprint PCS© | Pocket© | Century Tel[T] | Omnipoint© | Omnipoint© |
| Grand Rapids | AirTouch© | Century Tel[T] | AT&T Wireless[T] | Sprint PCS© | Pocket© | Century Tel[T] | Omnipoint© | Omnipoint© |
| Houghton | Buckhead Telephone | AirTouch© | Sprint PCS© | PrimeCo© | Northern Michigan PCS© | AT&T Wireless[T] | Century Tel[T] | Eldorado Comm© |
| Iron Mountain | Buckhead Telephone | AirTouch© | Sprint PCS© | PrimeCo© | Northern Michigan PCS© | AT&T Wireless[T] | Century Tel[T] | Metro Southwest PCS |
| Ironwood | | | Sprint PCS© | Aerial© | Northern Michigan PCS© | Century Tel[T] | Century Tel[T] | Metro Southwest PCS |
| Jackson | Centennial Cellular© | Century Tel[T] | AT&T Wireless[T] | Sprint PCS© | Pocket© | Century Tel[T] | Omnipoint© | Omnipoint© |
| Kalamazoo | Centennial Cellular© | Century Tel[T] | AT&T Wireless[T] | Sprint PCS© | Anishnabe Comm | Century Tel[T] | Message Express | Northcoast OpCo. |
| Lansing | AirTouch© | Century Tel[T] | AT&T Wireless[T] | PrimeCo© | Northern Michigan PCS© | Century Tel[T] | Century Tel[T] | Omnipoint© |
| Marquette | American Cellular | AirTouch© | Sprint PCS© | PrimeCo© | Fortunet Wireless | AT&T Wireless[T] | Century Tel[T] | VTel Wireless |
| Menominee | Buckhead Telephone | AirTouch© | Sprint PCS© | PrimeCo© | Northern Michigan PCS© | AT&T Wireless[T] | Century Tel[T] | Airadigm© |
| Mount Pleasant | Sterling Cellular | Century Tel[T] | AT&T Wireless[T] | Sprint PCS© | Anishnabe Comm | Century Tel[T] | Omnipoint© | Lite-Wave |
| Muskegon | AirTouch© | Century Tel[T] | AT&T Wireless[T] | Sprint PCS© | Pocket© | Century Tel[T] | Omnipoint© | Lite-Wave |
| Petoskey | Unitel | | AT&T Wireless[T] | Sprint PCS© | Noverr Publishing© | ACC-PCS | Lite-Wave | Alpine PCS© |
| Saginaw-Bay City | AirTouch© | Century Tel[T] | AT&T Wireless[T] | Sprint PCS© | Anishnabe Comm | Century Tel[T] | Omnipoint© | Alpine PCS© |
| Sault Ste. Marie | Mackinac Cellular | AirTouch© | AT&T Wireless[T] | Sprint PCS© | Northern Michigan PCS© | Century Tel[T] | Century Tel[T] | Alpine PCS© |
| Traverse City | Unitel | Century Tel[T] | AT&T Wireless[T] | Sprint PCS© | Noverr Publishing© | Century Tel[T] | Alpine PCS© | Lite-Wave |

| Market Name | Cellular Carriers | | PCS Carriers | | | | | |
| --- | --- | --- | --- | --- | --- | --- | --- | --- |
| | A Block | B Block | A Block | B Block | C Block | D Block | E Block | F Block |
| **Minnesota** | | | | | | | | |
| Bemidji | American Cellular | Rural Cellular | Sprint PCS[C] | Aerial[C] | Integrated Comm[C] | Western Wireless[C] | Century Tel[T] | Minnesota PCS |
| Brainerd | American Cellular | Rural Cellular | Sprint PCS[C] | Aerial[C] | Western Minnesota[C] | Minnesota PCS | Century Tel[T] | Redwood Wireless |
| Duluth | American Cellular | AirTouch[C] | Sprint PCS[C] | Aerial[C] | RLV-PCS I Ptshp[C] | AT&T Wireless[T] | Century Tel[T] | Minnesota PCS |
| Fairmont | Western Wireless | AirTouch[C] | Sprint PCS[C] | Aerial[C] | Fortunet Wireless | AT&T Wireless[T] | McLeod USA | Minnesota PCS |
| Fergus Falls | American Cellular | Rural Cellular | Sprint PCS[C] | Aerial[C] | Western Minnesota[C] | AT&T Wireless[T] | Touch America | Minnesota PCS |
| Mankato | American Cellular | AirTouch[C] | Sprint PCS[C] | Aerial[C] | Fortunet Wireless | AT&T Wireless[T] | McLeod USA | Minnesota PCS |
| Marshall | Western Wireless | AirTouch[C] | Sprint PCS[C] | Aerial[C] | Southwest Minnesota PCS | U S West[C] | Triad Cellular | Redwood Wireless |
| Minneapolis-St. Paul | AT&T Wireless[T] | AirTouch[C] | Sprint PCS[C] | Aerial[C] | Nextwave[C] | U S West[C] | AT&T Wireless[T] | Northcoast OpCo. |
| Rochester-Austin-Albert Lea | AT&T Wireless[T] | U.S. Cellular | Sprint PCS[C] | Aerial[C] | Fortunet Wireless | U S West[C] | McLeod USA | Minnesota PCS |
| St. Cloud | AT&T Wireless[T] | U.S. Cellular | Sprint PCS[C] | Aerial[C] | Redwood Wireless | AT&T Wireless[T] | U S West[C] | Wireless Comm[C] |
| Willmar | Western Wireless | AirTouch[C] | Sprint PCS[C] | Aerial[C] | Southwest Minnesota PCS | U S West[C] | Triad Cellular | Redwood Wireless |
| Winona | Cooper Cellular | AirTouch[C] | Sprint PCS[C] | PrimeCo[C] | Airadigm[C] | Century Tel[T] | PC PCS | Minnesota PCS |
| Worthington | Western Wireless | AirTouch[C] | Sprint PCS[C] | Aerial[C] | Western Wireless[C] | Triad Cellular | McLeod USA | Minnesota PCS |
| **Mississippi** | | | | | | | | |
| Biloxi-Gulfport-Pascagoula | Century Tel[T] | Mississippi Cellular | Sprint PCS[C] | PrimeCo[C] | Mobile Tri-States[C] | BellSouth[C] | Alltel[C] | Mercury PCS II |
| Columbus-Starkville | Century Tel[T] | Cellular South | Powertel[C] | Southwestern Bell[T] | Mobile Tri-States[C] | Sprint PCS[C] | BellSouth[C] | Mercury Mobility |
| Greenville-Greenwood | | Cellular South | Powertel[C] | Southwestern Bell[T] | MCG PCS | Sprint PCS[C] | BellSouth[C] | PCSouth |
| Hattiesburg | Cellular XL | Cellular South | Sprint PCS[C] | PrimeCo[C] | Mobile Tri-States[C] | Radiofone PCS | BellSouth[C] | Mercury PCS II |
| Jackson | Century Tel[T] | Alltel[C] | Powertel[C] | Southwestern Bell[T] | 21st Century Telesis[P] | Sprint PCS[C] | Bay Springs TelCo. | PCSouth |
| Laurel | Cellular XL | Cellular South | Sprint PCS[C] | PrimeCo[C] | Mobile Tri-States[C] | AT&T Wireless[T] | Mercury PCS II | Pine Belt PCS[C] |
| McComb-Brookhaven | Mississippi Cellular | Mississippi Cellular | Sprint PCS[C] | PrimeCo[C] | Reserve Telephone Co. | Alltel[C] | BellSouth[C] | Mercury PCS II |
| Meridian | Century Tel[T] | Alltel[C] | Powertel[C] | Southwestern Bell[T] | Mobile Tri-States[C] | Bay Springs TelCo. | Sprint PCS[C] | PCSouth |

| Market Name | Cellular Carriers A Block | Cellular Carriers B Block | PCS Carriers A Block | PCS Carriers B Block | PCS Carriers C Block | PCS Carriers D Block | PCS Carriers E Block | PCS Carriers F Block |
|---|---|---|---|---|---|---|---|---|
| Natchez | Mississippi Cellular | Cellular South | Powertel[C] | Southwestern Bell[T] | Reserve Telephone Co. | Sprint PCS | BellSouth[C] | Mercury Mobility |
| Tupelo-Corinth | Century Tel[T] | BellSouth[T] | Powertel[C] | Southwestern Bell[T] | Eldorado Comm[C] | Sprint PCS | PCSouth | Mercury Mobility |
| Vicksburg | Century tel[T] | Alltel[C] | Powertel[C] | Southwestern Bell[T] | PCSouth | Sprint PCS[C] | Century Tel[T] | Pinnacle Telecom |
| **Missouri** | | | | | | | | |
| Cape Girardeau-Sikeston | Ameritech[C] | Southwestern Bell[T] | AT&T Wireless[T] | Sprint PCS[C] | Roberts-Roberts[C] | AT&T Wireless[T] | Western Wireless[C] | Omnipoint[C] |
| Columbia | Ameritech[C] | U.S. Cellular | AT&T Wireless[T] | Sprint PCS[C] | Pocket[C] | Omnipoint[C] | Western Wireless[C] | Roberts-Roberts[C] |
| Hannibal | Ameritech[C] | U.S. Cellular | AT&T Wireless[T] | Sprint PCS[C] | Roberts-Roberts[C] | Western Wireless[C] | Omnipoint[C] | Polycell[C] |
| Jefferson City | Ameritech[C] | Southwestern Bell[T] | AT&T Wireless[T] | Sprint PCS[C] | Roberts-Roberts[C] | Western Wireless[C] | Alltel[C] | Omnipoint[C] |
| Joplin | AT&T Wireless[T] | U.S. Cellular | AT&T Wireless[T] | Aerial[C] | Nextwave[C] | Southwestern Bell[T] | Alltel[C] | DCC PCS[C] |
| Kansas City | CMT Partners[T] | Southwestern Bell[T] | Sprint PCS[C] | Sprint PCS[C] | Nextwave[C] | Southwestern Bell[T] | AT&T Wireless[T] | DCC PCS[C] |
| Kirksville | U.S. Cellular | U.S. Cellular | AT&T Wireless[T] | Sprint PCS[C] | R.F.W. Inc. | Omnipoint[C] | Western Wireless[C] | RLV-PCS I Ptshp[C] |
| Poplar Bluff | Ameritech[C] | Alltel[C] | AT&T Wireless[T] | Aerial[C] | Pocket[C] | Western Wireless[C] | Alltel[C] | Omnipoint[C] |
| Rolla | Ameritech[C] | Alltel[C] | Sprint PCS[C] | Sprint PCS[C] | Roberts-Roberts[C] | Western Wireless[C] | Alltel[C] | Omnipoint[C] |
| Sedalia | Ameritech[C] | Southwestern Bell[T] | AT&T Wireless[T] | Aerial[C] | Roberts-Roberts[C] | AT&T Wireless[T] | Alltel[C] | Integrated Comm[C] |
| Springfield | AT&T Wireless[T] | Mid-Missouri Cellular | Sprint PCS[C] | Sprint PCS[C] | Nextwave[C] | Southwestern Bell[T] | Alltel[C] | Omnipoint[C] |
| St. Joseph | AT&T Wireless[T] | Alltel[C] | Sprint PCS[C] | Sprint PCS[C] | RLV-PCS I Ptshp[C] | AT&T Wireless[T] | Triad Cellular | DCC PCS[C] |
| St. Louis | Ameritech[C] | Southwestern Bell[T] | AT&T Wireless[T] | Sprint PCS[C] | Pocket[C] | Omnipoint[C] | Western Wireless[C] | Nextwave[C] |
| West Plains | U.S. Cellular | Alltel[C] | AT&T Wireless[T] | Sprint PCS[C] | Roberts-Roberts[C] | Western Wireless[C] | Alltel[C] | Omnipoint[C] |
| **Montana** | | | | | | | | |
| Billings | Western Wireless | CommNet 2000 | GTE Wireless[C] | Sprint PCS[C] | Polycell[C] | Touch America | Western Wireless[C] | Montana PCS |
| Bozeman | Western Wireless | CommNet 2000 | GTE Wireless[C] | Sprint PCS[C] | Mountain Solutions[C] | Touch America | Western Wireless[C] | Montana PCS |
| Butte | Western Wireless | CommNet 2000 | GTE Wireless[C] | Sprint PCS[C] | MCG PCS | Western Wireless[C] | Touch America | Montana PCS |
| Great Falls | Western Wireless | CommNet 2000 | GTE Wireless[C] | Sprint PCS[C] | MCG PCS | Touch America | Western Wireless[C] | Montana PCS |
| Helena | Western Wireless | CommNet 2000 | GTE Wireless[C] | Sprint PCS[C] | Mountain Solutions[C] | Western Wireless[C] | Touch America | Montana PCS |

| Market Name | Cellular Carriers A Block | Cellular Carriers B Block | PCS Carriers A Block | PCS Carriers B Block | PCS Carriers C Block | PCS Carriers D Block | PCS Carriers E Block | PCS Carriers F Block |
|---|---|---|---|---|---|---|---|---|
| Kalispell | Western Wireless | Cellulink/Pactel | GTE Wireless[C] | Sprint PCS[C] | Mountain Solutions[C] | Western Wireless[C] | Century Tel[T] | Montana PCS |
| Missoula | Western Wireless | CommNet 2000 | GTE Wireless[C] | Sprint PCS[C] | USA Micro-Cellular | Western Wireless[C] | Touch America | Montana PCS |
| **Nebraska** | | | | | | | | |
| Grand Island-Kearney | Western Wireless | Nebraska Cellular | AT&T Wireless[T] | Sprint PCS[C] | 21st Century Telesis[P] | U S West[C] | Western Wireless[C] | Wireless II[C] |
| Hastings | Western Wireless | Nebraska Cellular | AT&T Wireless[T] | Sprint PCS[C] | USA Micro-Cellular | U S West[C] | Western Wireless[C] | 21st Century Telesis[P] |
| Lincoln | Western Wireless | Lincoln Telephone | AT&T Wireless[T] | Sprint PCS[C] | 21st Century Telesis[P] | U S West[C] | Western Wireless[C] | Polycel[C] |
| McCook | Western Wireless | Nebraska Cellular | AT&T Wireless[T] | Sprint PCS[C] | 21st Century Telesis[P] | Cambridge TelCo. | Western Wireless[C] | Tracy Corp. II |
| Norfolk | Western Wireless | Nebraska Cellular | AT&T Wireless[T] | Sprint PCS[C] | USA Micro-Cellular | Wireless II[C] | Western Wireless[C] | NE Nebraska TelCo. |
| North Platte | Western Wireless | Lincoln Telephone | AT&T Wireless[T] | Sprint PCS[C] | 21st Century Telesis[P] | U S West[C] | Western Wireless[C] | Montana PCS |
| Omaha | AirTouch[C] | Lincoln Telephone | AT&T Wireless[T] | Sprint PCS[C] | Pocket[C] | U S West[C] | McLeod USA | CM-PCS Partners |
| Scottsbluff | Gala | Nebraska Cellular | Sprint PCS[C] | Western Wireless[C] | Wireless Telecom[C] | U S West[C] | AT&T Wireless[T] | Tracy Corp. II |
| **Nevada** | | | | | | | | |
| Las Vegas | AT&T Wireless[T] | Alltel[C] | Sprint PCS[C] | PacBell Mobile[C] | Pocket[C] | AT&T Wireless[T] | Rivgam | Nextwave[C] |
| Reno | AT&T Wireless[T] | AirTouch[C] | Sprint PCS[C] | PacBell Mobile[C] | Clear-Comm | AT&T Wireless[T] | Rivgam | Aer Force |
| **New Hampshire** | | | | | | | | |
| Keene | Rural Cellular | U.S. Cellular | AT&T Wireless[T] | Sprint PCS[C] | New England Wireless | Omnipoint[C] | Omnipoint[C] | Devon Mobile[C] |
| Lebanon-Claremont | Rural Cellular | U.S. Cellular | AT&T Wireless[T] | Sprint PCS[C] | Omnipoint[C] | VTel Wireless | GST Wireless Comm | Devon Mobile[C] |
| Manchester-Nashua- | U.S. Cellular | GTE Wireless[C] | AT&T Wireless[T] | Sprint PCS[C] | Nextwave[C] | Omnipoint[C] | ACC-PCS | New Hampshire |
| Concord | Southwestern Bell[T] | GTE Wireless[C] | AT&T Wireless[T] | Sprint PCS[C] | Nextwave[C] | Omnipoint[C] | ACC-PCS | New Hampshire |
| **New Jersey** | | | | | | | | |
| Atlantic City | Comcast[C] | Bell Atlantic[C] | AT&T Wireless[T] | Sprint PCS[C] | Omnipoint[C] | Rivgam | Comcast PCS | Nextwave[C] |
| Trenton | Comcast[C] | Bell Atlantic[C] | AT&T Wireless[T] | Sprint PCS[C] | Omnipoint[C] | Comcast PCS | Rivgam | Nextwave[C] |
| **New Mexico** | | | | | | | | |
| Albuquerque | Bell Atlantic[C] | AirTouch[C] | Western Wireless[C] | AT&T Wireless[T] | Magnacom Wireless | Sprint PCS[C] | U S West[C] | Poka Lambro[C] |

| Market Name | Cellular Carriers | | PCS Carriers → | | | | | |
|---|---|---|---|---|---|---|---|---|
| | A Block | B Block | A Block | B Block | C Block | D Block | E Block | F Block |
| Carlsbad | Western Wireless | Cellular Three | Western Wireless[C] | AT&T Wireless[T] | High Country | Sprint PCS[C] | PVT Wireless[C] | PVT Wireless[C] |
| Clovis | | Cellular Three | PrimeCo[C] | Sprint PCS | Poka Lambro[C] | Triad Cellular | Western Wireless[C] | Mercury PCS II |
| Farmington | Alltel[C] | Century Tel[T] | Western Wireless[C] | AT&T Wireless[T] | PCS Plus | Sprint PCS[C] | Triad Cellular | Lite-Wave |
| Gallup | | | Western Wireless[C] | AT&T Wireless[T] | PCS Plus | Sprint PCS[C] | U S West[C] | Poka Lambro[C] |
| Hobbs | Western Wireless | Cellular Three | PrimeCo[C] | Sprint PCS[C] | Poka Lambro[C] | Western Wireless[C] | Mercury PCS II | Poka Lambro[C] |
| Las Cruces | Bell Atlantic[C] | GTE Wireless[C] | Western Wireless[C] | AT&T Wireless[T] | Nextwave[C] | Sprint PCS[C] | Rivgam | Poka Lambro[C] |
| Roswell | Western Wireless | Cellular Three | Western Wireless[C] | AT&T Wireless[T] | PVT Wireless[C] | Sprint PCS[C] | U S West[C] | Central Wireless |
| Santa Fe | Alltel[C] | AirTouch[C] | Western Wireless[C] | AT&T Wireless[T] | Magnacom Wireless | Sprint PCS[C] | U S West[C] | Poka Lambro[C] |
| **New York** | | | | | | | | |
| Albany-Schenectady | Albany Telephone | Bell Atlantic[C] | Omnipoint[C] | Sprint PCS[C] | Nextwave[C] | AT&T Wireless[T] | ACC-PCS | VTel Wireless |
| Binghamton | AT&T Wireless[T] | GTE Wireless[C] | Omnipoint[C] | Sprint PCS[C] | 21st Century Telesis[P] | AT&T Wireless[T] | AT&T Wireless[T] | Northcoast OpCo. |
| Buffalo-Niagara Falls | Buffalo Telephone | Bell Atlantic[C] | Sprint PCS[C] | AT&T Wireless[T] | Omnipoint[C] | Rivgam | | PCSouth |
| Corning-Hornell | Sygnet Comm | GTE Wireless[C] | Omnipoint[C] | Sprint PCS[C] | Personal Comm Ntwk[C] | AT&T Wireless[T] | AT&T Wireless[T] | Devon Mobile[C] |
| Elmira | AT&T Wireless[T] | GTE Wireless[C] | Omnipoint[C] | Sprint PCS[C] | Personal Comm Ntwk[C] | AT&T Wireless[T] | AT&T Wireless[T] | Devon Mobile[C] |
| Glens Falls | Albany Telephone | Bell Atlantic[C] | Omnipoint[C] | Sprint PCS[C] | Wireless Ventures[C] | AT&T Wireless[T] | ACC-PCS | 21st Century Telesis[P] |
| Ithaca | C-1 of Ithaca | | Omnipoint[C] | Sprint PCS[C] | 21st Century Telesis[P] | Harvey Leong | AT&T Wireless[T] | Devon Mobile[C] |
| Jamestown-Dunkirk | Sygnet Comm | Rochester Tel | Sprint PCS[C] | AT&T Wireless[T] | New England Wireless | AT&T Wireless[T] | Omnipoint[C] | Devon Mobile[C] |
| New York | AT&T Wireless[T] | Bell Atlantic[C] | Omnipoint[C] | Sprint PCS[C] | Nextwave[C] | Omnipoint[C] | AT&T Wireless[T] | Northcoast OpCo. |
| Olean | Sygnet Comm | Rochester Tel | Sprint PCS[C] | AT&T Wireless[T] | New England Wireless | Omnipoint[C] | Omnipoint[C] | Devon Mobile[C] |
| Oneonta | American Cellular | Bell Atlantic[C] | Omnipoint[C] | Sprint PCS[C] | 21st Century Telesis[P] | AT&T Wireless[T] | AT&T Wireless[T] | Delaware PCS |
| Plattsburgh | Rural Cellular | GTE Wireless[C] | Omnipoint[C] | Sprint PCS[C] | Wireless Ventures[C] | AT&T Wireless[T] | AT&T Wireless[T] | 21st Century Telesis[P] |
| Poughkeepsie-Kingston | American Cellular | Bell Atlantic[C] | Omnipoint[C] | Sprint PCS[C] | Nextwave[C] | AT&T Wireless[T] | AT&T Wireless[T] | Northcoast OpCo. |
| Rochester | Genessee Tel | Rochester Tel | Sprint PCS[C] | AT&T Wireless[C] | Omnipoint[C] | Omnipoint[C] | AT&T Wireless[T] | Northcoast OpCo. |
| Syracuse | C-1 of Syracuse | Bell Atlantic[C] | Omnipoint[C] | Sprint PCS[C] | 21st Century Telesis[P] | AT&T Wireless[T] | AT&T Wireless[T] | Northcoast OpCo. |
| Utica-Rome | C-1 of Syracuse | Rochester Tel | Omnipoint[C] | Sprint PCS[C] | 21st Century Telesis[P] | AT&T Wireless[T] | AT&T Wireless[T] | Holland Wireless |

| Market Name | Cellular Carriers A Block GMD Limited | Cellular Carriers B Block Bell Atlantic[C] | PCS Carriers A Block Omnipoint[G] | PCS Carriers B Block Sprint PCS[G] | PCS Carriers C Block 21st Century Telesis[P] | PCS Carriers D Block AT&T Wireless[T] | PCS Carriers E Block AT&T Wireless[T] | PCS Carriers F Block Sea Breeze Partners |
|---|---|---|---|---|---|---|---|---|
| Watertown | GMD Limited | Bell Atlantic[C] | Omnipoint[G] | Sprint PCS[G] | 21st Century Telesis[P] | AT&T Wireless[T] | AT&T Wireless[T] | Sea Breeze Partners |
| **North Carolina** | | | | | | | | |
| Asheville-Hendersonville | Bell Atlantic | U.S. Cellular | AT&T Wireless[T] | BellSouth[G] | Nextwave[C] | Sprint PCS[G] | Alltel[C] | Urban Comm[C] |
| Burlington | GTE Wireless[C] | Alltel[C] | AT&T Wireless[T] | BellSouth[G] | Urban Comm[C] | Sprint PCS[G] | Alltel[C] | Phoenix Wireless |
| Charlotte-Gastonia | Bell Atlantic[C] | Alltel[C] | AT&T Wireless[T] | BellSouth[G] | Nextwave[C] | Sprint PCS[G] | Alltel[C] | AirGate Wireless |
| Fayetteville-Lumberton | GTE Wireless[C] | Alltel[C] | AT&T Wireless[T] | BellSouth[G] | Urban Comm[C] | Sprint PCS[G] | Alltel[C] | Northcoast OpCo. |
| Goldsboro-Kinston | U.S. Cellular | Alltel[C] | AT&T Wireless[T] | BellSouth[G] | Urban Comm[C] | Sprint PCS[G] | Alltel[C] | Omnipoint[G] |
| Greensboro-Winston Salem-High Point | GTE Wireless[C] | Alltel[C] | AT&T Wireless[T] | BellSouth[G] | Nextwave[C] | Sprint PCS[G] | Alltel[C] | AirGate Wireless |
| Greenville-Washington | U.S. Cellular | U.S. Cellular | AT&T Wireless[T] | BellSouth[G] | Urban Comm[C] | Sprint PCS[G] | Alltel[C] | Phoenix Wireless |
| Hickory-Morganton | Bell Atlantic[C] | Alltel[C] | AT&T Wireless[T] | BellSouth[G] | Nextwave[C] | Sprint PCS[G] | Alltel[C] | AirGate Wireless |
| Lenoir | Bell Atlantic[C] | Alltel[C] | AT&T Wireless[T] | BellSouth[G] | Nextwave[C] | Sprint PCS[G] | Alltel[C] | AirGate Wireless |
| Jacksonville | GTE Wireless[C] | Alltel[C] | AT&T Wireless[T] | BellSouth[G] | Urban Comm[C] | Sprint PCS[G] | Alltel[C] | ComScape Telecomm |
| New Bern | U.S. Cellular | U.S. Cellular | AT&T Wireless[T] | BellSouth[G] | Urban Comm[C] | Sprint PCS[G] | Alltel[C] | ComScape Telecomm |
| Raleigh-Durham | GTE Wireless[C] | Alltel[C] | AT&T Wireless[T] | BellSouth[G] | Urban Comm[C] | Sprint PCS[G] | Alltel[C] | ComScape Telecomm |
| Roanoke Rapids | U.S. Cellular | | AT&T Wireless[T] | BellSouth[G] | Urban Comm[C] | Sprint PCS[G] | Alltel[C] | Phoenix Wireless |
| Rocky Mount-Wilson | U.S. Cellular | Alltel[C] | AT&T Wireless[T] | BellSouth[G] | Urban Comm[C] | Sprint PCS[G] | Alltel[C] | Phoenix Wireless |
| Wilmington | GTE Wireless[C] | Alltel[C] | AT&T Wireless[T] | BellSouth[G] | Urban Comm[C] | Sprint PCS[G] | Alltel[C] | ComScape Telecomm |
| **North Dakota** | | | | | | | | |
| Bismarck | Western Wireless | AirTouch | Sprint PCS[C] | Aeria[C] | MCG PCS | Touch America | Western Wireless[G] | N. Dakota Network |
| Dickinson | Western Wireless | CommNet 2000 | Sprint PCS[C] | Aeria[C] | MCG PCS | Consolidated Tel. | Consolidated Tel. | Consolidated Tel |
| Fargo | Western Wireless | AirTouch | Sprint PCS[C] | Aeria[C] | North Dakota PCS | Touch America | Western Wireless[G] | N. Dakota Network |
| Grand Forks | Western Wireless | AirTouch | Sprint PCS[C] | Aeria[C] | North Dakota PCS | Western Wireless[G] | N. Dakota PCS | Redwood Wireless |
| Minot | Western Wireless | CommNet 2000 | Sprint PCS[C] | Aeria[C] | MCG PCS | N. Dakota Network | N. Dakota PCS | N. Dakota Network |
| Williston | Western Wireless | CommNet 2000 | Sprint PCS[C] | Aeria[C] | Vincent McBride | N. Dakota PCS | N. Dakota PCS | N. Dakota PCS |

| Market Name | Cellular Carriers | | PCS Carriers | | | | | |
|---|---|---|---|---|---|---|---|---|
| | A Block | B Block | A Block | B Block | C Block | D Block | E Block | F Block |
| **Ohio** | | | | | | | | |
| Ashtabula | AirTouch[C] | GTE Wireless[C] | Ameritech[C] | AT&T Wireless[T] | Wireless Ventures[C] | Sprint PCS[C] | Western Wireless[C] | Northcoast OpCo. |
| Athens | AT&T Wireless[T] | Alltel[C] | AT&T Wireless[T] | Aerial[G] | Horizon Personal Comm[C] | Sprint PCS[C] | Sprint PCS[C] | Northcoast OpCo. |
| Canton | AirTouch[C] | GTE Wireless[C] | Ameritech[C] | AT&T Wireless[T] | R & S PCS | Sprint PCS[C] | Western Wireless[C] | Northcoast OpCo. |
| Chillicothe | American Cellular | U.S. Cellular | AT&T Wireless[T] | Aerial[G] | Horizon Personal Comm[C] | Sprint PCS[C] | Sprint PCS[C] | Northcoast OpCo. |
| Cincinnati | AirTouch[C] | Ameritech[C] | AT&T Wireless[T] | GTE Wireless[C] | Nextwave[C] | Sprint PCS[C] | Cincinnati Bell[C] | Western Wireless[C] |
| Cleveland-Akron | AirTouch[C] | GTE Wireless[C] | AT&T Wireless[T] | Ameritech[C] | Nextwave[C] | Sprint PCS[C] | Western Wireless[C] | Northcoast OpCo. |
| Columbus | AirTouch[C] | Ameritech[C] | AT&T Wireless[T] | Aerial[G] | Nextwave[C] | Sprint PCS[C] | Sprint PCS[C] | Northcoast OpCo. |
| Dayton-Springfield | AirTouch[C] | Ameritech[C] | AT&T Wireless[T] | GTE Wireless[C] | Nextwave[C] | Sprint PCS[C] | Western Wireless[C] | PCS Devco |
| East Liverpool-Salem | Sygnet Comm | Alltel[C] | Ameritech[C] | AT&T Wireless[T] | Americall[C] | Sprint PCS[C] | Western Wireless[C] | Northcoast OpCo. |
| Findlay | AirTouch[C] | Alltel[C] | AT&T Wireless[T] | Sprint PCS[C] | Miccom | Omnipoint[C] | Omnipoint[C] | Northcoast OpCo. |
| Lima | AirTouch[C] | Alltel[C] | AT&T Wireless[T] | Sprint PCS[C] | Pocket[C] | Omnipoint[C] | Omnipoint[C] | Telephone Service Co. |
| Mansfield | AirTouch[C] | Alltel[C] | Ameritech[C] | AT&T Wireless[T] | R & S PCS | Sprint PCS[C] | Western Wireless[C] | Northcoast OpCo. |
| Marietta | AT&T Wireless[T] | Alltel[C] | AT&T Wireless[T] | Aerial[G] | Horizon Personal Comm[C] | Sprint PCS[C] | Sprint PCS[C] | RLV-PCS I Ptshp[C] |
| Marion | AirTouch[C] | Alltel[C] | Ameritech[C] | Aerial[G] | Miccom | Sprint PCS[C] | Sprint PCS[C] | Northcoast OpCo. |
| New Philadelphia | American Cellular | U.S. Cellular | Ameritech[C] | AT&T Wireless[T] | R & S PCS | Sprint PCS[C] | Western Wireless[C] | Northcoast OpCo. |
| Portsmouth | American Cellular | U.S. Cellular | AT&T Wireless[T] | GTE Wireless[C] | Wireless Ventures[C] | Sprint PCS[C] | Sprint PCS[C] | Northcoast OpCo. |
| Sandusky | Dobson Comm | Alltel[C] | Ameritech[C] | AT&T Wireless[T] | Pocket[C] | Sprint PCS[C] | Western Wireless[C] | Urban Comm[C] |
| Steubenville | AT&T Wireless[T] | Alltel[C] | Sprint PCS[C] | Aerial[G] | Devon Mobile[C] | Omnipoint[C] | Omnipoint[C] | Northcoast OpCo. |
| Tiffin | Dobson Comm | Alltel[C] | AT&T Wireless[T] | Sprint PCS[C] | Miccom | Omnipoint[C] | Omnipoint[C] | Northcoast OpCo. |
| Toledo | AirTouch[C] | Alltel[C] | AT&T Wireless[T] | Sprint PCS[C] | Pocket[C] | Sprint PCS[C] | Western Wireless[C] | Northcoast OpCo. |
| Youngstown-Warren | Sygnet Comm | Alltel[C] | Ameritech[C] | AT&T Wireless[T] | R & S PCS | Sprint PCS[C] | Sprint PCS[C] | Northcoast OpCo. |
| Zanesville-Cambridge | American Cellular | Ameritech[C] | AT&T Wireless[T] | Aerial[G] | Horizon Personal Comm[C] | Sprint PCS[C] | | Northcoast OpCo. |

| Market Name | Cellular Carriers A Block | B Block | PCS Carriers A Block | B Block | C Block | D Block | E Block | F Block |
|---|---|---|---|---|---|---|---|---|
| **Oklahoma** | | | | | | | | |
| Ada | U.S. Cellular | | Western Wireless[C] | Sprint PCS[C] | Onque[C] | Triad Cellular | AT&T Wireless[T] | Central Wireless |
| Ardmore | U.S. Cellular | | Western Wireless[C] | Sprint PCS[C] | Onque[C] | Triad Cellular | AT&T Wireless[T] | Poka Lambro[C] |
| Bartlesville | AT&T Wireless[T] | Southwestern Bell[T] | Southwestern Bell[T] | Sprint PCS[C] | Western Wireless[C] | Alltel[C] | AT&T Wireless[T] | Mercury Mobility |
| Duncan | Western Wireless | U.S. Cellular | Western Wireless[C] | Sprint PCS[C] | Comtel PCS Mainstreet[C] | Triad Cellular | AT&T Wireless[T] | DCC PCS[C] |
| Enid | Dobson Comm | Enid Cellular | Western Wireless[C] | Sprint PCS[C] | National Telecom Holdings[C] | Triad Cellular | AT&T Wireless[T] | Poka Lambro[C] |
| Lawton | AT&T Wireless[T] | U.S. Cellular | Western Wireless[C] | Sprint PCS[C] | Comtel PCS Mainstreet[C] | Triad Cellular | AT&T Wireless[T] | DCC PCS[C] |
| McAlester | U.S. Cellular | OK Cellular | Western Wireless[C] | Sprint PCS[C] | Onque[C] | Southwestern Bell[T] | AT&T Wireless[T] | DCC PCS[C] |
| Miami | AT&T Wireless[T] | | Sprint PCS[C] | Aerial[C] | Nextwave[C] | Southwestern Bell[T] | Alltel[C] | MBO Wireless[C] |
| Muskogee | U.S. Cellular | OK Cellular | Southwestern Bell[T] | Sprint PCS[C] | Western Wireless[C] | Alltel[C] | AT&T Wireless[T] | DCC PCS[C] |
| Oklahoma City | AT&T Wireless[T] | Southwestern Bell[T] | Western Wireless[C] | Sprint PCS[C] | Nextwave[C] | Triad Cellular | AT&T Wireless[T] | DCC PCS[C] |
| Ponca City | AT&T Wireless[T] | Southwestern Bell[T] | Western Wireless[C] | Sprint PCS[C] | Mark M. Guest | Triad Cellular | AT&T Wireless[T], | DCC PCS[C] |
| Stillwater | AT&T Wireless[T] | Southwestern Bell[T] | Western Wireless[C] | Sprint PCS[C] | MBO Wireless[C] | Triad Cellular | AT&T Wireless[T] | WebTel Wireless |
| Tulsa | AT&T Wireless[T] | U.S. Cellular | Southwestern Bell[T] | Sprint PCS[C] | Western Wireless[C] | Alltel[C] | AT&T Wireless[T] | Nextwave[C] |
| **Oregon** | | | | | | | | |
| Bend | AT&T Wireless[T] | U.S. Cellular | Western Wireless[C] | Sprint PCS[C] | Aer Force | Central Oregon Cellular | U S West[C] | Westel |
| Coos Bay-North Bend | U.S. Cellular | Litchfield Cellular | Western Wireless[C] | Sprint PCS[C] | Polycel[C] | AT&T Wireless[T] | U S West[C] | Omnipoint[C] |
| Eugene-Springfield | AT&T Wireless[T] | AirTouch[C] | Western Wireless[C] | Sprint PCS[C] | Magnacom Wireless | AT&T Wireless[T] | U S West[C] | Point Enterprises |
| Grants Pass | U.S. Cellular | GTE Wireless[C] | Western Wireless[C] | Sprint PCS[C] | Americall[C] | Central Oregon Cellular | U S West[C] | Magnacom Wireless |
| Klamath Falls | AT&T Wireless[T] | U.S. Cellular | Western Wireless[C] | Sprint PCS[C] | Polycel[C] | Central Oregon Cellular | U S West[C] | Westel |
| Medford | AT&T Wireless[T] | U.S. Cellular | Western Wireless[C] | Sprint PCS[C] | Americall[C] | Central Oregon Cellular | U S West[C] | Magnacom Wireless |
| Pendleton | Blue Mountain Cellular | | GTE Wireless[C] | Sprint PCS[C] | Western Wireless[C] | Western Wireless[C] | U S West[C] | Magnacom Wireless |
| Portland | AT&T Wireless[T] | AirTouch[C] | Western Wireless[C] | Sprint PCS[C] | Nextwave[C] | AT&T Wireless[T] | U S West[C] | Magnacom Wireless |
| Roseburg | U.S. Cellular | GTE Wireless[C] | Western Wireless[C] | Sprint PCS[C] | Americall[C] | Central Oregon Cellular | U S West[C] | Magnacom Wireless |
| Salem-Albany-Corvallis | AT&T Wireless[T] | GTE Wireless[C] | Western Wireless[C] | Sprint PCS[C] | Magnacom Wireless | AT&T Wireless[T] | U S West[C] | Point Enterprises |

| Market Name | Cellular Carriers | | PCS Carriers | | | | | |
|---|---|---|---|---|---|---|---|---|
| | A Block | B Block | A Block | B Block | C Block | D Block | E Block | F Block |
| **Pennsylvania** | | | | | | | | |
| Allentown-Bethlehem-Easton | AT&T WirelessT | Bell AtlanticC | OmnipointC | Sprint PCSC | Nextwave | Comcast PCS | AT&T WirelessT | Northcoast OpCo. |
| Altoona | AT&T WirelessT | Telespectrum | Sprint PCSC | AerialC | Longstreet Comm | AT&T WirelessT | AT&T WirelessT | PCSouth |
| Bradford | AT&T WirelessT | Bell AtlanticC | Sprint PCSC | AT&T WirelessT | New England Wireless | OmnipointC | OmnipointC | Devon MobileC |
| Chambersburg | AT&T WirelessT | AlltelC | Sprint PCSC | AT&T WirelessT | NextwaveC | OmnipointC | Virginia PCSC | Virginia PCSC |
| Du Bois-Clearfield | Sygnet Comm | Bell AtlanticC | Sprint PCSC | AerialC | Devon MobileC | CM-PCS Partners | AT&T WirelessT | Sea Breeze Partners |
| Erie | AT&T WirelessT | GTE WirelessC | Ameritech | AT&T WirelessT | R & S PCS | Sprint PCSC | Western WirelessC | Devon MobileC |
| Harrisburg | AT&T WirelessT | Bell AtlanticC | AT&T WirelessT | Sprint PCSC | OmnipointC | Denver & Ephrata T&T | Comcast PCS | Nextwave |
| Indiana | Sygnet Comm | AlltelC | Sprint PCSC | AerialC | Devon MobileC | AT&T WirelessT | AT&T WirelessT | MCG PCS |
| Johnstown | AT&T WirelessT | AlltelC | Sprint PCSC | AerialC | MCG PCS | AT&T WirelessT | AT&T WirelessT | Central Wireless |
| Lancaster | AT&T WirelessT | AlltelC | AT&T WirelessT | Sprint PCSC | D&E Communications | Comcast PCS | OmnipointC | Nextwave |
| Meadville | Sygnet Comm | Bell AtlanticC | Ameritech | AT&T WirelessT | Devon MobileC | Sprint PCSC | Western WirelessC | Northcoast OpCo. |
| New Castle | Sygnet Comm | AlltelC | Sprint PCSC | AerialC | Devon MobileC | AT&T WirelessT | AT&T WirelessT | Northcoast OpCo. |
| Oil City-Franklin | Sygnet Comm | AlltelC | Sprint PCSC | AerialC | Devon MobileC | AT&T WirelessT | AT&T WirelessT | PolycellC |
| Philadelphia | ComcastC | Bell AtlanticC | AT&T WirelessT | Sprint PCSC | OmnipointC | Comcast PCS | Riygam | NextwaveC |
| Pittsburgh | AT&T WirelessT | Bell AtlanticC | Sprint PCSC | AerialC | NextwaveC | AT&T WirelessT | Radiofone PCS | Devon MobileC |
| Pottsville | Sunshine Cellular | U.S. Cellular | AT&T WirelessT | Sprint PCSC | OmnipointC | Conestoga Wireless | Comcast PCS | MFRI Inc. |
| Reading | AlltelC | Bell AtlanticC | AT&T WirelessT | Sprint PCSC | OmnipointC | Conestoga Wireless | Comcast PCS | NextwaveC |
| Scranton-Wilkes-Barre-Hazelton | AT&T WirelessT | Cellular Plus | OmnipointC | Sprint PCSC | Nextwave | AT&T WirelessT | AT&T WirelessT | 21st Century TelesisP |
| Sharon | Sygnet Comm | AlltelC | Ameritech | AT&T WirelessT | Devon MobileC | Sprint PCSC | Western WirelessC | CM-PCS Partners |
| State College | AT&T WirelessT | Cellular Plus | AT&T WirelessT | Sprint PCSC | OmnipointC | Comcast PCS | PCSouth | Devon MobileC |
| Stroudsburg | | | OmnipointC | Sprint PCSC | MFRI Inc. | Northcoast OpCo. | AT&T WirelessT | MFRI Inc. |
| Sunbury-Shamokin | Sunshine Cellular | U.S. Cellular | AT&T WirelessT | Sprint PCSC | OmnipointC | MFRI Inc. | Comcast PCS | Conestoga Wireless |

| Market Name | Cellular Carriers A Block | Cellular Carriers B Block | PCS Carriers → A Block | B Block | C Block | D Block | E Block | F Block |
|---|---|---|---|---|---|---|---|---|
| Warren | Sygnet Comm | Rochester Tel | | | | | | |
| Williamsport | AT&T Wireless(T) | U.S. Cellular | Ameritech(T) | AT&T Wireless(T) | New England Wireless | AT&T Wireless(T) | Omnipoint(C) | Devon Mobile(C) |
| York-Hanover | AT&T Wireless(T) | Alltel(T) | AT&T Wireless(T) | Sprint PCS(C) | Omnipoint(C); Omnipoint(C) | Conestoga Wireless; Comcast PCS | Comcast PCS; Denver & Ephrata T&T | Northcoast OpCo.; Nextwave(C) |
| **Rhode Island** | | | | | | | | |
| Providence | SNET(T) | Bell Atlantic(C) | AT&T Wireless(T) | Sprint PCS(C) | Nextwave(C) | ACC-PCS | Northcoast OpCo. | Omnipoint(C) |
| **South Carolina** | | | | | | | | |
| Anderson | Bell Atlantic(C) | Alltel(C) | AT&T Wireless(T) | BellSouth(C) | Carolina PCS I | Sprint PCS(C) | Alltel(C) | Public Service PCS |
| Charleston | GTE Wireless(C) | Alltel(C) | AT&T Wireless(T) | BellSouth(C) | Carolina PCS I | Sprint PCS(C) | Alltel(C) | Urban Comm(C) |
| Columbia | Bell Atlantic(C) | BellSouth(T) | AT&T Wireless(T) | BellSouth(C) | Carolina PCS I | Sprint PCS(C) | Alltel(C) | Nextwave(C) |
| Florence | GTE Wireless(C) | BellSouth(T) | AT&T Wireless(T) | BellSouth(C) | Carolina PCS I | Sprint PCS(C) | Alltel(C) | Urban Comm(C) |
| Greenville-Spartanburg | Bell Atlantic(C) | Alltel(C) | AT&T Wireless(T) | BellSouth(C) | Carolina PCS I | Sprint PCS(C) | Alltel(C) | Nextwave(C) |
| Greenwood | Bell Atlantic(C) | Alltel(C) | AT&T Wireless(T) | BellSouth(C) | Carolina PCS I | Sprint PCS(C) | Alltel(C) | AirGate Wireless |
| Myrtle Beach | AT&T Wireless(T) | BellSouth(T) | AT&T Wireless(T) | BellSouth(C) | Carolina PCS I | Sprint PCS(C) | Alltel(C) | Urban Comm(C) |
| Orangeburg | Bell Atlantic(C) | Alltel(C) | AT&T Wireless(T) | BellSouth(C) | Carolina PCS I | Sprint PCS(C) | Alltel(C) | Urban Comm(C) |
| Sumter | GTE Wireless(C) | BellSouth(T) | AT&T Wireless(T) | BellSouth(C) | Carolina PCS I | Sprint PCS(C) | Alltel(C) | Urban Comm(C) |
| **South Dakota** | | | | | | | | |
| Aberdeen | Western Wireless | CommNet 2000 | Sprint PCS(C) | Aerial(C) | MCG PCS | Western Wireless(C) | AT&T Wireless(T) | Montana PCS |
| Huron | Western Wireless | CommNet 2000 | Sprint PCS(C) | Aerial(C) | MCG PCS | Western Wireless(C) | | Redwood Wireless |
| Mitchell | Western Wireless | CommNet 2000 | Sprint PCS(C) | Aerial(C) | MCG PCS | Western Wireless(C) | | Redwood Wireless |
| Rapid City | Western Wireless | GTE Wireless(C) | Sprint PCS(C) | Western Wireless(C) | MCG PCS | U S West(C) | AT&T Wireless(T) | Montana PCS |
| Sioux Falls | Western Wireless | AirTouch(C) | Sprint PCS(C) | Aerial(C) | Brookings Municipal | Western Wireless(C) | McLeod USA | NE Nebraska TelCo. |
| Watertown | Western Wireless | Cellular 2000 | Sprint PCS(C) | Aerial(C) | Brookings Municipal | Western Wireless(C) | Minnesota PCS | Minnesota PCS |
| **Tennessee** | | | | | | | | |
| Chattanooga | GTE Wireless(C) | BellSouth(T) | AT&T Wireless(T) | Powertel(C) | Chase Telecomm(C) | Sprint PCS(C) | Alltel(C) | BTA Ventures II |
| Clarksville | GTE Wireless(C) | BellSouth(T) | Sprint PCS(C) | AT&T Wireless(T) | Chase Telecomm(C) | Powertel(C) | Powertel(C) | Tennessee LP 121 |

| Market Name | Cellular Carriers | | PCS Carriers | | | | | |
| --- | A Block | B Block | A Block | B Block | C Block | D Block | E Block | F Block |
| --- | --- | --- | --- | --- | --- | --- | --- | --- |
| Cleveland | GTE Wireless[C] | BellSouth[T] | AT&T Wireless[T] | Powertel[C] | Southern Comm Sys.[C] | Sprint PCS[C] | Alltel[C] | Troup EMC Comm |
| Cookeville | GTE Wireless[C] | U.S. Cellular | Sprint PCS[C] | AT&T Wireless[T] | Chase Telecomm[C] | Powertel[C] | Powertel[C] | Tennessee LP 121 |
| Dyersburg-Union City | GTE Wireless[C] | Yorkville Tel Co-op | Powertel[C] | Southwestern Bell[T] | Chase Telecomm[C] | Sprint PCS[C] | BellSouth[C] | PCSouth |
| Jackson | GTE Wireless[C] | BellSouth[T] | Powertel[C] | Southwestern Bell[T] | Chase Telecomm[C] | Sprint PCS[C] | Sprint PCS[C] | PCSouth |
| Kingsport-Johnson City | GTE Wireless[C] | Alltel[C] | AT&T Wireless[T] | BellSouth[C] | Chase Telecomm[C] | Sprint PCS[C] | Sprint PCS[C] | Virginia PCS[C] |
| Knoxville | GTE Wireless[C] | U.S. Cellular | AT&T Wireless[T] | BellSouth[C] | Chase Telecomm[C] | Sprint PCS[C] | Powertel[C] | Tennessee LP 121 |
| Memphis | GTE Wireless[C] | BellSouth[T] | Powertel[C] | Southwestern Bell[T] | Chase Telecomm[C] | Sprint PCS[C] | Alltel[C] | Telecorp Holding |
| Nashville | GTE Wireless[C] | BellSouth[T] | Sprint PCS[C] | AT&T Wireless[T] | Chase Telecomm[C] | Powertel[C] | Powertel[C] | Omnipoint[C] |

**Texas**

| Market Name | A Block | B Block | A Block | B Block | C Block | D Block | E Block | F Block |
| --- | --- | --- | --- | --- | --- | --- | --- | --- |
| Abilene | Western Wireless | Southwestern Bell[T] | PrimeCo[C] | Sprint PCS[C] | Poka Lambro[C] | Western Wireless[C] | Triad Cellular | Mercury PCS II |
| Amarillo | C-1 of Amarillo | Southwestern Bell[T] | PrimeCo[C] | Sprint PCS[C] | Omnipoint[C] | Western Wireless[C] | Triad Cellular | High Plains Wireless |
| Austin | AT&T Wireless[T] | GTE Wireless[C] | PrimeCo[C] | Sprint PCS[C] | Nextwave[C] | Western Wireless[C] | AT&T Wireless[T] | Poka Lambro[C] |
| Beaumont-Port Arthur | Centennial Cellular[C] | GTE Wireless[C] | Aerial[C] | PrimeCo[C] | Meretel | Sprint PCS[C] | AT&T Wireless[T] | Telecorp Holding |
| Big Springs | Western Wireless | Wes-Tex Telecom | PrimeCo[C] | Sprint PCS[C] | Poka Lambro[C] | Western Wireless[C] | AT&T Wireless[T] | Mercury PCS II |
| Brownsville-Harlingen | CenturyTel | Southwestern Bell[T] | Sprint PCS[C] | PrimeCo[C] | Nextwave[C] | Western Wireless[C] | AT&T Wireless[T] | America[C] |
| Brownwood | Prime Cellular | West Central Cellular | PrimeCo[C] | Sprint PCS[C] | Rosas[C] | Western Wireless[C] | AT&T Wireless[T] | Poka Lambro[C] |
| Bryan-College Station | AT&T Wireless[T] | GTE Wireless[C] | Aerial[C] | PrimeCo[C] | Nextwave[C] | Sprint PCS[C] | AT&T Wireless[T] | PCSouth |
| Corpus Christi | U.S. Cellular | Southwestern Bell[T] | Sprint PCS[C] | PrimeCo[C] | America[C] | Western Wireless[C] | AT&T Wireless[T] | Nextwave[C] |
| Dallas-Fort Worth | CMT Partners[T] | Southwestern Bell[T] | PrimeCo[C] | Sprint PCS[C] | Pocket[C] | AT&T Wireless[T] | AT&T Wireless[T] | Nextwave[C] |
| Eagle Pass-Del Rio | U.S. Cellular | | Sprint PCS[C] | PrimeCo[C] | Rosas[C] | Mercury PCS II | AT&T Wireless[T] | America[C] |
| El Paso | Bell Atlantic[C] | GTE Wireless[C] | Western Wireless[C] | AT&T Wireless[T] | Nextwave[C] | Sprint PCS[C] | Sprint PCS[C] | Telecorp Holding |
| Houston | BellSouth[T] | GTE Wireless[C] | Aerial[C] | PrimeCo[C] | Nextwave[C] | Sprint PCS[C] | AT&T Wireless[T] | Integrated Comm[C] |
| Laredo | U.S. Cellular | Cellular Info Systems | Sprint PCS[C] | PrimeCo[C] | America[C] | Western Wireless[C] | Elite[C] | Mercury Mobility |
| Longview-Marshall | AT&T Wireless[T] | Alltel[C] | PrimeCo[C] | Sprint PCS[C] | Pocket[C] | Southwestern Bell[C] | AT&T Wireless[T] | |

| Market Name | Cellular Carriers | | PCS Carriers | | | | | |
|---|---|---|---|---|---|---|---|---|
| | A Block | B Block | A Block | B Block | C Block | D Block | E Block | F Block |
| Lubbock | Western Wireless | Southwestern Bell[T] | PrimeCo[C] | Sprint PCS[C] | Poka Lambro[C] | High Plains Wireless | Triad Cellular | Mercury PCS II |
| Lufkin-Nacogdoches | U.S. Cellular | GTE Wireless[C] | Aerial[C] | PrimeCo[C] | Meretel | Sprint PCS[C] | AT&T Wireless[T] | Poka Lambro[C] |
| McAllen | CenturyTel | Southwestern Bell[T] | Sprint PCS[C] | PrimeCo[C] | Nextwave[C] | Western Wireless[C] | AT&T Wireless[T] | Integrated Comm[C] |
| Midland | Western Wireless | Southwestern Bell[T] | PrimeCo[C] | Sprint PCS[C] | Poka Lambro[C] | Western Wireless[C] | Western Wireless[C] | Mercury PCS II |
| Odessa | Cellular Info Systems | Southwestern Bell[T] | PrimeCo[C] | Sprint PCS[C] | Poka Lambro[C] | Western Wireless[C] | Western Wireless[C] | Mercury PCS II |
| Paris | AT&T Wireless[T] | Lamar County Cellular | PrimeCo[C] | Sprint PCS[C] | Onque[C] | Western Wireless[C] | AT&T Wireless[T] | Mercury Mobility |
| San Angelo | Western Wireless | West Central Cellular | PrimeCo[C] | Sprint PCS[C] | Poka Lambro[C] | Western Wireless[C] | AT&T Wireless[T] | Mercury PCS II |
| San Antonio | AT&T Wireless[T] | Southwestern Bell[T] | Sprint PCS[C] | PrimeCo[C] | Nextwave[C] | Western Wireless[C] | AT&T Wireless[T] | Omnipoint[C] |
| Sherman-Denison | AT&T Wireless[T] | Southwestern Bell[T] | PrimeCo[C] | Sprint PCS[C] | Western Wireless[C] | Alltel[C] | AT&T Wireless[T] | Onque[C] |
| Temple-Killeen | AT&T Wireless[T] | Alltel[C] | PrimeCo[C] | Sprint PCS[C] | Nextwave[C] | Southwestern Bell[T] | AT&T Wireless[T] | Western Wireless[C] |
| Texarkana | AT&T Wireless[T] | Century Cellunet | PrimeCo[C] | Sprint PCS[C] | Nextwave[C] | Alltel[C] | AT&T Wireless[T] | Mercury Mobility |
| Tyler | AT&T Wireless[T] | GTE Wireless[C] | PrimeCo[C] | Sprint PCS[C] | Pocket[C] | Southwestern Bell[T] | AT&T Wireless[T] | Nextwave[C] |
| Victoria | U.S. Cellular | Alltel[C] | Aerial[C] | PrimeCo[C] | Integrated Comm[C] | Sprint PCS[C] | AT&T Wireless[T] | Americall[C] |
| Waco | AT&T Wireless[T] | U.S. Cellular | PrimeCo[C] | Sprint PCS[C] | Aer Force | Southwestern Bell[T] | AT&T Wireless[T] | Omnipoint[C] |
| Wichita Falls | AT&T Wireless[T] | | PrimeCo[C] | Sprint PCS[C] | Western Wireless[C] | Triad Cellular | AT&T Wireless[T] | Poka Lambro[C] |
| **Utah** | | | | | | | | |
| Logan | AT&T Wireless[T] | AirTouch[C] | Western Wireless[C] | Sprint PCS[C] | ClearComm[CG] | AT&T Wireless[T] | U S West[C] | Integrated Comm[C] |
| Provo-Orem | AT&T Wireless[T] | AirTouch[C] | Western Wireless[C] | Sprint PCS[C] | ClearComm[CG] | AT&T Wireless[T] | U S West[C] | Nextwave[C] |
| Salt Lake City-Ogden | AT&T Wireless[T] | AirTouch[C] | Western Wireless[C] | Sprint PCS[C] | ClearComm[CG] | AT&T Wireless[T] | U S West[C] | Nextwave[C] |
| St. George | Western Wireless | CommNet 2000 | Western Wireless[C] | Sprint PCS[C] | PCS Plus | AT&T Wireless[T] | Triad Cellular | S. Cent. Utah Tel |
| **Vermont** | | | | | | | | |
| Burlington | Rural Cellular | GTE Wireless[C] | Omnipoint[C] | Sprint PCS[C] | Personal Comm Ntwk[C] | Devon Mobile[C] | AT&T Wireless[T] | VTel Wireless |
| Rutland-Bennington | Rural Cellular | GTE Wireless[C] | Omnipoint[C] | Sprint PCS[C] | Personal Comm Ntwk[G] | Devon Mobile[C] | AT&T Wireless[T] | VTel Wireless |
| **Virginia** | | | | | | | | |
| Charlottesville | U.S. Cellular | Alltel[C] | Sprint PCS[C] | AT&T Wireless[T] | Virginia PCS[C] | Devon Mobile[C] | Omnipoint[C] | Urban Comm[C] |
| Danville | GTE Wireless[C] | Alltel[C] | AT&T Wireless[T] | PrimeCo[C] | Southeast Wireless | Sprint PCS[C] | Western Wireless[C] | Devon Mobile[C] |

| Market Name | Cellular Carriers | | PCS Carriers | | | | | |
|---|---|---|---|---|---|---|---|---|
| | A Block | B Block | A Block | B Block | C Block | D Block | E Block | F Block |
| Fredericksburg | Southwestern Bell(T) | Bell Atlantic(C) | Sprint PCS(C) | AT&T Wireless(T) | Aer Force | Omnipoint(C) | Virginia PCS(C) | Urban Comm(C) |
| Harrisonburg | Virginia Cellular | CFW Cellular | Sprint PCS(C) | AT&T Wireless(T) | Devon Mobile(C) | Virginia PCS(C) | Virginia PCS(C) | Urban Comm(C) |
| Lynchburg | U.S. Cellular | Alltel(C) | AT&T Wireless(T) | Virginia PCS(C) | Southeast Wireless | Sprint PCS(C) | Western Wireless(G) | Devon Mobile(C) |
| Martinsville | U.S. Cellular | Alltel(C) | AT&T Wireless(T) | Virginia PCS(C) | Devon Mobile(C) | Sprint PCS(C) | Western Wireless(G) | Urban Comm(C) |
| Norfolk-Virginia Beach-Newport News | Alltel(C) | GTE Wireless(C) | AT&T Wireless(T) | PrimeCo(C) | Nextwave(C) | Sprint PCS(C) | Western Wireless(G) | Omnipoint(C) |
| Petersburg | Alltel(C) | GTE Wireless(C) | AT&T Wireless(T) | PrimeCo(C) | Nextwave(C) | Sprint PCS(C) | Western Wireless(G) | Urban Comm(C) |
| Richmond | BellSouth(T) | GTE Wireless(C) | AT&T Wireless(T) | PrimeCo(C) | Nextwave(C) | Sprint PCS(C) | Western Wireless(C) | Urban Comm(C) |
| Roanoke | U.S. Cellular | GTE Wireless(C) | AT&T Wireless(T) | Virginia PCS(C) | Nextwave(C) | Sprint PCS(C) | Western Wireless(C) | Urban Comm(C) |
| Staunton-Waynesboro | Virginia Cellular | CFW Cellular | AT&T Wireless(T) | Virginia PCS(C) | Devon Mobile(C) | Sprint PCS(C) | Devon Mobile(C) | Urban Comm(C) |
| Winchester | Southwestern Bell(T) | Shenandoah Cellular | Sprint PCS(G)(C) | AT&T Wireless(T) | Virginia PCS(C) | Shenandoah Mobile | Shenandoah Mobile | Devon Mobile(C) |
| **Washington, DC** | Southwestern Bell(T) | Bell Atlantic(C) | Sprint PCS(G)(C) | AT&T Wireless(T) | Nextwave(C) | Rivgam | Omnipoint(C) | Aer Force |
| **Washington** | | | | | | | | |
| Aberdeen | U.S. Cellular | AirTouch(C) | GTE Wireless(C) | Sprint PCS(C) | Western Wireless(G) | AT&T Wireless(T) | U S West(C) | Whidbey Telephone |
| Bellingham | AT&T Wireless(T) | AirTouch(C) | GTE Wireless(C) | Sprint PCS(C) | Nextwave(C) | AT&T Wireless(T) | Whidbey Telephone | Western Wireless(G) |
| Bremerton | AT&T Wireless(T) | AirTouch(C) | GTE Wireless(C) | Sprint PCS(C) | Western Wireless(G) | AT&T Wireless(T) | U S West(C) | Whidbey Tel |
| Kennewick-Pasco-Richland | AT&T Wireless(T) | U.S. Cellular | GTE Wireless(C) | Sprint PCS(C) | Onque(C) | Western Wireless(G) | U S West(C) | |
| Longview | AT&T Wireless(T) | U.S. Cellular | Western Wireless(G) | Sprint PCS(C) | Nextwave(C) | AT&T Wireless(T) | U S West(C) | Magnacom Wireless |
| Olympia-Centralia | AT&T Wireless(T) | AirTouch(C) | GTE Wireless(C) | Sprint PCS(C) | Nextwave(C) | AT&T Wireless(T) | Western Wireless(G) | Point Enterprises |
| Port Angeles | AT&T Wireless(T) | AirTouch(C) | GTE Wireless(C) | Sprint PCS(C) | Western Wireless(G) | AT&T Wireless(T) | Whidbey Tel | Whidbey Tel |
| Seattle-Tacoma | AT&T Wireless(T) | AirTouch(C) | GTE Wireless(C) | Sprint PCS(C) | Nextwave(C) | AT&T Wireless(T) | Western Wireless(G) | Western Wireless(G) |
| Spokane | AT&T Wireless(T) | AirTouch(C) | GTE Wireless(C) | Sprint PCS(C) | Nextwave(C) | AT&T Wireless(T) | AT&T Wireless(T) | Magnacom Wireless |
| Walla Walla | Blue Mountain Cellular | Inland Cellular | Western Wireless(G) | Sprint PCS(C) | Western Wireless(G) | Touch America | U S West(C) | Magnacom Wireless |
| Wenatchee | American Cellular | GTE Wireless(C) | GTE Wireless(C) | Sprint PCS(C) | Western Wireless(G) | Western Wireless(G) | Touch America | Northcoast OpCo. |
| Yakima | AT&T Wireless(T) | U.S. Cellular | GTE Wireless(C) | Sprint PCS(C) | Western Wireless(G) | AT&T Wireless(T) | U S West(C) | Magnacom Wireless |

| Market Name | Cellular Carriers | | PCS Carriers ↑ | | | | | |
| --- | --- | --- | --- | --- | --- | --- | --- | --- |
| | A Block | B Block | A Block | B Block | C Block | D Block | E Block | F Block |
| **West Virginia** | | | | | | | | |
| Beckley | Highland Cellular | Alltel[C] | AT&T Wireless[T] | GTE Wireless[C] | Devon Mobile[C] | Sprint PCS[C] | Sprint PCS[C] | Virginia PCS[C] |
| Bluefield | Highland Cellular | Alltel[C] | AT&T Wireless[T] | GTE Wireless[C] | Devon Mobile[C] | Sprint PCS[C] | Sprint PCS[C] | Northcoast OpCo. |
| Charleston | AT&T Wireless[T] | Alltel[C] | AT&T Wireless[T] | GTE Wireless[C] | ComScape Telecomm | Sprint PCS[C] | Sprint PCS[C] | MCG PCS |
| Clarksburg | Mountaineer Mobile | U.S. Cellular | Sprint PCS[C] | Aerial[C] | Polycell[C] | AT&T Wireless[T] | Virginia PCS[C] | Northcoast OpCo. |
| Elkins | Rural Cellular | U.S. Cellular | Sprint PCS[C] | Aerial[C] | Polycell[C] | AT&T Wireless[T] | Virginia PCS[C] | Northcoast OpCo. |
| Fairmont | Mountaineer Mobile | U.S. Cellular | Sprint PCS[C] | Aerial[C] | Quantum Comm Group[C] | AT&T Wireless[T] | Virginia PCS[C] | Virginia PCS[C] |
| Huntington | AT&T Wireless[T] | Alltel[C] | AT&T Wireless[T] | GTE Wireless[C] | Horizon Personal Comm[C] | Sprint PCS[C] | Sprint PCS[C] | Northcoast OpCo. |
| Logan | ClearComm[T] | Alltel[C] | AT&T Wireless[T] | GTE Wireless[C] | Devon Mobile[C] | Sprint PCS[C] | Sprint PCS[C] | RLV-PCS I Ptshp[C] |
| Morgantown | Mountaineer Mobile | U.S. Cellular | Sprint PCS[C] | Aerial[C] | MCG PCS | AT&T Wireless[T] | PC PCS | Virginia PCS[C] |
| Parkersburg | AT&T Wireless[T] | Alltel[C] | AT&T Wireless[T] | Aerial[C] | Horizon Personal Comm[C] | Sprint PCS[C] | Sprint PCS[C] | RLV-PCS I Ptshp[C] |
| Weirton | AT&T Wireless[T] | Alltel[C] | Sprint PCS[C] | Aerial[C] | Devon Mobile[C] | Sprint PCS[C] | Western Wireless[G] | Urban Comm[C] |
| Wheeling | AT&T Wireless[T] | Alltel[C] | Sprint PCS[C] | Aerial[C] | Americall[C] | AT&T Wireless[T] | Virginia PCS[C] | Northcoast OpCo. |
| Williamson | AT&T Wireless[T] | Alltel[C] | AT&T Wireless[T] | GTE Wireless[C] | SouthEast Telephone[G] | Sprint PCS[C] | Sprint PCS[C] | Omnipoint[G] |
| **Wisconsin** | | | | | | | | |
| Appleton-Oshkosh | BellSouth[T] | Cellulink/Pactel | Sprint PCS[C] | PrimeCo[C] | Airadigm[G] | AT&T Wireless[T] | Century Tel[T] | Metro Southwest PCS |
| Eau Claire | American Cellular | Cellulink/Pactel | Sprint PCS[C] | Aerial[G] | Airadigm[G] | AT&T Wireless[T] | Century Tel[T] | Minnesota PCS |
| Fond du Lac | BellSouth[T] | Cellulink/Pactel | Sprint PCS[C] | PrimeCo[C] | Airadigm[G] | AT&T Wireless[T] | Century Tel[T] | Metro Southwest PCS |
| Green Bay | BellSouth[T] | Cellcom | Sprint PCS[C] | PrimeCo[C] | Airadigm[G] | AT&T Wireless[T] | Century Tel[T] | PCS One |
| Janesville-Beloit | BellSouth[T] | Ameritech[C] | Sprint PCS[C] | PrimeCo[C] | Airadigm[G] | AT&T Wireless[T] | Century Tel[T] | Nextwave[C] |
| La Crosse | U.S. Cellular | Century Tel[T] | Sprint PCS[C] | PrimeCo[C] | Airadigm[G] | Century Tel[T] | PC PCS | Minnesota PCS |
| Madison | BellSouth[T] | Ameritech[C] | Sprint PCS[C] | PrimeCo[C] | Airadigm[G] | AT&T Wireless[T] | Nextwave[C] | PCS Wisconsin |
| Manitowoc | BellSouth[T] | Cellcom | Sprint PCS[C] | PrimeCo[C] | Airadigm[G] | AT&T Wireless[T] | Century Tel[T] | Metro Southwest PCS |
| Marinette | BellSouth[T] | Cellcom | Sprint PCS[C] | PrimeCo[C] | Fortunet Wireless | AT&T Wireless[T] | Century Tel[T] | Airadigm[G] |
| Milwaukee | BellSouth[T] | Ameritech[C] | Sprint PCS[C] | PrimeCo[C] | Indus[T] | AT&T Wireless[T] | Western Wireless[G] | Nextwave[C] |
| Rhinelander | American Cellular | Cellulink/Pactel | Sprint PCS[C] | PrimeCo[C] | Airadigm[G] | AT&T Wireless[T] | Century Tel[T] | Metro Southwest PCS |

| Market Name | Cellular Carriers | | PCS Carriers → | | | | | |
|---|---|---|---|---|---|---|---|---|
| | A Block | B Block | A Block | B Block | C Block | D Block | E Block | F Block |
| Sheboygan | BellSouth[T] | Ameritech[C] | Sprint PCS[C] | PrimeCo[C] | Airadigm[C] | AT&T Wireless[T] | Century Tel[T] | Metro Southwest PCS |
| Stevens Point-Marshfield | U.S. Cellular | U.S. Cellular | Sprint PCS[C] | PrimeCo[C] | Airadigm[C] | Century Tel[T] | Wisconsin RSA #7 | PCS Devco |
| Wausau | American Cellular | U.S. Cellular | Sprint PCS[C] | PrimeCo[C] | Airadigm[C] | AT&T Wireless[T] | Century Tel[T] | Metro Southwest PCS |
| **Wyoming** | | | | | | | | |
| Casper-Gillette | Western Wireless | AirTouch[C] | Sprint PCS[C] | Western Wireless[G] | High Country | U S West[C] | RT Comm. | RT Comm. |
| Cheyenne | Western Wireless | AirTouch[C] | Sprint PCS[C] | Western Wireless[G] | High Country | U S West[C] | RT Comm. | RT Comm. |
| Riverton | CommNet 2000 | Union Cellular | Sprint PCS[C] | Western Wireless[G] | RT Comm | U S West[C] | AT&T Wireless[T] | Polycell[C] |
| Rock Springs | HBF Cellular | Cell-Tel Comm | Sprint PCS[C] | Western Wireless[G] | Mountain Solutions[G] | U S West[C] | AT&T Wireless[T] | Silver Star |
| **American Samoa** | | | South Seas Satellite | Communications Int'l | Westel | AT&T Wireless[T] | AT&T Wireless[T] | Westel |
| **Guam** | Guam Cellular | Guam T.A. | Guam Net | Guam Communications | Pocket[C] | IT&E Overseas | Guam T.A. | Longstreet Comm |
| **Northern Mariana Islands** | Western Airwave | Micronesian Telecom | Guam Net | Guam Communications | Pocket[C] | IT&E Overseas | Guam T.A. | Longstreet Comm |
| **Puerto Rico** | Cel Comm of P.R. | Puerto Rico TelCo | AT&T Wireless[T] | Centennial Cellular[C] | ClearComm[C][G] | Sprint PCS[C] | Puerto Rico TelCo | Omnipoint[G] |
| **Puerto Rico** | Cel Comm of P.R. | Puerto Rico TelCo | AT&T Wireless[T] | Centennial Cellular[C] | ClearComm[C][G] | Puerto Rico TelCo | Sprint PCS[C] | Pegasus PCS |
| **U.S. Virgin Islands** | U.S. Virgin Islands Tel | Vitelcom | AT&T Wireless[T] | Centennial Cellular[C] | Windkeeper Comm[P] | Sprint PCS[C] | Vitelcom | Westel |

# Carrier Name Abbreviations

The following list is comprised of companies whose names were too long to fit in the Carriers by Market, Channel Block, and Technology table. The abbreviated name used is on the left, with the full name of the carrier on the right.

| | |
|---|---|
| 21st Century Telesis | 21st Century Telesis Joint Venture |
| Aer Force | Aer Force Communications |
| American Personal | American Personal Communications |
| Anishnabe Comm | Anishnabe Communications |
| Bay Springs TelCo. | Bay Springs Telephone Co. |
| Brookings Municipal | Brookings Municipal Utilities |
| Central Wireless | Central Wireless Partnership |
| Chase Telecomm | Chase Telecommunications |
| Comcast PCS | Comcast PCS Communications |
| Comm Venture PCS | Communications Venture PCS |
| ComScape Telecomm | ComScape Telecommunications |
| Consolidated Comm | Consolidated Communications |
| Consolidated Tel | Consolidated Telephone Cooperative |
| Denver & Ephrata T&T | Denver & Ephrata Telephone & Telegraph Co. |
| Devon Mobile | Devon Mobile Communications |
| Eldorado Comm | Eldorado Communications |
| Enterprise Comm | Enterprise Communications Partnership |
| Fairbanks Muni | Fairbanks Municipal Utilities System |
| Georgia Ind. PCS | Georgia Independent PCS |
| Global Info Tech | Global Information Technologies |
| GST Wireless Comm | GST Wireless Communications |
| Horizon Personal Comm. | Horizon Personal Communications |
| Integrated Comm | Integrated Communications Group |
| Kansas PCS | Kansas Personal Communication Services |
| Lite-Wave | Lite-Wave Communications |
| Longstreet Comm | Longstreet Communication International |
| Mobile Tri-States | Mobile Tri-States LP130 |
| Montana PCS | Montana PCS Alliance |
| N. Dakota Network | North Dakota Network Co. |
| N. Dakota PCS | North Dakota PCS Alliance |
| NE Nebraska TelCo. | Northeast Nebraska Telephone Co. |

New England Wireless . . . New England Wireless Communications
New Hampshire . . . . . . . . New Hampshire Wireless
NextWave . . . . . . . . . . . . NextWave Power Partners
NH Wireless . . . . . . . . . . New Hampshire Wireless
Northcoast OpCo. . . . . . . . Northcoast Operating
Northern Michigan PCS . . Northern Michigan PCS Consortium
Panhandle Telecom . . . . . Panhandle Telecommunication Systems
Personal Comm Ntwk . . . . Personal Communications Network
Phoenix Wireless . . . . . . . The Phoenix Wireless Group
Pine Belt PCS. . . . . . . . . . Pine Belt PCS Partnership
Pinnacle Telecom . . . . . . . Pinnacle Telecom of Jackson, Miss.
Pioneer Tel . . . . . . . . . . . Pioneer Telephone Association
Poka Lambro . . . . . . . . . . Poka Lambro/PVT Wireless
Polycell Comm . . . . . . . . . Polycell Communications
Quantum Comm Group. . . Quantum Communications Group
Rivgam. . . . . . . . . . . . . . Rivgam Communicators
RLV-PCS I Ptshp . . . . . . . RLV-PCS I Partnership
Roberts-Roberts . . . . . . . . Roberts-Roberts & Associates
S.Cent. Utah Tel . . . . . . . . South Central Utah Telephone Association
Savannah Ind. PCS . . . . . Savannah Independent PCS
SNET . . . . . . . . . . . . . . . Southern New England Telephone
South Seas Satellite . . . . . South Seas Satellite Communications
Southeast Wireless. . . . . . Southeast Wireless Communications
Southern Comm Sys. . . . . Southern Communications Systems
Sowega Wireless Comm. . Sowega Wireless Communications
Troup EMC Comm . . . . . . Troup EMC Communications
Urban Comm . . . . . . . . . . Urban Communicators
Virginia PCS . . . . . . . . . . Virginia PCS Alliance
Windkeeper Comm. . . . . . Windkeeper Communications
Wireless Telecomm. . . . . . Wireless Telecommunications Co.

# Frequency Charts

**G**

**Appendix**

| | |
|---:|:---|
| Nextel: | 806-821 MHz |
| | 851-866 MHz |
| | |
| 800 MHz Cellular: | 824-849 MHz |
| | 869-894 MHz |
| | |
| GSM900 (Europe): | 890-915 MHz |
| | 935-960 MHz |
| | |
| GSM1800 (Europe): | 1710-1785 MHz |
| | 1805-1880 MHz |
| | |
| GSM-NA 1900 MHz PCS: | 1850-1910 MHz |
| | 1930-1990 MHz |
| | |
| LMDS: | 27.5-28.35 GHz |
| | 29.1-29.25 GHz |
| | 31.0-31.15 GHz |
| | 31.15-31.30 GHz |

# 800 MHz Cellular Frequencies Chart

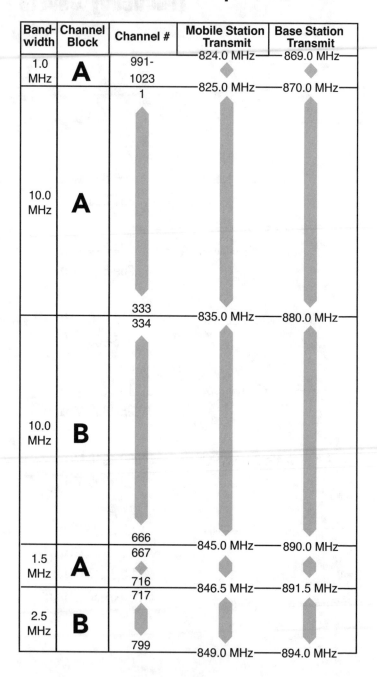

| Band-width | Channel Block | Channel # | Mobile Station Transmit | Base Station Transmit |
|---|---|---|---|---|
| 1.0 MHz | A | 991-1023 | 824.0 MHz | 869.0 MHz |
| 10.0 MHz | A | 1 ... 333 | 825.0 MHz | 870.0 MHz |
| 10.0 MHz | B | 334 ... 666 | 835.0 MHz | 880.0 MHz |
| 1.5 MHz | A | 667 716 | 845.0 MHz | 890.0 MHz |
| 2.5 MHz | B | 717 799 | 846.5 MHz | 891.5 MHz |
| | | | 849.0 MHz | 894.0 MHz |

# 1900 MHz PCS Frequencies Chart

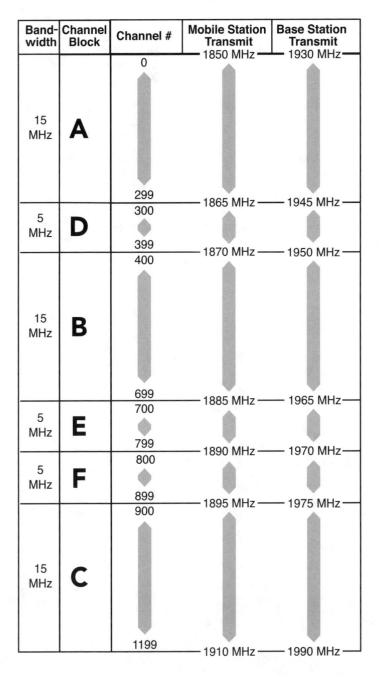

| Band-width | Channel Block | Channel # | Mobile Station Transmit | Base Station Transmit |
|---|---|---|---|---|
| | | | 1850 MHz | 1930 MHz |
| 15 MHz | A | 0 ⋯ 299 | | |
| | | | 1865 MHz | 1945 MHz |
| 5 MHz | D | 300 ⋯ 399 | | |
| | | | 1870 MHz | 1950 MHz |
| 15 MHz | B | 400 ⋯ 699 | | |
| | | | 1885 MHz | 1965 MHz |
| 5 MHz | E | 700 ⋯ 799 | | |
| | | | 1890 MHz | 1970 MHz |
| 5 MHz | F | 800 ⋯ 899 | | |
| | | | 1895 MHz | 1975 MHz |
| 15 MHz | C | 900 ⋯ 1199 | | |
| | | | 1910 MHz | 1990 MHz |

## Nextel Frequencies Chart

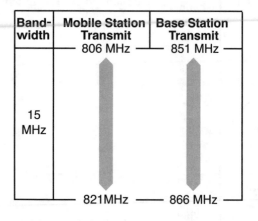

| Band-width | Mobile Station Transmit | Base Station Transmit |
|---|---|---|
| | 806 MHz | 851 MHz |
| 15 MHz | | |
| | 821MHz | 866 MHz |

# A

**A block**  A set of channels designated by the FCC to be used by certain carriers. In cellular, this is one of two sets of channels, each consisting of 25 MHz of spectrum. Channel block A initially referred to RCC-type, or non-wireline, cellular carriers. PCS divides its spectrum into six sets of channels, designated frequency blocks A through F. Frequency block A in PCS is 30 MHz of spectrum licensed to operate in MTA service areas.

**access channel**  One of the carrier's control channels used to continuously transmit information about itself, as well as instructions to wireless phones, in what is called an overhead signal.

**access fee**  See **interconnect fee** and **monthly access fee**.

**access overload class**  Part of the NAM programming, this two-digit (00 to 15) code is used to control access to the wireless network in times of emergency or overload. Most carriers in the U.S. do not have a structure for using this feature.

**activation fee**  This is a one-time charge from the carrier to set up your service. Some carriers have promotions to waive this fee.

**adaptive answer**  This feature, available on newer modems, allows the phone to detect whether the incoming call is a voice call, a fax, or data, and answer accordingly. Some modems use this feature to provide caller ID benefits, usually through software on a computer.

**airtime** This refers to your actual usage, not how long the phone is turned on. Airtime is usually broken down into two billing times: peak time and off-peak time.

**air interface** Refers to the type of technology used by a wireless system—AMPS, NAMPS, TDMA, CDMA, PACS, GSM, or GSM-NA.

**A-key** A 26-character identifier encoded in the wireless handset that is shared only with the service provider. It is used for authentication.

**alphanumeric** A term that describes the display of a wireless handset that uses both letters (alphabetical characters) and numbers. Alphanumeric displays allow you to store directory phone numbers alphabetically, as well as into a number location, with easy retrieval via the keypad or special button. Phones with alphanumeric capability are also user-friendly and can usually provide caller ID with name when you subscribe to this service.

**amplitude modulation (AM)** The flow of electromagnetic energy waves is regulated or controlled by altering the transmitter's power. See also **modulation**.

**AMPS** Advanced Mobile Phone Service is the analog system used in North, Central, and South America, the Caribbean, parts of Southern Asia and Russia, as well as Australia and New Zealand. It uses a total of 50 MHz of spectrum: 25 MHz at 824-849 MHz for transmission from the mobile phone to the cell site, and 25 MHz at 869-894 MHz for transmission from the cell site to the mobile phone. The FCC divided the 832 channels available into two blocks, A and B. AMPS uses 30 kHz channel separation.

**analog signal** An RF transmission that is adjusted or modulated proportionally. An example of proportional adjustment is tuning into a radio station using a rotating dial, which is often difficult to tune exactly and sometimes staticky. This not as accurate as finding a specific radio frequency using a digital tuner. The rotating dial is proportional, using rotations to try to hone in on the signal. The digital tuner is able to dial directly to a specific signal. In cellular, analog is a continuous transmission wave, whereas pulse code modulation (digital) breaks the information down into digital ones and zeros for transmission. It then reassembles the signal on the other end back into analog form so that we humans can understand the information being transmitted. See also **modulation**.

**answer mode** Enabling this option in your modem allows you to receive an incoming call to your data device.

**ANSI** The American National Standards Institute.

**ASCII (American Standards Committee on Information Interchange)** A standard representation of 127 characters on your computer keyboard, including numbers 0 to 9, the alphabet, punctuation, and certain special characters. An ASCII (pronounced "askee") file is commonly referred to as a text file and enables you to transfer information to someone with incompatible computer software or hardware. Most software applications offer you the option to save a file as "text."

**asymmetric transmission** This is where the transmission speed differs from the receiving speed.

**asynchronous mode** The space between character transmissions is not regulated by a specified length of time, resulting in the need for start bits and stop bits for proper interpretation by the receiving modem.

**authentication** A protocol to reduce or eliminate fraud in AMPS technology by using an A-key. The 26-character A-key is only known by the phone and the carrier. Unlike the mobile phone number and ESN, the A-key is not transmitted. Both the phone and the system must be capable of authentication for this technology to work.

**auto answer** If you have a modem and computer capable of voice mail, this setting will answer an incoming call and, with **adaptive answer**, either record a voice message, accept a fax, or save a data file transfer.

**automatic call delivery** A service offered by most carriers whereby they automatically forward your calls to the market you are visiting so that you don't miss an incoming call.

**autonomous registration** In order to maintain call processing efficiency, the carrier asks the wireless phone to identify itself when you first turn it on, and thereafter every five to fifteen minutes. This allows the system to page your phone only at a small number of cell sites, such as your last known site and the adjacent cells, within a time/distance travel ratio that is feasible.

# B

**baud rate** The signals per second transmitted between two modems, or the connection rate. Baud rate is different from bps because more than one bit can be represented per signal.

**B block** A set of channels designated by the FCC to be used by certain carriers. In cellular, this is one of two sets of channels, each consisting of 25 MHz of spectrum. Channel block B initially referred to landline companies offering cellular service, or wireline carriers. PCS divides its spectrum into six sets of channels, designated frequency blocks A through F. Frequency block B in PCS is 30 MHz of spectrum licensed to operate in MTA service areas.

**bandit mobile**  A subscriber unit whose mobile phone number and ESN do not match the information in the wireless switch, whether at home or roaming. This user will be denied service until the problems are corrected.

**bandwidth**  A range of spectrum or contiguous frequencies used to transmit radio signals; also referred to as a pipe. In cellular, the bandwidth is 30 kHz per channel, or 30 kHz channel separation. In PCS, the bandwidth used by CDMA networks is 1,250 kHz or 1.25 MHz.

**base station**  This is the term for the building at the base of a cell site that houses the electronic equipment used to relay incoming and outgoing transmissions between the phone and the MTSO. The infrastructure of a wireless network consists of cell sites, base stations, and the MTSO. The base station uses either wirelines or microwaves to transmit information to and from the MTSO.

**Basic Trading Area (BTA)**  A geographic division of the United States used to define PCS 1900 MHz wireless phone service areas for frequency blocks C, D, E, and F. Based on information from Rand McNally, the FCC designated 493 BTAs.

**bps**  See **bits per second**.

**binary**  A numbering system used by computers that consists of the digits 0 and 1. Also called a base 2 numbering system.

**bit**   One of two numerals in the binary numbering system, either 0 or 1. Computers reduce all of their information or data into bits.

**bits per second (bps)**   The rate, or speed, data bits are transmitted between modems; the throughput speed.

**broadband**   The use of a wide range of contiguous frequencies, or wide "pipe," for voice, data, or video communication services.

**Broadband PCS**   Broadband Personal Communications Services designated by the FCC to operate in the 1900 MHz frequency range for voice and data communications. One hundred and twenty MHz of spectrum is divided into six channel blocks: A, B, and C blocks are 30 MHz each; D, E, and F blocks are 10 MHz each. PCS operates at 1850-1910 MHz for transmission from the mobile phone to the cell site, and at 1930-1990 MHz for transmission from the cell site to the mobile phone.

**BTA**   See **Basic Trading Area**.

**bundling**   This term is used in two instances. One meaning is where a carrier ties the sale of the wireless phone to the airtime service package. Another meaning is where a service provider is able to bundle landline and wireless phone service with long distance, and perhaps paging and Internet services, all from one company and possibly all on one bill.

**busy signal**   In wireless telephony, if the number you dial from your wireless phone is busy, you will hear a busy signal, just as you do on your home phone.

**busy transfer**   This call diversion feature is a switch-based function where you can designate an alternate phone number to receive your calls if your wireless phone is busy. This feature can't be used at the same time as voice mail.

# C

**CALEA (Communications Assistance to Law Enforcement Act)** A law enacted in 1994 that requires both landline and wireless phone companies to accommodate eavesdropping equipment on their new digital networks, and grants law enforcement agencies the ability to wiretap these networks.

**call detail** The carrier offers this option for you to see a record of all your outgoing and incoming calls, as well as your roaming activity. Some carriers charge a nominal fee for call detail.

**call diversion** See **no-answer transfer** and **busy transfer**.

**caller ID** A service enhancement showing the number (and sometimes the name) of the person calling on the display of your phone. This feature works the same as on your home phone service. There is often an additional charge per month from your wireless carrier.

**call forwarding** This switch-based feature, which works the same as on landline phones, directs an inbound call intended for the wireless phone to an alternate number. The inbound call will not ring on the wireless phone. Also see **no-answer transfer** and **busy transfer**.

**call waiting** A switch-based feature alerting you that you have a new incoming call while you are on an existing call. You can answer the new call using a switchhook function, the same way as you do on your home phone. You can alternate between the calls, but you can't create a three-way conversation. See **three-way calling**. You are charged for the airtime on both connections.

**calling party pays (CPP)** As the name implies, the person calling the wireless phone pays the airtime charges of the call. This concept usually increases wireless usage, as the financial burden isn't borne wholly by the subscriber, who only pays for outgoing calls. Inbound call charges are spread among the various callers. CPP is very popular in other parts of the world and is slowly being implemented across the U.S.

**calling signal (CNG)** When a fax machine or fax modem is sending a fax, it transmits a calling signal to alert the receiver that a fax is on its way. This signal is used by the receiving fax machine to automatically connect. Small offices and home offices (SOHO) often use a switching device to minimize the number of phone lines they need. If the calling fax device doesn't transmit this tone, these switches won't detect a fax and, therefore, won't switch to the fax machine.

**carrier** This term usually refers to a service provider, or system operator, in your area. This term also is used to describe the nature of a wireless network, which uses a carrier wave to transmit the audio signal.

**C block** In PCS, this is one of six sets of channels into which the PCS spectrum is divided, and it consists of 30 MHz of spectrum. Frequency block C was reserved for entrepreneurial businesses and is licensed to operate in BTA service areas.

**CCITT (Comité Consultatif International Télégraphique et Téléphonique)** The International Telegraph and Telephone Consultative Committee is an international standards-setting body. The CCITT changed their name on March 1, 1993 to the

International Telecommunication Union—Telecommunication Standardization Sector (ITU-T).

**CDMA** See **code division multiple access**.

**cdmaOne** A brand name for CDMA technology.

**CDPD** See **cellular digital packet data**.

**cell** The designated geographic area covered by a cell site (antenna and base station) to provide coverage in a wireless system. A CGSA consists of multiple cells to complete the system. As you travel through the CGSA, you will be handed off from one cell to another to provide you with continuous service. The size of a cell varies according to use. AMPS and 800 MHz digital networks have cells ranging from four to twenty miles, while PCS 1900 MHz networks range in size from 200 feet to six miles.

**cell site** The cell site consists of an antenna and a base station, usually at the center of a cell. Some antennas at cell sites are directional and will not provide coverage of a circular design.

**cellular** A wireless telephone network that provides a link from a mobile subscriber to a cell site and MTSO, which ultimately connects to the public switched telephone network (PSTN). The wireless telephone network is divided into overlapping, circular-shaped areas called cells. Each cell has an antenna at its center.

**cell splitting** This refers to the concept of dividing an existing wireless network into smaller cells. Its purpose is to create greater potential for channel separation and thereby increase the capacity of the network. See **frequency reuse**.

**cellular digital packet data (CDPD)** CDPD was originally intended to take advantage of unused airtime at the beginning and end of every call (while the call is being set up and after you hang up) before the channel is reassigned. CDPD provides data-only access to the 800 MHz cellular network, transmitting information at 19,200 bps by breaking the information down into small "packets" and then reassembling them at the receiving side. CDPD provides Internet Protocol (IP) connectivity through specific devices such as laptop computers and PDAs. Today, most CDPD service providers designate a specific channel for this data transmission.

**Cellular Geographic Service Area (CGSA)** A CGSA is the geographic area covered by a wireless service provider. The FCC designates a CGSA using MSAs, RSAs, MTAs, and BTAs to determine service area boundaries. These areas are usually matched to major metropolitan areas and to county borders. In rural areas, several counties may be lumped together and considered one RSA or BTA.

**channel** A frequency or frequency range assigned by the FCC that is used by your phone to communicate with the wireless network.

**channel reuse** When networks are designed, the engineers first look at the geography to be covered. The size of the cells is determined by the anticipated capacity. Smaller cells will be required in heavy usage areas. There is a limited quantity of channels or frequencies, but these channels can be reused within the system. However, there must be sufficient distance between the cells using the channels so as not to cause any interference.

**channel seizure** After entering the number you are calling and pressing SEND, your phone is assigned a channel by the MTSO. The phone seizes the channel before you hear audio feedback that the call is processing. Some wireless phone companies start their billing from the time the channel is seized. Most, however, don't start charging you until the person you're calling answers.

**channel separation** When engineers design a wireless network, they create a physical distance and regulate power levels between the channels so that no channel will be reused within the cell and in the six contiguous cells. This prevents co-channel interference.

**churn** The term the carriers use when you leave your current provider to sign up with service at another company.

**CLEC (competitive local exchange carrier)** This term refers to a company—either landline or wireless—that is offering you an alternative to your existing local phone company.

**clone** A thief uses scanning equipment to acquire your mobile phone number and ESN, programs it into an older phone and sells this phone, or the use of it, for a fee. The buyer uses this phone with your information (though not usually in your home market as that is easily detected), and in a month, you get a gigantic phone bill calling cities you've never heard of from places you've never been to! This process is called cloning, because the thief duplicated or cloned your phone information. Only older phones can be cloned, as phones manufactured since 1995 are unalterable by law. This type of wireless fraud is not possible on digital equipment and is declining among users who have authenticating equipment where analog carriers offer authentication.

**co-branding** This term applies to an item that has two brand names on it, such as the phone that carries the name of both the manufacturer and the service provider.

**co-channel interference** Improperly managed power levels or a wireless phone used from an aircraft can cause interference among channels within a terrestrial network. The result is cross talk, where your connection is interrupted by the sound of one or both sides of another conversation.

**code division multiple access (CDMA)** CDMA is a technology used in both cellular and PCS wireless telephony that assigns unique matching codes to each pair of listeners and speakers and is then able to transmit them over the same channel. CDMA combines several smaller channels into one larger channel by using **spread spectrum** technology. The channels are large or "wide," occupying 1,250 MHz, versus the 30 kHz used in AMPS. The CDMA channel is more than 40 times the size of the AMPS channel, and it is capable of transmitting 64 different voice circuits at one time through the use of vocoders. In addition, by using code assignments and converting the audio into ones and zeros, different conversations can be transmitted over the same frequency spectrum. This provides approximately ten times more capacity to the carrier than the existing AMPS technology.

**collocation** Rather than dotting our landscape with more and more antennas, many carriers are choosing to collocate, or share, an existing site. Zoning and economic issues are also reasons wireless companies are choosing collocation, as this expedites construction of their networks. For example, a wireless telephony carrier may ask a police station erecting a new antenna to add 25 to 50 feet to the top of the new tower for the wireless antenna so that a second antenna doesn't need to be erected in the neighborhood.

**command** You can use your computer to communicate with your modem via AT (attention) commands. Hayes developed a standard set of commands with which modem manufacturers comply. Your modem must be in a command mode to accept them. Command mode is also called "escape mode" or "online mode."

**compatible** A modem that is compatible **may** work at any speed in the established standard.

**compliant** A compliant modem **must** work at any speed in the established standard.

**configuration** The process of setting parameters in the modem that will allow it to communicate with another modem successfully. This is usually accomplished by entering an initialization string into the software you are using to operate the modem.

**control channel** Carriers need a way for the phone and the system to talk to each other. They do this on a control channel, which is either a paging channel or an access channel. Depending on the network, there may be as many as 21 channels designated for these functions. The phone scans the control channels for instructions. In the call setup, the control channel assigns the voice channels that will be used for your conversation. During a call, the cell site may tell your phone to increase or decrease the amount of power it is using to transmit. The cell site also uses control channels to give instructions to your phone to change to a different channel when you are moving from one cell to another.

**cross talk** Hearing one or both sides of another wireless conversation, and losing your call, is usually the result of co-channel interference.

**C-scan** Some telephones have this negative-scan feature, where you can program the phone with system IDs that you don't want to access. This feature is handy if you want to be sure you don't roam in your home market. Just enter the SID of the carrier(s) you didn't subscribe to.

**CTIA** The Cellular Telecommunications Industry Association is an organization comprised of wireless telephone companies operating at 800 MHz and 1900 MHz.

# D

**D-AMPS** Digital AMPS is the term Ericsson, Inc. uses to describe time division multiple access (TDMA) at 800 MHz.

**data** Information that is converted into binary form when used by a computer.

**data compression** When transmitting data, it is best to minimize or condense it as much as possible. There are standards for compressing data, equivalent to substitution codes, which reduce the amount of data being sent. The modems agree up front on which standard to use so the data can be reconstructed at the receiving end. See the **modem standards** at the end of this glossary.

**data device** Any device capable of communicating in binary format: computers, PDAs, fax machines, etc.

**D block** In PCS, this is one of six sets of channels into which the PCS spectrum is divided, and it consists of 10 MHz of spectrum. Frequency block D is licensed to operate in BTA service areas.

**DCS1800** Digital Cellular Service (DCS)—or GSM— is available in the 1800 MHz range in Europe and other parts of the world. This spectrum is an addition to the services offered at 900 MHz, allowing competition and increased capacity. These networks operate at less power than the 900 MHz networks, similar to the way that the 1900 MHz networks in the U.S. operate at less power than the 800 MHz systems.

**digital modulation** The system and the phone communicate by converting your voice sounds into bits (ones and zeros) used by computers. Because the information is sent digitally, humans can't eavesdrop, so you have privacy. Transmitting digitally is also more efficient than transmitting your voice because more people can use the same channel by using multiple access schemes such as TDMA and CDMA. The digital capabilities of the network and the phone have presented new service options such as messaging and paging. See also **modulation**.

**digital signal** Modems convert information on your laptop into binary information. Then a modem uses analog audio signals to communicate or transmit this information. These audio signals can be transmitted as analog sound waves over the AMPS network.

**directory listing** Your home phone number is probably listed in your local white pages phone directory. You may choose **not** to list your wireless phone number in your local directory (as most wireless phone users do) because you are charged for incoming calls.

**diversity reception** This is a two-antenna system that is used by installed 3-watt mobile phones. One antenna is designated as the primary antenna, the other is secondary. When the phone detects the signal weakening from the first antenna, it then asks the second antenna to see if it has a stronger signal. If the second antenna's signal is stronger, then the phone switches to the second antenna. The phone continues to monitor which antenna is providing the stronger signal and continually transfers to the best one.

**dropped call** This phenomenon, which you'll recognize as silence on your wireless phone, occurs when the connection between your phone and the cell site is interrupted. If the cell site and phone aren't able to reestablish communications within five seconds, the call will be lost completely. At this point, you may hear a loud hiss. Dropped calls can occur during a handoff or when the signal spirals. A signal can spiral when you travel in hilly terrain or among tall buildings. You will also experience a dropped call if you travel beyond the coverage area.

**DTMF (dual tone multifrequency)** You know this as touch tones. When you dial a phone number on your home phone, you will hear tones for as long as you press the buttons, and they will be transmitted over the line. Wireless phones don't use DTMF to process calls. DTMF is included in a wireless phone for two reasons: 1) to provide audio feedback to you and 2) to allow you access to systems that do use DTMF, such as voice mail and long-distance services. However, unless you have long tone DTMF activated in your wireless phone, when you press on a number key, it will transmit a timed burst of DTMF tone regardless of how long you hold down the button. For some services, such as voice mail, this timed burst isn't long enough for the system to recognize the signal. If you find that you are having trouble with services that use DTMF, look in your manual to see whether you have long tone DTMF and how to activate it.

**dual NAM** Subscribing to two different wireless systems is called dual registration, dual system, or dual NAM. Some phones have the capability to register to more than two systems. Dual registration can provide a local number in a market you visit frequently, as well as reduce wireless charges because you are local instead of roaming. Police, fire, and rescue departments can benefit from dual registration because it provides maximum coverage in markets with hilly terrain.

# E

**E 9-1-1 (Enhanced 9-1-1)** A wireless 9-1-1 service that transmits the wireless phone number and the caller's location (within 125 meters). This is expected to be implemented nationwide by October of 2001, and it is required to be accurate two-thirds of the time.

**E block** In PCS, this is one of six sets of channels into which the PCS spectrum is divided, and it consists of 10 MHz of spectrum. Frequency block E is licensed to operate in BTA service areas.

**echo (a.k.a. local echo)** Setting your modem to echo what is being transmitted is helpful if you are "talking" on line with someone before or after a file transfer. It allows you to see on your computer screen what you are typing on your keyboard, as well as the other person's communication to you. If you have the local echo turned off, you will only see what the other person types, not what you are typing to them. This is not good for high-speed data transmission. It is easy to turn on and off. Just change the setting of the number after the E in the initialization string to 1 (on) or 0 (off). After a transmission with echo off, you can reactivate local echo by typing +++ followed by the return key (to tell the modem to obey the next command you type), and then typing ATE1 followed by a return.

**e.i.r.p. (equivalent isotropically radiated power)** The measurement of antenna transmission gain in a given direction from power supplied to the antenna as relative to an isotropic antenna (a theoretical concept of an omnidirectional antenna that is used as a reference to measure gain).

**electronic serial number (ESN)** The ESN is a unique, unalterable 32-bit code assigned to each wireless phone, usually expressed in decimal (11-digit) or hexadecimal (8-character) format. The ESN and mobile ID are transmitted each time a call is placed and matched to the information in the carrier's database to ensure the user's validity. If the ESN and mobile ID in the phone don't match the information the carrier has, you won't be able to make a call.

**encryption** The technique of scrambling or encoding a digital signal to prevent interception of conversations. The information is unusable without special decrypting equipment and may take days to decode.

**error correction/control** When a modem transmits data, it is broken down into blocks of information. In order for the receiving modem to know for sure if it got the entire block, a checksum is calculated by the sending modem and sent at the end of the data block for verification by the receiving modem. If all the data didn't arrive intact, the modems know to retransmit that block of data. This process is better than sending the entire file and then saying, "Did you get it all?" There are different error correction protocols. See the **modem standards** at the end of this glossary. The modems agree on which one to use during the setup—part of all that screeching you hear at the beginning of a modem connection.

**e.r.p. (effective radiated power)** The measurement of antenna gain in a given direction when power is supplied to the antenna, relative to a half-wave dipole. A 3-watt mobile with a 3 dB antenna will transmit at a maximum of 3 watts. However, a 3-watt mobile with a 5 dB gain antenna will transmit up to 5 watts e.r.p. Don't forget that the system tells the phone to reduce power if the signal is too strong, so using a 5 dB antenna won't make the signal received by the cell site more than 3 watts, but it helps boost your signal when you are at the edge of the system.

**ESMR (enhanced specialized mobile radio)** Digital wireless phone and data services that are offered on channels previously offering only two-way radio communications. Nextel Communications, Inc. dominates this area of spectrum. It offers wireless telephony, paging, two-way radio, and data services.

**ETACS (Enhanced Totally Accessed Communications System)** Operating in the 900 MHz band, this analog technology was and is used in some European and East Asian countries.

**E-TDMA** This enhancement to TDMA digital technology was proposed by Hughes Network Systems and offers a capacity increase eight to ten times that of AMPS.

**ETSI (European Telecommunications Standards Institute)** Sets the standards for wireless telecommunications in Europe.

# F

**F block** In PCS, this is one of six sets of channels into which the PCS spectrum is divided, and it consists of 10 MHz of spectrum. Frequency block F was reserved for entrepreneurial businesses and is licensed to operate in BTA service areas

**FCC (Federal Communications Commission)** The FCC manages the spectrum for radio frequency (RF) in the United States, both commercial and private. It determines allocation, and it develops and enforces regulations governing spectrum use. Regulations for wireless telephony in the U.S. are delineated in the Code of Federal Regulations (CFR) 47, parts 20-39.

**FDMA (frequency division multiple access)** This technology, used in AMPS analog cellular, assigns one entire channel (30 kHz of spectrum) to one direction of a conversation. This means that in order to have a full-duplex conversation, you need two channels, one for transmitting from the phone to the switch and one for receiving from the switch to the phone. AMPS networks have 416 channels per carrier. Allowing for some control channels, this means that the system can handle a maximum of about 200 conversations at any given moment. This is not accounting for channel reuse, of course.

**FH (frequency hopping)** The transmission of a call jumps over several different frequencies known by both the transmitter and the receiver, and this reduces co-channel interference. GSM combines TDMA with frequency hopping.

**flow control** Signals between the modems control the rate at which the data is transmitted and received, regardless of your computer's connection rate.

**FM (frequency modulation)** The flow of electromagnetic energy waves is regulated, or controlled, by changing the transmitter's frequency. See also **modulation**.

**Follow-Me-Roaming** The brand name for automatic call delivery provided by GTE Telecommunications Services, Inc.

**forward channel** This term designates the direction of the call from the base station to your phone. It can refer to a control channel (FOCC) or a voice channel (FOVC). The opposite is the **reverse channel** from your phone to the base station.

**full duplex**   Simultaneous two-way signal transmission, which allows you to hear the listener trying to interrupt you while you are talking. In AMPS, full-duplex conversations use two different channels, one to transmit and one to receive, to accommodate simultaneous two-way conversations.

# G

**GEO (geosynchronous earth orbit)**   A satellite in a fixed orbit around the earth at an altitude of approximately 22,000 miles is in a geosynchronous earth orbit. GEO satellite systems are used for high-speed data and television. It can take as few as three GEOs to cover the earth.

**GPS (global positioning system)**   A constellation of satellites that communicates with a ground control system and GPS devices installed in planes and ships (as well as cars and handheld devices) to provide instantaneous latitude, longitude, altitude, time, and bearing 24 hours a day worldwide. GPS was developed by the Department of Defense and has been fully operational since July 17, 1995.

**group ID mark**   Used in NAM programming, this two-digit (00 to 15) number indicates how the phone will recognize and respond to the local system ID information.

**GSM (Groupe Speciale Mobile a.k.a. Global Systems for Mobile communications)**   In the late 1980s, GSM was developed for European countries, where roaming was all but impossible due to incompatible systems. Since then, it has been widely adopted globally. In the U.S., this technology is being used at PCS 1900 MHz frequencies. Elsewhere around the world, GSM operates at 900 MHz. GSM is a digital technology that uses digital modulation and frequency hopping.

# H

**handoff**   As you travel through a wireless system, your phone doesn't stay on the same channel. Within one cell there are different channels to which your phone may be handed off, and, of course, handoffs will occur as you travel from cell to cell. The MTSO and base station coordinate the handoff by monitoring the strength of the signal from your phone to the base station you are using as well as adjacent base stations. The MTSO then sends instructions to the base station and the phone to tune in to the proper channels.

With CDMA technology, there are three types of handoffs: soft, softer, and hard. CDMA uses three rake receivers that are always looking for stronger signals. Soft and softer handoffs operate on the premise of a "make before break" concept, where a new connection is made before the old one is broken. Hard handoffs operate on the premise of "break before make." This is the kind of handoff used by AMPS technology, which is why there is often static before the signal gets stronger again. The channels in CDMA are quite large, and a soft handoff occurs when the CDMA phone changes cells without changing channels. A softer handoff occurs when the CDMA phone is handed off to another sector within the same cell, but remains on the same channel. A hard handoff occurs when the CDMA phone changes channels or hands off to the analog mode. CDMA/AMPS phones can hand off from CDMA mode to AMPS, but there is no handoff from AMPS up to CDMA. TDMA also hands off to AMPS, but AMPS can't hand off to any digital technology.

**hands-free**   The use of an external microphone and speaker that allows you to use a wireless phone without holding it in your hands. Originally conceived for installed mobile phones, this concept is now available for portables by attaching a headset to your wireless phone or by installing a hands-free car kit to plug your portable into. Hands-free accessories are ideal for driving or any time you need both hands free.

**hardware handshake** A flow control protocol between a computer and a modem so they know when to stop and start sending data. Your computer may have the capabilities to send information faster than the modem can process it. The hardware handshake regulates the flow. These are the settings: RTS (request to send) and CTS (clear to send).

**Hertz (Hz)** Named after Heinrich Hertz for his work in the late 1880s, a Hertz is the measurement of frequency where one cycle ( ⁓ ) is completed in one second. One kiloHertz (1 kHz) is one thousand cycles per second; one MegaHertz (1 MHz) is one million cycles per second; and one GigaHertz (1 GHz) is one billion cycles per second.

**hexadecimal (HEX)** Hexadecimal is a base 16 numbering system that uses 16 characters (the digits 0 to 9 plus the letters A to F). The letters have the following equivalents: A=10; B=11; C=12; D=13; E=14; F=15. The decimal system is a base 10 numbering system that uses the digits 0 to 9. For example, the number 12 in a decimal system equals C in a hexadecimal system. The number 25 in a decimal system equals 19 in a hexadecimal system.

**home location register (HLR)** The database used by the carrier to confirm the validity of local subscribers in their home market.

**home system** The market you subscribe to.

**hookflash** To activate a switchhook feature, such as call waiting or three-way calling, you must perform a hookflash action. Your home phone may have a flash button. On your wireless phone, you can use your SEND or TALK key to perform this function.

**host modem** This refers to the modem at the other end of your connection, such as a bulletin board, online service, mainframe, or Internet service provider.

# I

**iDEN (integrated digital enhanced network)** This is a digital wireless technology developed by Motorola, Inc. and used in the U.S. on ESMR frequencies by Nextel Communications, Inc. It incorporates wireless telephony with two-way radio and paging technologies.

**incoming call** A call ringing in to your wireless phone.

**incomplete call** When the call you make doesn't answer or the number you dialed is busy, this is considered an incomplete call. Some carriers charge for incomplete calls.

**infrastructure** There are two elements that make wireless telephony work: the phone, or subscriber unit, and the infrastructure. The infrastructure is the actual hardware and software that comprise the wireless system, including the cell sites, base stations, and the MTSO.

**initial paging channel** When your wireless phone is paged by the system to alert it to an incoming call, the phone has a channel designated as the first channel to page, which is tied to a specific channel block. For example, in 800 MHz cellular, the initial paging channel for block A is 0333, and the initial paging channel for block B is 0334.

**initialization**   The computer software programs that interface with your modem sometimes need to impart specific instructions to set up your modem. This process is called initialization and is done through initialization strings.

**initialization string (a.k.a. init string)**   A group of instructions strung together that follow the AT, or attention, command. This string of commands must follow a certain order, or syntax, for the modem to properly understand the instructions.

**interconnect fee**   This is a surcharge by the local phone company for calls that connect from the mobile telephone switching office to its public switched telephone network.

**international calling**   The ability to make international calls. This is often denied by default, especially when roaming, but can be activated by special request.

**International Telecommunication Union (ITU-T)** The International Telecommunication Union–Telecommunication Standardization Sector, formerly the CCITT, is a United Nations agency headquartered in Geneva, Switzerland. This organization is involved in worldwide telecommunications development that oversees future use allocation of spectrum globally. It also helps to establish worldwide telecommunications standards.

**interim standard (IS)**   The American National Standards Institute (ANSI) establishes industry protocol that is designated IS followed by a number, e.g., IS-41.

**IP**   Internet protocol.

**ISDN (integrated services digital network)**   A digital landline technology that combines high-capacity voice with high-speed data transfer.

# J

**JTACS (Japanese Totally Accessed Communications System)** A 900 MHz analog system operating in Japan.

# L

**landline** Your local phone company, which is connected to the public switched telephone network (PSTN) or worldwide wired phone system.

**LEC (local exchange carrier)** This refers to your local phone company.

**LEO (low earth orbit)** Any orbit around the earth at an altitude between 100 and 1,000 miles. Little LEO further defines this orbit's use by satellites for data, such as paging and e-mail. Big LEO satellites add voice capabilities and access to mobile phone networks globally. Broadband LEO satellites offer high-speed, broad bandwidth communications for data to allow advanced wireless communications such as videoconferencing.

**LMDS (local multipoint distribution services)** This emerging technology is a broadband wireless service intended to provide voice, data, and video communications in the 28 to 31 GHz spectrum.

**local calling area** Wireless carriers provide greater local dialing privileges than your local phone company. Sometimes, it is less expensive to make wireless calls within your CGSA than it is to make a long-distance call.

**local modem** This refers to **your** modem, as opposed to the host modem, and is the modem you dial from.

**local number portability (LNP)** This subscriber benefit, expected to be available on wireless services by the spring of 2000, will allow you to retain your phone number regardless of how often you switch your service among LECs (for your landline service) or wireless carriers (for your wireless service).

# M

**macrocell**   Refers to the size of a cell. Macrocells are the largest cells in a wireless network at six to twenty miles in diameter.

**Major Trading Area (MTA)**   The FCC adopted Rand McNally's organization of the United States into 51 major trading areas to define the service areas for the block A and B carriers that are offering PCS 1900 MHz wireless phone service.

**MEO (middle earth orbit)**   A compromise between GEOS (requiring only three to six satellites, but subject to disruptive time delays in conversations) and LEOS (requiring 66 or more satellites that provide superior voice quality), middle earth orbit occupies an altitude of 1,000 to 22,000 miles and needs only seven to twenty satellites to cover the earth.

**memory effect**   Memory effect results when a battery is partially used, say about 80 percent, but not fully drained. The battery recharges, but thinks that 80 percent is 100 percent. The next time it is used 80 percent and recharged, it charges 80 percent of 80 percent, which is really only 64 percent. As this decline in recharge continues to occur, due to the battery not being fully drained and fully recharged, the usable amount of charge in the battery becomes less and less. This is called memory effect.

**Metropolitan Service Area (MSA)**   The Office of Management and Budget defined, and the FCC modified, 306 metropolitan geographic areas for cellular coverage in the U.S. Each MSA has two carriers: a channel block A system and a channel block B system.

**microcell**   Refers to the size of a cell. Microcells are a mile or less in diameter.

**microwave**   Encompasses frequencies 2 GHz or higher.

**MIN (mobile identification number)**   The 10-digit mobile number programmed into your wireless phone, represented by a 34-bit binary code called a MIN. The MIN and the ESN are transmitted when you initiate a phone call and are validated in the carrier's database to allow your call to process. The MIN and ESN are also transmitted every time the phone autonomously registers, which can be as frequently as five minutes.

**MID (mobile ID)**   This is the last seven digits (excluding the area code) of the mobile number of your wireless handset.

**MNP (Microcom Networking Protocol)**   Error correction and data compression standards devised by Microcom. They are identified by the letters MNP preceding a number. For example, MNP 5 refers to a compression scheme that will reduce the data to half its size.

**mobile attenuation**   The cell site is constantly monitoring the transmit power level of your wireless phone. As the system detects a weaker signal from your phone, it instructs your phone to increase its power. If the power levels of your phone are getting stronger and could possibly cause interference, the system instructs your phone to reduce power.

**mobile directory number (MDN)**   This term is currently the equivalent of your mobile telephone number. With the implementation of local number portability (LNP), this will be the number you want to keep. It is the number people will dial to call you, and it is the number you would list in a phone directory if you wanted your wireless phone number listed.

**mobile station (a.k.a. mobile unit)** There are two components that make wireless telephony work: the phone, or mobile station, and the infrastructure. As the subscriber, you use a mobile unit, or handset.

**mobile telephone number** The 10-digit number (3-digit area code plus 7-digit phone number) assigned to your wireless handset by the wireless carrier.

**modem** A device that is capable of modulating and demodulating information from its binary form into signal tones that can be transmitted or received over either wired or wireless communication networks. Some modems are capable of using faxing protocol to communicate with fax machines and other fax modems.

**modulation** The altering or regulating of an RF signal. Amplitude modulation (AM) modulates a signal by amplifying the signal. Frequency modulation (FM) modulates a signal by varying the frequency used to transmit the signal. Pulse code modulation (digital modulation) changes the signal into digital ones and zeros, or bits, and transmits signal pulses that get decoded at the receiving end.

**monthly access fee** This is the fee you pay to the wireless provider to ensure local service, similar to the monthly fee paid to your local landline phone company. Some wireless companies offer bundled rate plans that include local minutes at a discount if you pay for them up front.

**MSA**   See **Metropolitan Service Area**.

**MSC (mobile switching center)**   See **MTSO**.

**MSN (mechanical serial number)**   The actual serial number of your handset is the number usually needed to file a police report if your equipment is lost or stolen.

**MSS**   Mobile Satellite Service

**MTA**   See **Major Trading Area**.

**MTSO (mobile telephone switching office)**   The heart of the wireless phone system, the MTSO uses hardware and software to interface with all the base stations within its network. It also monitors usage for billing, validates users, coordinates handoffs, and connects calls to and from the local telephone company.

**multipath**   Radio frequencies often reflect off buildings and bounce around creating ghost signals or multiple paths. This can also happen in hilly terrain. It is sometimes referred to as signal spiraling. In an AMPS network, multipath can result in a dropped call because the phone doesn't know whether to listen to the signal or the reflection. So it decides to do neither. In CDMA technology, multipath is used to enhance the signal.

**multipath fading**   An idiosyncrasy of FM that you might be familiar with from your car radio. You pull up to a traffic light, and your favorite song starts to fade. Then you roll forward a foot or two, and the signal comes back. This is multipath fading, and it can also occur in wireless telephony. Sometimes putting the phone up to the other ear will correct the problem.

# N

**NAM (number assignment module)** Your phone needs certain information in order to work on a wireless phone system. The carrier assigns the wireless phone number, or MIN, and provides other information for use on its network, such as the system ID (SID), the access overload class, the group ID, and the initial paging channel. As the user of the phone, you decide what your unlock code and security code will be. All this information is stored in a special place in your phone called the NAM.

**NAMPS (Narrowband Advanced Mobile Phone Service)** NAMPS is a form of frequency division multiple access (FDMA) developed by Motorola, Inc. that increases the capacity of a regular AMPS network threefold by dividing the 30 kHz channel into three 10 kHz channels. Both the phone and the switching equipment must support NAMPS in order for this technology to be accessed.

**negotiation** When your modem dials up a host modem, you can hear lots of screeching tones as the modems agree on a baud rate and which protocols to use. This is the setup, or negotiation.

**NMT (Nordic Mobile Telephone)** A wireless analog phone service available at two frequency bands: 450 MHz and 900 MHz. Countries in parts of Europe and Asia use NMT-450 or NMT-900 or both.

**no-answer transfer** This call diversion feature is a switch-based function where the call rings into the wireless unit and, if not answered within a specific number of rings (usually four), will transfer to a predesignated number. No-answer transfer cannot be used at the same time as a voice mail feature because this is how the calls are transferred to the voice mail system.

**non-wireline**  When the FCC licensed the 800 MHz cellular spectrum, channel block A was licensed to companies that had not previously been in the telephone business. See also **wireline**.

**North American Numbering Plan (NANP)**  The numbering plan in North America that designates the area code (NPA) and exchange (NXX) of telephone numbers, and determines where new area codes are needed.

**NPA (numbering plan area code)**  This is usually referred to as the area code and is comprised of three digits, NXX, where N represents any number 2 to 9 and X represents any number 0 to 9.

**NXX**  The exchange part of a phone number. It is the three digits immediately following the area code (NPA) and is comprised of three digits, NXX, where N represents any number 2 to 9 and X represents any number 0 to 9.

**NPA restriction**  Denies outbound calls made to other area codes. Most carriers offer this option. This is useful if you give a wireless phone to someone, and you don't want them making long-distance calls while you're paying the bill.

**NTIA**  National Telecommunications and Information Administration

# O

**off-hook**  This is the equivalent of lifting up the receiver of, or answering, your home phone. On a wireless unit, you can go off-hook by pressing the SEND button or TALK button.

**off-peak time**  The carrier typically charges a lower rate per minute to use the wireless phone during nonbusiness hours, or off-peak time. Each carrier sets its own peak and off-peak times, but they are different than your working day. Off-peak time is often 9:00 P.M. to 6:00 A.M. Monday through Friday, weekends, and holidays. Some carriers offer unlimited night and weekend calls for a nominal fee or as part of a promotion to sign up new customers.

**on-hook**  This is the equivalent of hanging up your home phone. On a wireless unit, you can go on-hook by pressing the END key.

**opposing carrier**  Cellular 800 MHz service has two types of carriers: block A, or A system, and block B, or B system. Because these carriers used opposite sets of cellular channels, they are often referred to as opposing carriers. If you are an A system subscriber, then the B system is the opposing carrier for you, and vice versa.

**outgoing call**  A call dialed or originated from your wireless phone.

**overhead signal**  This is a signal containing information and instructions for phones that is constantly transmitted by a carrier. For example, the carrier includes information about itself, such as its system ID. The overhead signal also includes instructions telling the phone to "register" itself by transmitting its mobile identification number and electronic serial number.

# P

**page**  When the carrier receives a call for your wireless phone, it sends out a page message to alert your phone to the call. Your phone responds to the page by ringing, so that you can answer the call.

**parity**  Used by modems and digital networks, parity is either 0 or 1. If the transmission has an odd number of ones in the binary digits, the parity bit is set to one (1). If the transmission has an even number of ones in the binary digits, the parity bit is set to zero (0). The parity bit is set in the software modem configuration, which you would set to 0 or 1, depending on what the host modem requires.

**PC card** This removable credit-card-sized device (formerly called a PCMCIA card) can be used in laptops and PDAs as RAM memory, a modem, or a hard drive, as well as to connect devices such as cameras or CD-ROM drives to your laptop.

**PCMCIA (Personal Computer Memory Card International Association)** This acronym, which used to refer to a credit-card-sized device that plugged into laptop computers and PDAs, has been shortened to **PC card**. Now called a PC card, the PCMCIA organization sets the standards for PC cards to be used as modems, RAM cards, hard drives, and other input/output devices.

**PCS** See **Personal Communications Services**.

**PDA (personal digital assistant)** Small, hand-held computer devices commonly used for maintaining appointment schedules and electronic phone directories, PDAs are like electronic DayRunners or FiloFaxes.

**peak time** The carrier typically charges a higher rate per minute to use the wireless phone during business hours or peak time. Each carrier sets its own peak time schedule, but the hours are longer than your working day, often Monday through Friday 6:00 A.M. to 9:00 P.M.

**Personal Communications Industry Association (PCIA)** An industry trade group whose members operate narrowband and broadband PCS networks, Specialized Mobile Radio services, and paging and other wireless companies.

**Personal Communications Services (PCS)** The FCC has allocated 140 MHz of spectrum at 1810-1950 MHz for use as broadband PCS networks. The spectrum is divided into six blocks: three blocks of 30 MHz each, designated blocks A, B, and C, and three blocks of 10 MHz each, designated blocks D, E, and F. Frequency blocks A and B are licensed to operate in the 51 MTAs. Frequency blocks C, D, E, and F are licensed to operate in the 493 BTAs. The 20 MHz of spectrum between 1910-1930 MHz is temporarily unassigned.

**picocell** Refers to the size of a cell. Picocells are the smallest cells in a wireless network usually one-quarter mile or less in diameter.

**pigtail antenna** Installed cellular (800 MHz) phones use antennas that have a coiled section, the phasing coil, which resembles a pigtail. Ergo the name.

**postorigination dialing** Most landline phone systems use a postorigination dialing system. You take the phone off the hook first, wait for a dial tone, and then you enter the number you are calling.

**preorigination dialing** Wireless phones use a preorigination dialing system. You enter the number first. You will hear DTMF tones as you enter the numbers only to provide you with auditory feedback. Then you take the phone off-hook by pressing SEND. You don't hear a dial tone because wireless doesn't use one. The numbers you entered will be processed by the system. Notice that when you press SEND on your wireless phone, you don't hear the DTMF tones sound because wireless doesn't use DTMF.

**prepaid wireless service** Wireless services typically send you a bill each month for the airtime you use. This is considered postpaid because you pay after you've used the phone. An alternative is being offered that allows you to pay in advance for a predetermined amount of use. This prepaid service is available to all applicants, with no credit checks required. It's great if you want to budget your use.

**propagation** Propagation refers to moving RF energy from one point in space to another, such as from the switch to the phone, and vice versa. Different levels of power, or electrical energy, are required to propagate, or move, an RF signal different distances. Higher frequencies need more power for the RF signal to travel the same distance as that of lower frequencies. Because power levels are regulated by the government, one way to compensate is to reduce the distance the RF energy needs to travel. This is why 1900 MHz networks have smaller cells than 800 MHz networks.

**protocol** When two modems connect, they create an agreement on how they will communicate with each other. Specifically, they establish which standards will be used for speed, compression, and error correction. This is their protocol.

**public switched telephone network (PSTN)** The worldwide wired phone system or landline phone system.

**pulse code modulation** Pulse code modulation (digital modulation) changes a wireless phone signal into digital ones and zeros, or bits, and transmits signal pulses that are decoded at the receiving end.

**public safety answering point (PSAP)** The 9-1-1 call center that receives the emergency calls for both landline and wireless calls.

# R

**radio frequency (RF)**  Electromagnetic frequencies above 20,000 Hertz. Audio frequencies, also called mechanical frequencies, range from 20 to 20,000 Hertz, which is the frequency range of the human ear.

**regional Bell operating company (RBOC)**  When American Telephone and Telegraph (AT&T) was divested in the late 1970s, it kept the long-distance part of its business. The 23 Bell operating companies were combined into seven regional Bell operating companies (RBOCs): Bell Atlantic, Southwestern Bell, BellSouth, Ameritech, U.S. West, Pacific Telesis, and Nynex. Today there are five RBOCs. Pacific Telesis merged with Southwestern Bell, and Nynex merged with Bell Atlantic. At the time of this writing, Southwestern Bell and Ameritech were merging, as were Bell Atlantic and GTE Mobilnet.

**radio common carrier (RCC)**  The FCC established this class of wireless carrier to ensure competition for the wireline companies, thereby providing the consumer with options for wireless phone service. During the initial licensing phase of cellular, RCCs licensed channel block A.

**receiver**  Both the base station and the wireless phone must be capable of receiving signals from each other. They do this by using an antenna and electronics that interpret the RF signal and then translate it into audio sounds you can understand. Your phone is actually a combination transmitter and receiver, called a transceiver.

**remote modem**  Also called the **host modem**, this is the modem you call to.

**repeater**  An antenna that intercepts, amplifies, and retransmits an RF signal.

**repertory memory**   Your wireless phone has the ability to store numbers in its repertory memory. The number of memory locations will vary from three to ninety-nine, or more. Some phones have the added benefit of being able to store an alphabetical nametag along with the phone number, storing the information alphabetically in addition to numerically. Dialing from repertory memory is easy. Just press the one- or two-digit memory location and follow with the SEND key. Handset manufacturers may have different ways to access the repertory memory, such as Motorola's Smart Key™ and Sony's Jog Dial™.

**reseller**   A company that buys time and numbers from the carrier at wholesale and then resells them to consumers at retail prices. The FCC currently mandates resellers in an effort to encourage competition and provide greater options for consumers. The PCIA has requested that the FCC provide relief from this mandate in markets with four or more wireless carriers.

**reverse channel**   This term designates the direction of the call from your phone to the base station. It can refer to a control channel (RECC) or a voice channel (REVC). The opposite is the **forward channel** from the base station to your phone.

**RF fingerprinting**   This high-tech fraud deterrent is based on a unique electronic "fingerprint" generated by each phone's RF transmission. This RF fingerprint is matched at the switch, along with the mobile number and ESN. Cloned phones may have the correct mobile number and ESN, but the fraudulent caller will be disconnected when the RF fingerprint doesn't match.

**roamer**   When you use a system that is not the one you subscribe to, you are considered a roamer.

It is possible for your phone to try to roam in your home market.

**RSA (Rural Service Area)**   Once the 306 MSAs were defined, the FCC established geographic divisions for the rural areas of the United States, designating 428 RSAs. Each RSA has at least two carriers: a channel block A carrier and a channel block B carrier.

**RSSI (relative signal strength indicator)**   The RSSI is a measure of the signal strength the phone receives from the cell site. This information is used by both the phone and the cell site to adjust power levels in the phone or to determine when handoffs should occur.

# S

**security code**   This a number four to six digits long, depending on the manufacturer of the phone. It is used to program or reprogram your wireless phone.

**selectable system registration (a.k.a. network registration)**   This feature allows you to control your phone by forcing it to scan a particular type of system. You can change settings in the phone to Scan A, Scan B, Home only, etc. This is helpful if you travel into several markets frequently, and prefer A systems in some markets and B systems in others. Sometimes it helps you to roam. One of my analog customers who subscribed to Altoona A system could roam on the A system in Philadelphia, but had to change to the B system to use his phone in Wilmington, Delaware.

**serial communication**   Sending data single file over a single wire. Compare this to parallel communication, which sends multiple bits of data over more than one wire.

**serial connection** Most modems use the serial port on your computer or PDA, sometimes called an RS-232-C, DB-9, or Mini DIN-8.

**service area** The geographic area served by your wireless carrier, which is usually larger than the service boundaries of your local landline phone company.

**signaling tone (ST)** A tone sent on a voice channel from the phone to the cell site that communicates information, including hookflash activity, ringing, and disconnecting.

**SIM (subscriber identification module)** Used by GSM phones, this card is the size and shape of a credit card and slides into the phone. You can't use a GSM handset without a SIM card, which contains the phone number and other subscriber information that makes the GSM phone work. Some SIM cards are Smart cards, which allow you to store directory phone numbers, short messages, and even prepaid service.

**Smart card** A SIM card can be a Smart card, but Smart cards are lots more than SIM cards. For example, Smart cards can keep track of usage on prepaid cards, or track charges and payments on credit cards in real time.

**SMR** See **Specialized Mobile Radio**.

**short messaging service (SMS)** Digital phones offer you enhanced services. Among them is the ability to send and receive short messages using the display and keypad of your digital wireless phone, similar to text messages on pagers. Two other benefits, offshoots of SMS, provide you with notification of a voice mail message, even while you're on a call, and storage of pager-like alpha and numeric messages when your phone is turned off. When you turn on your phone, the message appears and, if it is a numeric message, is predialed for automatic callback.

**Specialized Mobile Radio (SMR)** The FCC has allocated portions of spectrum in the 200 MHz, 800 MHz, and 900 MHz bands that are used for paging, dispatch, and data services for businesses.

**spectrum** A continuous range of radio frequencies. For example, the 800 MHz spectrum contains the frequencies for both Nextel and for conventional cellular.

**spread spectrum** A method of transmission that takes a specific bandwidth signal, separates it, and transmits it over an even broader bandwidth, essentially spreading the signal out over more spectrum. The receiver gathers up the signal and reassembles it to match the original bandwidth. The jamming resistance and interference tolerance inherent in spread spectrum technology made it ideal for use by the military, for which it was originally devised. For instance, 800 MHz CDMA channels are 1,250 kHz in size, instead of the 30 kHz chunks of spectrum used by 800 MHz AMPS technology, allowing the signals to be spread over more bandwidth.

**SS7 (signaling system 7)** A high-speed signaling protocol used by the public switched telephone network to provide enhanced features such as caller ID.

**standby** The mode your portable phone is in when it is turned on and ready to make or receive calls.

**standby time** The length of time a phone will remain in standby mode from the time the battery is fully charged until it is fully discharged, or drained. Standby times quoted by battery manufacturers are usually exclusive of any talk time use and can vary if either the phone or the system has "sleep" capabilities.

**start bit/stop bit** Bits used to indicate the beginning and end of a character set in asynchronous modem transmissions.

**station class mark** This piece of information is included in the NAM programming. It tells the wireless system whether the wireless phone you are using is a 3-watt mobile unit or a .6-watt portable unit, and whether it is capable of voice operated transmission (VOX).

**subscriber** In order to use a wireless phone network, you must subscribe to it. Therefore, you become a subscriber.

**subscriber fraud** The act of subscribing for service with no intention of paying the bill.

**subscriber profiling** As wireless phone fraud continues to be a $1 million-a-day problem, carriers have taken a proactive approach to prevent fraud by creating a profile of your usage habits. If your call patterns change (increase), the carrier may temporarily suspend your number until it can verify that you were using the phone, and not a thief or clone.

**subsidy lock** Carriers who don't want you using anybody else's systems but theirs can create an algorithmic lock code, similar to the security code of analog phones. This makes it impossible for another carrier to reprogram your phone for its service without the specific code for your phone.

**supervisory audio tone (SAT)** One of three tones used by the cell site to communicate with your wireless phone and confirm correct channel assignment.

**switchhook function** To access certain features available at the network's switch, your phone must give the switch an indication. On your home phone, this is usually accomplished by pressing a flash key or quickly pressing the button that disconnects your call. With a wireless phone, pressing the SEND or TALK button emulates the flash key to access features such as call waiting and three-way calling. Some "flip" phones have partial switchhook capabilities in that a call can be answered or disconnected using the flip cover.

**synchronous mode**   When two modems initially establish communication, they agree that a set of characters, or a block of data, will always take a specified amount of time to transmit. Therefore, start bits and stop bits are not needed.

**system busy**   When your phone is unable to access the network, you will hear a fast busy signal, about twice the rate of a regular busy signal and pitched a little bit higher. You will hear this sound when there is no network, or when there is a network, but no channel available for you to use.

**system identification (SID)**   Each wireless system has a unique identification code, which is transmitted in the carrier's overhead signal. The SID of your service provider is also programmed into your wireless phone to designate your home market. The phone compares the SID in the phone with the SID transmitted by the carrier to determine if you are roaming or not. In 800 MHz cellular, an even SID indicates a B system, and an odd SID indicates the A carrier.

# T

**TACS (Totally Accessed Communications System)**   This 900 MHz band technology is used in Europe and in a few countries in Asia.

**talk time**   The amount of time your battery will last during continuous conversation. Talk times quoted by battery manufacturers are usually exclusive of any standby time.

**TDMA (time division multiple access)** As the name implies, this digital technology divides your conversation into packets of digital information and time-shares it with two other conversations on the same channel, thereby providing a threefold increase in system capacity.

**telephone answering device (TAD)** This refers to an answering machine. Although you can connect an answering machine to a wireless telephone, it is more practical to use the voice mail offered by the service provider or to buy a wireless phone with a built-in answering machine.

**terminal emulation** Connection to some mainframe computers that require your computer to act as a "dumb" video terminal rather than an actual computer. Some communication software programs allow you to emulate a video terminal by choosing a setting of VT-100 or VT-320.

**3G** A wireless industry term used to describe technology that is expected to be the third generation of wireless telephony. Availability is anticipated around the year 2001. Some say it will be an adoption of wide-CDMA, using the same spectrum globally. Others feel that the technology will be GSM. It may ultimately consist of multiple technologies.

**three-way calling** A switch-based feature that allows you to create a three-way conversation between yourself and two other parties. The conference call can be set up by calling one party and then calling the second party. Conversely, if someone calls you, then you can put them "on hold" while you establish the third party connection. The conference call is completed by bringing the first party back online. You will pay airtime charges for both calls.

**throughput** This term refers to the amount of data you are actually receiving in bits per second, but not necessarily your connect speed, or baud rate. Throughput accounts for data compression when calculating the speed of the transmission. This means that a 28,800 bps connection with MNP 5 invoked, which provides two to one compression, will actually have a throughput of 57,600 bps.

**TIA** Telecommunications Industry Association

**transceiver** The base station may physically have the room for a separate transmitter and receiver, but you want to carry around the smallest possible communication device. Handset manufacturers design wireless phones to contain both a transmitter and a receiver in one unit, called a transceiver.

**transmitter** Both the base station and the wireless phone must be capable of transmitting signals to each other, using an antenna and electronics that transform your voice into an RF signal for transmission. Your phone is actually a combination transmitter and receiver, called a **transceiver**.

**tri-mode handset** A tri-mode phone, also called dual mode/dual frequency, operates in digital mode at both 1900 MHz and 800 MHz. It can also revert to 800 MHz AMPS when digital services are not available or accessible.

**24/7** This term means twenty-four hours a day, seven days a week. Many carriers are implementing customer service programs that provide you with support 24/7 as opposed to Monday through Friday 8:30 A.M. to 5:00 P.M.

**2G** A wireless industry term used to describe the second generation of wireless telephony, which includes the digital technology as well as the PCS frequencies. The first generation is considered analog AMPS.

# U

**UHF (ultrahigh frequency)** Refers to the 300 MHz to 3,000 MHz range.

**unlock code** This is a three- or four-digit number that will unlock your wireless phone. Check your user manual for complete information.

**unregistered phone** A call placed from a phone that has not been signed up for service will not validate in the carrier's switch. Service will be denied **unless the call is to 9-1-1**, which must be processed per an FCC ruling in the spring of 1998.

**usage** See **airtime**.

**user friendly** A description of how easy the wireless phone is to use.

# V

**validation** When you place a call from your wireless phone, the carrier validates your mobile number and ESN by comparing them to its **home location register**, ensuring that you are a registered user in good standing. Service will be denied otherwise.

**VHF (very high frequency)** Refers to the 30 MHz to 300 MHz range.

**visitor location register (VLR)** The database used by the carrier to confirm the validity of roaming, or visiting, wireless users.

**voice-activated dialing** Voice activation is the ultimate in hands-free. This feature allows you to speak to the phone, telling it the number you're calling, rather than to manually dial it. Although it is usually a switch-based feature, some phones have a variation of voice activation built in.

**vocoder** Digital wireless phone technology uses voice coders, or vocoders, to encode your voice so it can be transmitted digitally, and then decode it so you will be understood by the person on the other end.

**voice mail** Similar to an answering machine, this electronic service can answer more than one call at a time with your outgoing message. Some services allow callers to designate if a message is urgent. Some voice mail services will even alert your pager to a new message.

**VOX (voice-operated transmission)** A phone has different levels of power usage. Transmitting is the most power intensive; receiving doesn't take as much power; and standby mode drains your battery even less. With VOX, the phone reduces power during a conversation when you are listening to someone, and then boosts it back up when you want to talk. This is usually an option in the phone that must be supported by the carrier in order to work. This feature causes voice clipping (each time you talk, the beginning of your first word is cut off), so most carriers don't support this. It would be perceived as poor service.

# W

**WAP (Wireless Applications Protocol)** People using wireless telephony for voice are also demanding wireless data capabilities for Internet connectivity, etc. Therefore, protocols must be established to create a common ground. A forum was created to devise and delineate those standards in the spring of 1998. Details are available at the WAP Web site (*www.wapforum.org*).

**W-CDMA (wideband code division multiple access)** This is the technology expected to provide greater capacity than CDMA, with high-speed data transfer rates of 2 megabits. Use of this technology is proposed to accommodate global roaming, providing that a worldwide spectrum can be agreed upon.

**wireless telephone** A device that uses RF to transmit or receive voice or data signals to a system that is connected to the public switched telephone network, or local phone company.

**wireline** When the FCC licensed the 800 MHz cellular spectrum, channel block B was licensed to companies that were already in the telephone business—companies that were regional Bell operating companies (RBOCs). See also **non-wireline**.

**wireless local loop (WLL)** The traditional method for you to obtain phone service to your home is from your local phone company, which runs wires to your house. With WLL, the wiring inside your home stays the same, but there are no outside wires. A wireless switch box with an antenna replaces the network interface box inside your home that currently interfaces with a landline phone company. Wireless carriers implement channel and frequency reuse patterns to maximize usage of their spectrum. WLL service adds to the growing choices of competitive local phone company providers instead of being limited to only one local phone company as in the past.

# Y

**Y2K** Computers were invented in the 1900s. Most date information in the United States is entered into computers as MM/DD/YY, where the M stands for the month, the D for the day, and the Y for the year. The year 2000 presents a software logistics problem for many computers because they don't have a reference for the century. Until now, computers assumed it was 1900. Solutions are being implemented so that a date entered as 01/01/00 for January 1, 2000 will not be seen by the computer as January 1, 1900. You will notice that most date entries on forms that you complete today are formatted MM/DD/YYYY to include century information.

# Modem Standards
## Communication

| Name | Speed |
|------|-------|
| Bell 103 | 300 bps |
| ITU-TSS V.21 | 330 bps |
| Bell 212A | 1,200 bps |
| ITU-TSS V.22 | 1,200 bps |
| ITU-TSS V.22 bis | 2,400 bps |
| ITU-TSS V.32 | 4,800, 9,600 bps |
| ITU-TSS V.32 bis | 4,800, 7,200, 9,600, 12,000, 14,400 bps |
| ITU-TSS V.FC | 14,400, 16,800, 19,200, 24,000, 26,400, 28,800 bps |
| ITU-TSS V.34 | 2,400, 4,800, 7,200, 9,600, 12,000, 14,400, 16,800, 19,200, 24,000, 26,400, 28,800, 31,200, 33,600 bps |
| K56 Flex | 32,000, 34,000, 36,000, 38,000, 40,000, 42,000, 44,000, 46,000, 48,000, 50,000, 52,000, 54,000, 56,000 bps |
| ITU-TSS V.90 | 28,000, 29,333, 30,667, 31,200, 32,000, 33,333, 33,600, 34,000, 34,667, 36,000, 37,333, 38,000, 38,667, 40,000, 41,333, 42,000, 42,667, 44,000, 45,333, 46,000, 46,667, 48,000, 49,333, 50,000, 50,667, 52,000, 53,333, 54,000, 54,667, 56,000 bps |

# Modem Standards
*continued*

## Compression

| Name | Ratio |
|------|-------|
| MNP-5 | 2:1 Compression |
| ITU-TSS V.42 bis | 4:1 Compression |

## Error Correction

| Name | |
|------|------|
| ITU-TSS V.42 | Public Domain |
| MNP Class 2 | Public Domain |
| MNP Class 3 | Public Domain |
| MNP Class 4 | Public Domain |
| MNP Class 10 | Proprietary, Enhanced for Wireless |

# Index

.6-watt portable 33, 314

1-800-Batteries 186

1.9 GHz 2, 13, 166

1900 MHz 1-2, 4, 9-10, 16, 31, 34-35, 48, 77, 102, 105, 108-113, 148, 163, 165, 207, 211, 235, 269, 271, 277-278, 281, 286, 293, 299, 308, 317

21st Century Telesis ii, 17, 236

24/7 317

2G 318

3-watt car kit 63, 73

3-watt phone 33

3Com ii, 130, 181

3G 316

800 MHz 1-2, 9, 12-14, 18, 23, 31, 34-36, 48, 50, 56, 71, 77, 97, 102, 104, 106, 112, 115, 146, 148, 153, 159, 162-163, 166, 170, 172, 187, 196, 235, 269-270, 281, 286, 296, 304, 307-308, 313, 317, 320

## A

A block 108, 242, 273

A-key 121, 274, 276

access channel 273, 285

access fee 43, 47, 60, 69, 76, 79-80, 86, 92, 148, 167-168, 173, 273

access overload class 157, 167, 273, 303

accessories 44, 55, 57, 59, 63, 73, 133, 142, 295

Action Cellular 181

activation fee 47, 51, 88, 273

waived 60

Acura 53

adaptive answer 273, 276

AeroVironment, Inc. 25

agent 46, 49, 51-52

air interface 274

airtime 19, 44, 47, 49, 51, 60, 74, 76, 79, 81, 84, 88, 114, 123, 146, 159, 172, 274, 278, 280, 281, 307, 317-318

free off-peak 47, 75, 78-79

off-peak 75, 79, 86, 88, 274, 304

peak 77-78, 86, 88, 162, 274, 304, 306

AirTouch 12-13, 45, 49, 94, 105, 236

alarm clock 63, 70

Alltel 93, 236

alphanumeric 10, 67, 78, 83, 274

alphanumeric directory 62, 66

America Online 129

American Wireless 52

Ameritech 12, 29, 49, 94, 105, 131, 237, 309

amplitude modulation 274, 301

AMPS 9, 11-12, 14, 17, 21, 23, 30, 33-34, 56, 68, 93, 103, 106, 110, 115, 125, 131, 148, 164, 168, 170, 236, 274, 276, 281, 284, 291, 294, 302, 313, 317

analog signal 275

Angel Technologies Corp. 24

ANSI 156, 275, 297

answer mode  275

answering machine  63, 69, 83, 145, 316, 319

antenna  2, 18, 22, 29, 31-32, 57, 58, 139, 155, 172, 281, 284, 287, 289-290, 307, 309, 317, 320

ASCII  275

asymmetric transmission  275

asynchronous mode  275

AT&T Ventures  21

AT&T Wireless  24, 48, 50, 85, 112, 130, 171, 237

atmospheric satellite  25

Audiovox  175

authentication  14, 67, 121, 123, 274, 276, 283

auto answer  276

automatic answer  63, 71

autonomous registration  32-33, 39, 276

**B**

B block  108, 242, 277

bag phone  54, 56, 58, 139, 156, 172

bandit mobile  277

bandwidth  28, 277, 298, 313

base station  17, 31-32, 147, 277, 281, 292, 294, 309-310, 317

Basic Trading Area  211, 277-278

battery  34, 42, 44, 47, 57, 63, 68, 73, 133, 136, 138, 141-142, 160, 170, 299, 313, 315, 319

lithium ion  63, 73, 135, 138

nickel cadmium  63, 73, 133, 136, 138, 141

nickel metal hydride  63, 73, 134, 138

battery meter  62, 68

baud rate  276, 303, 317

BearCom  52

Belkin Components  142, 182

Bell 103  322

Bell Atlantic Mobility  12, 45, 50, 106, 131, 237

Bell Laboratories  11, 152

Best Buy  49, 51-53

Bin Talal, Prince Alwaleed  24

binary  80, 278, 286, 300, 305

bit  128, 276, 278, 290, 300, 305, 314

bits per second  277-278, 317

Boeing  24

bps  128, 132, 276-278, 282, 317, 322

briefcase  23, 58

broadband  17, 166, 180, 278, 298, 306

Broadband PCS  17, 278, 306

brownout: see roaming

BTA  10, 17, 46, 211, 242, 277, 278, 280, 282, 286, 289, 291

bundling  278

busy signal  96, 161, 278, 315

busy transfer  83, 279

**C**

C block  108, 242, 278, 280

C-scan  285

Cadillac  53

CALEA  150, 279

call detail  70, 75, 84, 279

call diversion  83, 279, 303

call forwarding  75, 78, 82, 279

call restriction  63, 71

call termination  41

call timers  63, 70

call waiting  75, 78, 81, 279, 295, 315

caller ID  4, 75, 78, 83, 148, 154, 157, 274, 279, 313

calling party pays  75, 84, 280

calling signal  280

cancellation penalties  60, 64

carrier  43, 66, 72, 74, 76, 79, 81, 83, 93, 95, 99, 106, 108, 111, 115, 119, 122-123, 137, 147, 149, 151, 153, 157, carrier, *continued,* 159, 161, 164, 166, 168-169, 235, 273, 276, 278, 280, 284, 290, 292, 300-301, 305, 310, 312, 315, 318

carrier channel 53-54

carry phone: see bag phone

CCITT 280, 297

CDMA 3, 10, 14, 17, 21, 32, 35, 37, 56, 105, 109, 112, 115, 137, 165, 236, 242, 274, 281, 284, 294, 302, 313, 316, 320, see also code division multiple access

cdmaOne 281

CDPD 125, 129, 131, 281, see also cellular digital packet data

cell 281

cell site 2, 28-29, 31, 33, 39, 41, 121, 160, 274, 277, 281, 285, 288, 300, 311-312, 314

cell splitting 281

cellular 27, 31, 51, 56, 69, 80, 93, 100, 114, 117, 119, 122, 125, 129, 146, 159, 163, 166, 169-170, 172, 174, 184, 281

cellular digital packet data 281

Cellular Geographic Service Area 46, 282

Cellular Networking Perspectives 183

Cellular Travel Guide 184

CGSA: see Cellular Geographic Service Area

channel 8, 13, 19, 21, 30, 32-33, 41, 110, 112, 160, 242, 277-278, 282-284, 287, 292, 294, 296, 303, 314, 316

channel block A 9, 11-12, 44, 112, 117, 207, 273, 278, 300, 304, 309, 311

channel block B 9, 11-12, 44, 207, 276-278, 300, 311, 320

channel reuse 12, 22, 31, 282, 292, 320

channel seizure 282

channel separation 274, 277, 281, 283

charger 42, 63, 73, 133, 135, 137-138, 141, 170

Chase Capital Partners 21

churn 283

cigarette lighter adapter 44, 47, 63, 73, 142, 161

Circuit City 49, 51-53

CLEC: see competitive local exchange carrier

clock 63, 70

clone 119, 123, 283, 310, 314

CNG: see calling signal

co-branding 283

co-channel interference 30, 32, 283-285, 292

code division multiple access 3, 10, 14, 37, 281, 284

collocation 284

Columbia Capital 21

command 284, 297

communications satellites 25

compatible 170, 285

competitive local exchange carrier 283

competitive rates 87

compliant 117, 136, 147, 285

Comsat Corporation 23, 179

configuration 285, 306

Consumer Reports 4

control channel 40, 285, 292, 310

cordless phones 2-3, 16, 146, 148

cost of airtime 75-76

coverage area 44, 46, 68, 78, 103, 108-109, 130, 162, 288

CPP: see calling party pays

cross talk 285

CTIA ii, 56, 183, 286

**D**

D block 106, 108-109, 242, 278, 286

D-AMPS 286

data 16, 21-22, 40, 121, 125-126, 129-131, 173, 273, 275, 278, 281-282, 286, 289-291, 293, 295, 297, 300, 311, 313, 315, 317, 319

data compression 286, 300, 317

data device 126, 275, 286

DCS1800 286

dead air 34

deal of the day 47, 52

dealer 29, 39, 46, 49, 51-52, 54, 118, 125, 158

DH Brothers 52

dialing
credit card 62, 66, 67
password 62, 67

Diamond Multimedia Systems 182

digital footprint 77, 103, 163

digital indicator 103

digital messaging service: see DMS

digital modulation 287, 293, 301, 308

digital network 80, 103, 162

digital signal 287, 290

digital switch 103

Dillard's 52

dip 36, 161

directory listing 287

display 57
dot matrix 62, 68
LCD with backlighting 62, 68
LED 62, 68
one-line 62, 67
segmented 62, 67
two-line 62, 67

diversity reception 140, 287

DMS 13

dropped call 35-36, 160, 288, 302

DTMF 40, 126, 288, 307
long tone DTMF 63, 69, 288

dual frequency 63, 69, 72, 105, 164

dual mode 56, 63, 68, 103, 105-107, 111, 125, 162-164

dual mode/dual frequency 72, 105-106, 109, 111, 168, 317

dual NAM 167, 169, 288

dual registration 63, 69, 167-168, 288

dual tone multifrequency: see DTMF

**E**

E 9-1-1 148, 150, 289

E block 108, 242, 278, 289

E-TDMA 291

e.i.r.p. 289

e.r.p. 140, 290

echo: see local echo

electronic serial number: see ESN

emergency use 60, 75, 134, see also user, security

encryption 15, 290

END 41-42, 162, 305

Enhanced 9-1-1: see E 9-1-1

enhanced specialized mobile radio: see ESMR

Ericsson 81, 132, 175, 286

error correction/control 290

ESMR 19, 48, 291, 296

ESN 28, 38, 40, 119-121, 158, 169, 276, 277, 283, 290, 300, 310, 318

ETACS 291

ETSI 291

Everything Wireless ii, 49, 142, 185

**F**

F block 108, 242, 278, 291

Famous Barr 52

FCC 8-9, 11, 18, 27, 44, 46, 48, 56, 120, 149, 152, 155, 165, 171, 183, 273, 274, 276, 278, 282, 291, 299, 304, 307, 309-311, 313, 318, 320

FDMA 13, 292, 303

features 1, 3, 10, 13, 42, 53, 58, 60, 62, 64, 75, 78, 81, 114, 138, 141, 148, 158, 313-314

Federal Communications Commission: see FCC

Filene's 52

first-time buyer 5, 61

flow control 292, 295

FM 34, 140, 292, 301-302

Foley's 52

Follow-Me-Roaming 114-117, 292

forward channel 292, 310

free phone 1, 44, 59, 64

frequency block A 17, 273

frequency block B 17, 277

frequency block C 17, 280

frequency block D 17, 286

frequency block E 17, 289

frequency block F 17, 291

frequency division multiple access: see FDMA

frequency hopping 292-293

frequency modulation: see FM

Fujitsu 175

full duplex 7-8, 12, 19, 293

**G**

Gates, Bill 24

GEO 22-23, 179-180, 293

geostasis 25

geosynchronous earth orbit: see GEO

global positioning system: see GPS

Global Systems for Mobile communications: see GSM

Globalstar 24, 179

GoAmerica ii, 130, 182

GPS 149, 173, 293

GPRS 132

group ID mark 293

Groupe Speciale Mobile 15, 293

GSM 10, 15, 17, 23, 108, 132, 171, 235-236, 242, 269, 274, 286, 292-293, 312, 316

GSM-NA 3, 15-16, 113, 163, 269, 274

GSM1800 21, 269

GTE Wireless 12, 48-49, 105, 114, 117, 131, 171, 182, 238, 242

**H**

HALO 24

handheld phone 56, 58

handoff 14, 32, 34, 128, 288, 294, 302, 311

analog 34

digital 35

hard handoff 15, 294

soft handoff 14, 294

softer handoff 15, 294

hands-free 18, 42, 57-58, 63, 73, 142, 156, 294-295, 318

handset 2, 4, 7, 17, 51, 53, 56-57, 68, 113, 142, 147, 274, 300, 302, 310, 312, 317

hardware handshake 295

headset 42, 57, 63, 71, 73, 143, 156, 295

health and safety 57, 139, 156

Hecht Company 52

helium blimps 25

Hello Direct ii, 49, 52, 142, 185

Hertz 27, 295, 309

Hertz, Heinrich 27

HEX: see hexadecimal

hexadecimal 290, 295

high-altitude long-operation: see HALO

HLR: see home location register

hole: see system hole

home 3, 29, 39, 46, 60, 69, 71, 80, 89, 91-92, 94, 97, 104, 107, 109, 114-115, 118-119, 121, 151, 159-160, 164-165, 168, 283, 286, 295, 304, 311, 315

Home Depot 52

home location register 32, 39, 41, 295, 318

home system 71, 91, 295

hookflash 295

host modem 296, 298, 303, 306, 309

Hughes Network Systems 291

Hz: see Hertz

**I**

ICO Global Communications Services, Inc. 24, 179

iDEN 19, 296

ILLUMINET 118, 182

Improved Mobile Telephone Service: see IMTS

IMTS 7, 8, 10, 12

incoming call 41, 70, 81, 273, 275-276, 279, 296

incoming call notification 63, 70

incomplete call 296

Independence Recycling 19-20

Infinity 53

infrastructure 17-18, 28-29, 146, 148, 277, 296, 301

init string: see initialization string

initial paging channel 157, 167, 296, 303

initialization string 285, 289, 297

Inmarsat Communication Systems 23, 179

insurance 63, 72

integrated digital enhanced network: see iDEN

integrated services digital network: see ISDN

Intelsat 23, 179-180

interconnect fee 273, 297

interim standard 115, 297

internal fast charger 54, 142

international calling 113, 117, 171, 297

International Telecommunication Union 281, 297

Internet 24, 50, 52, 54, 82, 130, 132, 173, 278, 282, 296, 319

Internet Protocol 282

InTouch USA 181

ion-propulsion system 25

IP 129, 132, 282, 297

Iridium, Inc. 23, 180

ISDN 297

ITU-T: see International Telecommunication Union

**J**

JTACS 298

**K**

K56 Flex 322

Kaufmann's 52

keypad 40, 42, 57, 65, 71, 83, 129, 274, 312

KMart 51, 53

**L**

landline 11, 16, 22, 28, 30, 40, 77, 80, 82, 126-128, 147, 149, 153, 277-279, 283, 297-298, 301, 307-308, 312, 320

LandSea Communications 23, 180

last number redial 65

lease program 59

least-cost-per-minute 75, 78-79

least-cost-per-month 75, 78-79

LEC 148, 298

LEO 23-24, 179-180, 298

Lexus 53

lightweight 58, 73

Lincoln 53

line of sight 35, 161

LMDS 21, 269, 298

LNP: see local number portability

loaner phone 63, 72

local calling area 298

local echo 289

local exchange carrier: see LEC

local modem 298

local multipoint distribution services: see LMDS

local number portability 153, 298

lock 63, 70, 72, 160, 314
  automatic 63, 70
  keypad 63, 71
  manual 63, 70
long distance 20, 43, 46, 66, 69-70, 76, 84-85, 96, 98, 100, 102, 151, 169, 173, 288, 298, 304
Loral Space 24
low earth orbit: see LEO

**M**

macrocell 299
Major Trading Area: see MTA
Matra Marconi 24
May Company 52
McCaw, Craig 24
MCI WorldCom 48, 186
MCSI: see Motorola Cellular Service, Inc.
MDN: see mobile directory number
mechanical serial number: see MSN
Meier & Frank 52
MEIN 15
memory effect 133-135, 136, 138, 141, 299
MEO 24, 179, 299
Mercedes 53
Metropolitan Service Area 8-9, 44, 187, 299, 302
microcell 300
Microcom Networking Protocol: see MNP
microphone 42, 57, 71, 129, 142, 294
microwave 2, 27, 32, 277, 300
MID: see mobile ID
middle earth orbit: see MEO
MIN: see mobile identification number
Mitsubishi 175
MNP 300, 317, 323
MNP-5 323

MNP10 323
mobile attenuation 300
mobile directory number 153, 300
mobile electronic identity number: see MEIN
mobile ID 290, 300
mobile identification number 153, 157, 300, 305
mobile phone 7, 18, 56, 58, 73, 139, 274, 278, 298
mobile phone number 15, 33, 41, 119, 153, 154, 158, 276, 277, 283
Mobile Satellite Service: see MSS
mobile station 301
mobile telephone number 300-301
Mobile Telephone Service: see MTS
mobile telephone switching office: see MTSO
mobile unit 56, 301, 314
modem 126, 129-130, 132, 275-276, 280, 284-285, 287, 289-290, 295-298, 301, 303, 306, 309, 314, 322
modulation 274-275, 287, 292, 301, 308
Montgomery Ward 51, 53
monthly access fee 43, 47, 76, 86, 87, 92, 148, 167, 173, 273, 301
Motorola 13, 19, 24, 37, 54, 126-127, 146, 148, 155, 172, 176
Motorola Cellular Service, Inc. 48, 171, 186
Motorola VIP Sales 54
MSA 8, 10, 44, 187, 302, 311, see also Metropolitan Service Area
MSC: see MTSO
MSN 158, 302
MSS 302

MTA 10, 17, 45, 108, 207, 211, 273, 277, 282, 299, 302, 307

MTS 7

MTSO 2, 28-29, 32, 34, 41, 102, 121, 277, 281, 294, 296, 302

multipath 35, 302

multipath fading 35, 302

mute 63, 71

**N**

NACN 117, 184

NAM 28, 38, 69, 153, 157, 159, 169, 273, 293, 303, 314

NAMPS 13, 21, 23, 34, 37, 115, 274, 303

NANP: see North American Numbering Plan

NANPA: see North American Numbering Plan Administrator

narrowband 37, 306

Narrowband Advanced Mobile Phone Service: see NAMPS

NASA 25

National Cellular Rentals 181

NEC 176

negotiation 303

network 2, 7, 12, 15, 18-19, 22-23, 28-29, 33, 35, 40, 50, 52, 66, 72, 97, 103, 105, 110, 114, 118, 132, 137, 146, 157, 160, 162, 164, 172, 273, 277, 280, 282, 284, 287, 299, 302-303, 307, 314, 320

network ID: see NID

network registration 311

network selection 92, 164

Next Wireless 52

Nextband Communications LLC 21

Nextel 2-3, 9-10, 19, 21-22, 27, 50, 52, 77, 80, 114, 182, 225, 269, 272, 291, 296, 313

NID 39

NMT 303

NO SERVICE 29, 38, 96, 160, 161

no-answer transfer 83, 279, 303

Nokia 176

non-wireline 7, 11, 273, 304, 320

North American Cellular Network: see NACN

North American Numbering Plan 152, 304

North American Numbering Plan Administrator ii, 152, 184

Novatel 182

NPA 93, 152, 164, 304

NPA restriction 304

NTIA 304

number assignment module: see NAM

numbering plan area code: see NPA

NXX 93, 152, 164, 304

**O**

O'Gara Satellite Networks 23, 180

OEM: see Original Equipment Manufacturer

off-hook 40, 304, 307

off-peak time 79, 86, 88, 274, 304-305

Office Depot 51-53

Office Max 51, 53

OKI 176

Omnipoint 132, 239

on-hook 305

one phone, one number, anywhere 22, 146, 147

one-rate plan 78, 85, 168

one-rate roaming 75, 80, 169

one-touch button 62, 65

opposing carrier 93, 164, 305

Original Equipment Manufacturer 53

outgoing call 84, 280, 305

over-the-air activation 39, 50

overhead signal 28, 32, 41, 118, 159, 161, 273, 305, 315

## P

PACS 3, 10, 16-17, 108, 113, 236, 242, 274

page 3, 10, 33, 38-39, 41, 77, 83, 86, 131, 145, 276, 296, 305, 312, 319

Panasonic 176

parity 305

PBX: see private branch exchange

PC card 126, 130, 132, 306

PCIA 48, 184, 306, 310

PCMCIA 130, 306

PCS 2, 4, 9-10, 13, 16-17, 21, 27, 31, 37, 39, 48, 50, 52, 69, 72, 82, 106, 108, 111, 114, 148, 159, 163, 165, 185, 207, 211, 235, 242, 306-307, 318

PDA 130, 131, 306, 312

peak time 88, 274, 306

penalty fees 44

Personal Access Communications Systems: see PACS

Personal Communications Industry Association: see PCIA

Personal Communications Services: see PCS

Personal Computer Memory Card International Association: see PCMCIA

personal digital assistant: see PDA

personal phones 57, 138

Philips Consumer 177

picocell 307

pigtail antenna 307

pipe 21, 277-278

portable phone 36, 57-58, 73, 133, 140, 155, 313

postorigination dialing 40, 307

power levels 12, 18, 31, 33-34, 57, 172, 283-284, 300, 308, 311

power steps 33

preorigination dialing 40, 307

prepaid wireless service 1, 75, 84, 307, 312

private branch exchange 146

propagation 308

protocol 115, 129, 276, 282, 290, 295, 297, 301, 303, 308, 313, 319

PSAP 148, 150, 154, 308

PSTN 2, 28, 38, 40-41, 152, 281, 298, 308

public safety answering point: see PSAP

public switched telephone network: see PSTN

pulse code modulation 275, 301, 308

purse 58, 71, 130

## Q

Qualcomm 24, 177

## R

radio common carrier: see RCC

radio frequency: see RF

Radio Shack® 49, 52-53

rake receivers 14, 294

Rand McNally 45-46, 277, 299

rate plan analysis 86

RBOC 309, 320

RCC 7-8, 11, 273, 309

RCR Global Wireless 185

RCR Weekly 185

real estate agent 57

receiver 14, 40, 57, 280, 292, 304, 309, 313, 317

regional Bell operating company: see RBOC

registration 32, 72, 165, 288, see also system registration, see also dual registration

relative signal strength indicator: see RSSI

remote modem 309

rental program 59, 170-171, 181

repeater 309

repertory memory  42, 62, 66, 310

reseller  1, 48-49, 52, 172, 186, 310

residuals  47

retail channel  53

reverse channel  292, 310

RF  18, 35, 67, 121, 155, 275, 291, 301, 308-309, 317, 320

RF fingerprinting  67, 121, 310

ringer notification  63, 70

ringer tone selection  63, 69

ROAM  29, 38, 93, 104, 111, 159

roamer  72, 78, 92, 95, 102, 310

roaming

  800 MHz analog cellular  97

  automatic call delivery  39, 95, 97, 100-101, 115, 117, 276, 292

  brownout  93, 164

  dialing pattern  95

    one plus the area code and phone number (1 +10)  96

    seven (7) digits  95

    ten (10) digits  95

    zero plus the area code and phone number (0 +10)  96

  digital roaming  102

    1900 MHz  108

      1900 MHz CDMA  109

      1900 MHz GSM-NA  113

      1900 MHz PACS  113

      1900 MHz TDMA  111

    800 MHz  102

      800 MHz CDMA  104

      800 MHz TDMA  106

  inbound roaming calls  97

  Nextel roaming  114

  nonlocal automatic call delivery  101

  nonlocal traditional roaming  102

  outbound roaming calls  95

  reduced roaming rates  92

  roaming charges  92

  roaming rules  93

  traditional roaming  97

roaming partners  39

Robinson's May  52

Rolls Royce  53

RSA  10, 44, 196, 282, 311

RSSI  311

Rural Service Area:  see RSA

**S**

Samsung  177

SAT:  see supervisory audio tone

satellite phones  2, 5, 22, 24, 179, 293, 298-299, 302

Sears  49, 51, 53

secure communications  75, 80

security code  157-158, 167, 303, 311, 314

selectable system registration  311

SEND  40, 41-42, 65-67, 71, 81, 122, 162, 282, 296, 304, 307, 310, 315

serial communication  311

serial connection  312

service area  18, 37, 46, 84, 91, 162, 166, 282, 299, 311-312

service contract  43

shopping for a phone  61

short messaging service  75, 83, 312,  see also SMS

SID  28, 38-39, 45, 157, 159, 167, 286, 303, 315

Siemens  ii, 183

signal strength meter  62, 68

signaling system 7: see SS7

signaling tone  312

SIM  15, 113, 312

Sky Station International  25

sliding scale  46-47

Smart card  312

SMR  19, 312-313

SMS 4, 77-78, 83, 131, 164, 312

Sony ii, 177

Southwestern Bell 12, 148, 240, 309

speaker 18, 42, 53, 57, 73, 129, 142-143, 284, 294

Specialized Mobile Radio 313, see also SMR

spectrum 1, 3, 8-9, 16, 21-22, 27, 45, 102, 113, 146, 242, 273-274, 276, 278, 280, 284, 286, 289, 291-292, 297-298, 304, 307, 313, 316, 320

Spectrum Equity Investors 21

speed dial 62, 65

spread spectrum 185, 284, 313

Sprint PCS 50, 52, 82, 106, 109-110, 157, 165, 240

SRS 183

SS7 313

standby 137, 313, 319

standby time 136-137, 313, 316

start bit 275, 314-315

static 34, 128, 162, 275, 294

station class mark 33, 167, 314

stop bit 314

subscribe 28, 43, 46, 82, 91, 94, 103, 104, 108, 111, 114, 151, 167, 274, 286, 295, 310, 314

subscriber 1, 12, 15, 23, 56, 71, 92, 94, 102, 110, 114, 121-122, 146, 164, 280, 295, 298, 301, 305, 312, 314

subscriber fraud 122, 314

subscriber identification module: see SIM

subscriber profiling 120, 314

subscriber units 28, 277, 296, 301

subsidy 51

subsidy lock 159, 165, 166, 314

supersystem 45

supervisory audio tone 314

switch 19, 22, 34, 41, 50, 81, 82, 83, 98, 99, 119, 121, 137, 147, 169, 277, 278, 280, 292, 299, 303, 308, 310, 314, 316, 318, 319, 320

switchhook function 81, 279, 314

synchronous mode 315

system busy 315

system hole 35

system identification: see SID

system registration 63, 71, 72, 165, 167, 168

**T**

TACS (Totally Accessed Communications System) 315

TAD: see telephone answering device

TALK: see SEND

talk time 135-136, 313, 315

TDMA 3, 10, 13, 15, 17, 19, 37, 56, 103, 106, 108, 111, 115, 125, 131, 148, 163, 274, 286-287, 292, 294, 316

Technocel 183

Teledesic 24, 180

telephone answering device 316

Telular 183

terminal emulation 316

The Good Guys 52

The Sharper Image 52

three-way calling 78, 81, 280, 295, 315, 316

throughput 278, 317

TIA 317

TIC 52

time division multiple access: see TDMA

transceiver 7-8, 32, 57, 140, 309, 317

transmitter 57, 274, 292, 309, 317

tri-mode handset 317

two-way radio 3, 7, 19-20, 38, 75, 77, 80, 171, 291, 296

**U**

ubiquitous roaming  75, 79, 111

UHF  8, 27, 140, 318

ultrahigh frequency:  see UHF

Uniden  177

unlock code  70, 157-158, 167, 303, 318

unregistered phone  318

usage  5, 20, 23, 43, 46-47, 74, 76, 84, 86, 92, 117, 120, 147, 167, 274, 280, 302, 312, 314, 318

user

  heavy  75, 77, 85

  high-volume  57, 135

  light  75, 77

  medium  75, 77, 134, 142

  power  75, 78, 85

  security  58, 65, 75-76, 79, 85

user friendly  42, 318

USOP  52

**V**

V.21  322

V.22  322

V.22 bis  322

V.32  322

V.32 bis  322

V.34  322

V.42  323

V.42 bis  323

V.90  322

V.FC  322

validation  121, 318

very high frequency:  see VHF

VHF  7, 27, 318

vibration notification  63, 70, 145

videoconferencing  24

visitor location register  318

VLR:  see visitor location register

vocoder  284, 319

voice-activated dialing  318

voice channel  13, 34, 40-41, 162, 285, 292, 310, 312

voice mail  4, 69, 75, 78, 84, 127, 148, 276, 279, 288, 303, 312, 319

voice-operated transmission: see VOX

volume control  65

VOX  314, 319

**W**

W-CDMA  21, 320

Wal-Mart  51, 53

Walt Disney World  109

WAP  319

warranty  55, 62, 64, 136

wideband code division multiple access:  see W-CDMA

Wireless Applications Protocol: see WAP

Wireless Dimensions  49, 183

wireless local loop:  see WLL

Wireless Review  185

wireless telephone  1, 2, 4, 9, 15, 19, 23, 28, 33-35, 38-41, 42-43, 45-46, 49, 53, 56, 58, 64, 74, 81, 91, 95, 106, 117, 120, 125, 133, 139, 145, 148, 153, 281, 286, 316, 320

Wireless Week  185

wireline  7, 11, 277, 304, 309, 320

WLL  16, 22, 320

WNP Communications, Inc.  21

**Y**

Y2K  320

**Z**

Z-modem  129